THE SPANISH RIGHT
AND THE JEWS,
1898–1945

The Cañada Blanch / Sussex Academic Studies on Contemporary Spain

General Editor: Professor Paul Preston, London School of Economics

Published

Cristina Palomares, *The Quest for Survival after Franco: Moderate Francoism and the Slow Journey to the Polls, 1964–1977.*

Soledad Fox, *Constancia de la Mora in War and Exile: International Voice for the Spanish Republic.*

Isabelle Rohr, *The Spanish Right and the Jews, 1898–1945: Antisemitism and Opportunism.*

Forthcoming

Richard Wigg, *Churchill and Spain: The Survival of the Franco Regime, 1940–45* (paperback edition).

Published by the Cañada Blanch Centre for Contemporary Spanish Studies in conjunction with Routledge / Taylor & Francis

1. Francisco J. Romero Salvadó, *Spain 1914–1918: Between War and Revolution.*
2. David Wingeate Pike, *Spaniards in the Holocaust: Mauthausen, the Horror on the Danube.*
3. Herbert Rutledge Southworth, *Conspiracy and the Spanish Civil War: The Brainwashing of Francisco Franco.*
4. Angel Smith (editor), *Red Barcelona: Social Protest and Labour Mobilization in the Twentieth Century.*
5. Angela Jackson, *British Women and the Spanish Civil War.*
6. Kathleen Richmond, *Women and Spanish Fascism: The Women's Section of the Falange, 1934–1959.*
7. Chris Ealham, *Class, Culture and Conflict in Barcelona, 1898–1937.*
8. Julián Casanova, *Anarchism, the Republic and Civil War in Spain 1931–1939.*

9 Montserrat Guibernau, *Catalan Nationalism: Francoism, Transition and Democracy.*

10 Richard Baxell, *British Volunteers in the Spanish Civil War: The British Battalion in the International Brigades, 1936–1939.*

11 Hilari Raguer, *The Catholic Church and the Spanish Civil War.*

12 Richard Wigg, *Churchill and Spain: The Survival of the Franco Regime, 1940–45.*

13 Nicholas Coni, *Medicine and the Spanish Civil War.*

14 Diego Muro, *Ethnicity and Violence: The Case of Radical Basque Nationalism.*

15 Francisco J. Romero Salvadó, *Spain's Revolutionary Crisis, 1917–1923.*

Numbers 11, 13, 14 and 15 are forthcoming.

THE SPANISH RIGHT AND THE JEWS, 1898–1945

Antisemitism and Opportunism

ISABELLE ROHR

Cañada Blanch Centre
for Contemporary
Spanish Studies

sussex
ACADEMIC
PRESS

Brighton • Portland • Toronto

2 4 6 8 10 9 7 5 3

First published 2007 in hardcover, and 2008 in paperback, in Great Britain by
SUSSEX ACADEMIC PRESS
PO Box 139
Eastbourne BN24 9BP

Distributed in North America by
SUSSEX ACADEMIC PRESS
ISBS Publisher Services
920 NE 58th Ave #300, Portland, OR 97213, USA

British Library Cataloguing in Publication Data
A CIP catalogue record for this book is available from the British Library.

Library of Congress Cataloging-in-Publication Data
Rohr, Isabelle.
The Spanish right and the Jews,1898–1945 : antisemitism and
opportunism / Isabelle Rohr.
p. cm.
Includes bibliographical references and index.
ISBN 978-1-84519-181-8 (h/c : alk. paper)
ISBN 978-1-84519-182-5 (pbk : alk. paper)
1. Jews—Spain—Politics and government—19th century. 2. Jews—
Spain—Politics and government—20th century. 3. Jews—Morocco —
P olitics and government—20th century. 4. Antisemitism—Spain—
History—20th century. 5. Conservatism—Spain—History—20th century.
6. Sephardim—History—20th century. 7. World War, 1939–1945—
Jews—Rescue—Spain. 8. Spain—Ethnic relations. 9. Spain—Politics and
government—1886–1931. 10. Spain—Politics and government—
1931–1939. 11. Spain—Politics and government—1939–1945. I. Title.

DS135.S7.R64 2007
305.892′404609041—dc22

2006102345

Typeset and designed by SAP, Brighton & Eastbourne.
Printed by TJ International, Padstow, Cornwall.
This book is printed on acid-free paper.

Contents

Illustrations

The author and publisher gratefully acknowledge the following for permission to reproduce copyright material:

1   Students of the Alliance Israélite Universelle (AIU) School in Tetuan, Spanish Morocco c. 1900. The AIU is a French-Jewish organization which operated day schools for Jewish children in Muslim countries. The fact that the language of instruction was French led graduates to identify culturally with France. The AIU schools were denounced by Spanish officials as a tool for French cultural expansion in Spanish Morocco. Gérard Sylvain Collection, Paris. Courtesy of Beth Hatefutsoth, Photo Archive, Tel Aviv.

2   The writer and propagandist Ernesto Giménez Caballero. during a meeting of General Franco's single party, the Falange Española Tradicionalista de las JONS (5 June 1939). Giménez Caballero, who had become interested in the Sephardic Jews as a young conscript of Morocco, had been an ardent philosephardite in the 1920s. He espoused fascism in 1929 and during the Spanish Civil War he advocated the re-establishment of traditional forms of religious persecution such as "auto-da-fe" "to purify" Spain from the Jews who had "infiltrated" the country. Copyright © EFE, HERMES PATO.

3   Page from the *Botwin* the newspaper of the Jewish Botwin unit in the International Brigades. The newspaper was published in Yiddish. The first issue stressed that the Jewish Brigadiers had come to Spain to fight not only Spanish Nationalists but also "to defy" the Nazis. Copyright © Beth Hatefutsoth Photo Archive.

4   Group portrait of the members of the Jewish Botwin company in the International Brigades fighting in Spain. The unit was named after Naftali Botwin, a Jewish trade-unionist from Lvov, who was arrested and hanged in Poland in 1926. It included Jews from Poland, various European countries, and Palestine, but also a Greek and two Palestinian Arabs in addition to Spaniards. The unit had a Yiddish marching song and newspaper. Copyright © Centre de Documentation Juive Contemporaine.

5   Franco and on the left Ramon Serrano Suñer. Franco had just made a speech to the national council of the Falange in the monastery de las

Huelgas (26 September 1939). Copyright © EFE, HERMES PATO.

6 *Arriba España*, 2 February 1937.

7 Cartoon from *Los Hijos del Pueblo*, 26 January 1933.

8 Page of a passport with stamped French, Portuguese and Spanish visas issued to Raya Markon, a Jewish emigré from Vilna, and her son, Alain. Copyright © United States Holocaust Memorial Museum.

9 *Reichsführer SS* Heinrich Himmler meets with the Minister of Foreign Affairs, Ramon Serrano Suñer during his visit to Madrid (20 October 1940). Suñer invited Himmler to Madrid to give him advice on the liquidation of opponents and the capture of political refugees. Copyright © EFE, HERMES PATO.

10 Investiture of José Felix de Lequerica as Foreign Minister (12 August 1944). In his previous position as Spanish Ambassador in Vichy, Lequerica had been unwilling to defend Spanish Jews in Vichy France on the grounds that they were Spain's "eternal enemies". Copyright © EFE, Vidal.

11 The Oskenhandler family, Jewish refugees from Poland, receiving clothing from the Joint Distribution Committee distribution centre in Tangier (1944). Copyright © American Jewish Joint Distribution Committee Photo Archives.

The publishers apologize for any errors or omissions in the above list and would be grateful to be notified of any corrections that should be incorporated in the next edition or reprint of this book.

The Cañada Blanch Centre for Contemporary Spanish Studies

In the 1960s, the most important initiative in the cultural and academic relations between Spain and the United Kingdom was launched by a Valencian fruit importer in London. The creation by Vicente Cañada Blanch of the Anglo-Spanish Cultural Foundation has subsequently benefited large numbers of Spanish and British scholars at various levels. Thanks to the generosity of Vicente Cañada Blanch, thousands of Spanish schoolchildren have been educated at the secondary school in West London that bears his name. At the same time, many British and Spanish university students have benefited from the exchange scholarships which fostered cultural and scientific exchanges between the two countries. Some of the most important historical, artistic and literary work on Spanish topics to be produced in Great Britain was initially made possible by Cañada Blanch scholarships.

Vicente Cañada Blanch was, by inclination, a conservative. When his Foundation was created, the Franco regime was still in the plenitude of its power. Nevertheless, the keynote of the Foundation's activities was always a complete open-mindedness on political issues. This was reflected in the diversity of research projects supported by the Foundation, many of which, in Francoist Spain, would have been regarded as subversive. When the Dictator died, Don Vicente was in his seventy-fifth year. In the two decades following the death of the Dictator, although apparently indestructible, Don Vicente was obliged to husband his energies. Increasingly, the work of the Foundation was carried forward by Miguel Dols whose tireless and imaginative work in London was matched in Spain by that of José María Coll Comín. They were united in the Foundation's spirit of open-minded commitment to fostering research of high quality in pursuit of better Anglo-Spanish cultural relations. Throughout the 1990s, thanks to them, the role of the Foundation grew considerably.

In 1994, in collaboration with the London School of Economics, the Foundation established the Príncipe de Asturias Chair of Contemporary Spanish History and the Cañada Blanch Centre for Contemporary Spanish Studies. It is the particular task of the Cañada Blanch Centre for

Contemporary Spanish Studies to promote the understanding of twenti-eth-century Spain through research and teaching of contemporary Spanish history, politics, economy, sociology and culture. The Centre possesses a valuable library and archival centre for specialists in contemporary Spain. This work is carried on through the publications of the doctoral and post-doctoral researchers at the Centre itself and through the many seminars and lectures held at the London School of Economics. While the seminars are the province of the researchers, the lecture cycles have been the forum in which Spanish politicians have been able to address audiences in the United Kingdom.

Since 1998, the Cañada Blanch Centre has published a substantial number of books in collaboration with several different publishers on the subject of contemporary Spanish history and politics. A fruitful partner-ship with Sussex Academic Press began in 2004 with the publication of Cristina Palomares's fascinating work on the origins of the Partido Popular in Spain, *The Quest for Survival after Franco. Moderate Francoism and the Slow Journey to the Polls, 1964–1977*. More recently, this has been followed by the deeply moving biography of one of the most intriguing women of 1930s Spain, *Constancia de la Mora in War and Exile: International Voice for the Spanish Republic*. This collaboration is now continued with the publica-tion of Isabelle Rohr's path-breaking study of anti-Semitism in Spain.

Series Editor's Preface

There are many contradictory opinions held about the Franco regime and most of them derive from the thorough-going myth-making of the Caudillo and his propaganda apparatus. Franco himself began to re-invent his own past from a very early stage in his military career and, as his power increased, so did his capacity to add weight to the myths that he created. He wrote two autobiographical works and in both missed no opportunity to speak highly of himself. Both directly in his speeches and articles, and through published interviews with journalists or in private conversations with his hagiographers, he constantly managed to rewrite and, of course, adorn his own biography. Had he not wanted to be projected as the el Cid, Carlos V or Philip II of the twentieth century, he could easily have issued orders restraining his more enthusiastic sycophants. It is reasonable to assume that he was happy with the exaggerations of his own image-makers. When his close friend and first propaganda chief during the Spanish Civil War, General José Millán Astray, declared that 'Franco is the envoy of God sent to lead Spain to freedom and greatness' or that 'Franco is the greatest strategist of the century' or simply, as he did repeatedly, that 'Franco never makes mistakes', the Caudillo betrayed no embarrassment.

Among a myriad of minor myths there have been five which, although thoroughly dismantled by serious historical scholarship, have persisted in Spain among his admirers. These outrageous fabrications are as follows. Franco won the Spanish Civil War by dint of brilliant generalship worthy of Napoleon. During the Second World War, Franco saved Spain from destruction by dint of courageously resisting Hitler's demands that he enter the conflict on the Axis side. After 1945, Franco saved Spain from the consequence of an economic blockade mounted by the democratic powers in an effort to destroy a regime of which they were jealous. Franco was the architect of Spain's economic miracle in the 1960s. Franco foresaw and fostered Spain's transition to democracy between 1976 and 1981.

There is a broad scholarly consensus that none of these claims can be sustained. Franco won the Civil War, despite his own mediocrity, thanks to international factors. Spain remained neutral, despite Franco's constant efforts to negotiate a profitable entry into the war, thanks to Hitler's reluctance to acquire another impecunious ally. The Western Powers did little or nothing to remove Franco between 1945 and 1953 beyond a symbolic withdrawal of ambassadors. Spain's economic miracle was the result of the intervention of the World Bank and the International Monetary Fund after Franco had admitted the disastrous failure of his own economic policies, and was based on foreign investment, tourism and remittances sent home by Spanish migrant workers. Until his dying day, Franco was declaring publicly and privately that the dictatorship would not be changed after his death. Despite the views of the scholarly community, all five myths are still fervently believed on the Spanish Right and most of them, especially that regarding Spanish neutrality during the Second World War, are still accepted among the Caudillo's foreign admirers.

In the case of neutrality, the fact that Spain was not a belligerent in the war is frequently and understandably cited as underpinning Franco's claim, despite the overwhelming evidence regarding Franco's overtures to Hitler. Moreover, in support of the notion of 'Franco, silent ally' (to quote the words of Willard L. Beaulac), there has emerged a subsidiary claim. This is that, in addition to quietly supporting the allies with his courageously guarded neutrality, Franco pursued a benevolent policy towards Jewish refugees during the Holocaust. Because of the incontrovertible fact that a significant numbers of Jews were able to escape via Spain, there has been a tendency to romanticize Franco's attitude towards the refugees, attributing it to the Caudillo's disinterested benevolence. In the United States, this view was widely popularized by Trudi Alexy's bestselling 1994 memoir *The Mezuzah in the Madonna's Foot.* It is the object of this important book by Isabelle Rohr to explain the paradox of how the Francoist regime's allegedly humanitarian attitude to Jewish refugees from all over Europe sat comfortably with the pro-Nazi policies and virulently anti-Semitic rhetoric of the Caudillo in particular and of the Spanish Right in general.

On the basis of meticulous archival research in Britain, Spain, the United States and France, Dr Rohr shows that, to the extent that the Franco regime did help Jewish refugees, it was out of shameless opportunism rather than being built on any ethical stance. As far as the Spanish Right was concerned, and particularly after the loss of empire in the course of the nineteenth century, the Jews were ferocious enemies committed to bringing Spain down, allied in the peninsula with Liberals, leftists and Catalan separatists, and abroad with the Moors of Morocco, the French, the Soviets, the English and the Americans. As Dr Rohr brilliantly demonstrates, the bizarre belief in the existence of a Jewish-Bolshevik-Masonic conspiracy was seized upon by the extreme Right during the years of the Second Republic (1931–1936) to justify violence against the left. In the aftermath of the Spanish Civil War, the

Franco regime refused to give shelter to persecuted Jews from Nazi Germany and Fascist Italy even when they had Spanish nationality.

Indeed, the Caudillo's own speeches were imbued with a fierce anti-Semitism. It was only the belief, shared by Franco himself, that the Jews controlled the politics and the economy of the United States and Great Britain, which would lead after 1943 to improved treatment of Jewish refugees. After the fall of Mussolini, Franco began to suspect that, in the unlikely event of Hitler losing the war, his regime would need the good will of the Anglo-Saxon Powers. Accordingly, as an insurance policy, he began to contemplate the idea of currying favour with the international Jewish community. In one of the most original sections of this path-breaking work, Dr Rohr demonstrates that, concerned about its image in the foreign press, which Franco believed to be under Jewish control, he accepted suggestions from his advisors that it was time to improve relations with the World Jewish Congress as a first step to creating the myth of Spain's rescue of Jewish refugees. But as she also reveals, the regime's fundamental policy towards Jewish refugees was unchanged. Jewish refugees, even those with Spanish nationality, were allowed to pass through Spain but were not permitted to settle there.

This fascinating and compelling work moves some considerable way beyond the existing literature on the Franco regime's treatment of Jewish refugees during the Second World War. In an entirely original way, it combines a lucid analysis of the historical origins of Spanish anti-Semitism with a revealing dissection of the ideological and strategic (indeed cynical) motives underlying the contradictory policies adopted by the Franco regime after 1943. This unique work is an extremely important contribution to the history of contemporary Spain, to the post-Inquisition history of the relationship between Spain and the Jews, and to an important dimension both of the Holocaust and of the Second World War.

Acknowledgments

This book could not have been written without the invaluable guidance and encouragement of Professor Paul Preston, who supervised the PhD thesis on which it is based. First and foremost, I wish to thank him.

I would also like to thank Professor Helen Graham and Dr Michael Richards, my examiners, for the time they took to read and comment on my thesis as well as for their useful suggestions. I am also deeply grateful to the Vidal Sassoon Centre for the Study of Antisemitism at the Hebrew University of Jerusalem, which provided support in the form of the Felix Posen doctoral fellowship. In addition, the department of International History at the London School of Economics provided a stimulating intellectual climate, which nurtured this project.

Others to whom I would like to express my gratitude include Mercedes Sanz Bachiller for her willingness to provide me access to the correspondence of her late husband Javier Martinez Bedoya; the late Egon Wolf for kindly sharing with me memories of his passage through Spain during World War II; Gerald Howson and Maite Ojeda Mata for their useful feedback on some parts of the manuscript; and Dr Francisco Romero for some inspirational conversations. My thanks also go to Anthony Grahame at Sussex Academic Press for his suggestions, which have helped improve this book immeasurably. I am also indebted to Dr Soledad Fox, Dr Cristina Palomares and Dr Manfred Böcker, who provided assistance with the photographs and illustrations. I would also like to thank the American Jewish Joint Distribution Committee, Beth Hatefutsoth, the Centre de Documentation Juive Contemporaine, EFE and the United States Holocaust Museum for granting permission to reproduce photographs.

A book of history stands on its research in primary documents, which would not exist without the ceaseless efforts of innumerable archivists and librarians. My work is no exception, and I am indebted to the staff of the Archivo General de la Administración (Alcalá de Henares), Archivo Historico Nacional (Madrid), Ministerio de Asuntos Exteriores (Madrid), United States National Archives (Baltimore), United States Holocaust Museum (Washington, DC), Archives de l'Alliance Israélite Universelle (Paris), Archives du Centre de Documentation Juive Contemporaine (Paris), University Library (Cambridge), British Public Library (London), Marx

Memorial Library (London), Wiener Library (London), University Library (Southampton), Archives of the American Jewish Joint Distribution Committee (New York), Columbia University, Rare Book and Manuscript Library (New York), Center for Jewish Studies (New York).

Special thanks to Robin D. Wear from the Alderman Library University of Virginia Manuscripts and Rare Books (Charlottesville), for sending me complementary copies of the J. Rives Childs materials.

I would like to take this opportunity to thank my family and all my friends for their constant support and encouragement throughout this project. My heartfelt thanks go to Dr Tatjana Kraljic for her meticulous proofreading and for her warm friendship. Finally, I am deeply grateful to Emil Varda for being there and for making it seem worth it.

Some of the ideas presented in Chapter 1 were introduced in "Philosephardism and Antisemitism in Turn-of-the-Century Spain," *Historical Reflections/Réflexions Historiques*, Vol. 31, No. 3 (Fall 2005): 374–92.

An earlier version of Chapter 3 was published as "The Use of Antisemitism during the Spanish Civil War", *Patterns of Prejudice*, Vol. 37, No. 2 (June 2003): 195–211. I acknowledge with thanks *Historical Reflections/Réflexions Historiques* and Routledge for permission to use this material here.

Abbreviations

AAIU	Archives of the Alliance Israélite Universelle, Paris, France.
AGA	Archivo General de la Administración, Alcalá de Henares, Spain.
AIU	Alliance Israélite Universelle.
CEDA	Confederación Española de Derechas Autonómas.
DGS	Dirección General de Seguridad.
JDC	Joint Distribution Committee.
LBI	Leo Baeck Institute, New York, USA.
MAEE	Ministerio de Asuntos Exteriores, Madrid, Spain.
MAEF	Ministère des Affaires Etrangères Français, Paris, France.
NARA	United States National Archives and Records Administration, College Park, MD, USA.
PRO	Public Record Office, Kew Gardens, Surrey (now the National Archives).
WJC	World Jewish Congress.
YIVO	Institute for Jewish Research, New York, USA.

In memory of my grand-father,
Josef Rohr,
who made it possible

Introduction

The Interplay of Political Myths, Foreign Policy and Colonial Ambitions

The interplay of political myths, foreign policy and colonial ambitions determined the Spanish radical right's attitude towards the Jews between 1898 and 1945. There are three main dimensions of the Spanish–Jewish relationship. The first has an internal focus as it touches on the myths that were embedded in the ideology of the Spanish radical right, most notably the myth of the *Reconquista* and the myth of a Judeo-Masonic conspiracy. The second concerns Spanish imperialism in Morocco and the role it assigned to the Jews. The third dimension of Spanish–Jewish relations has an external focus as it sets the topic within the broader context of Spain's foreign policy, particularly during World War II.

It is this last aspect of the Spanish–Jewish axis that has attracted the most interest among academics. The question of the Franco regime's attitude towards the Jews first emerged in the immediate aftermath of World War II. It was brought up by the dictatorship itself. Ostracized in the international arena and excluded from the newly formed United Nations on the grounds that he had collaborated with the Axis powers, Franco sought to acquit himself by claiming that he had secretly supported Great Britain and the United States throughout the war. Throwing itself into the task of rewriting Spain's war record, the Francoist propaganda machine was quick to have recourse to Spain's alleged Holocaust record. In April 1946, a proposal by the Polish delegate to the UN Security Council, Oscar Lange, to suspend diplomatic relations with Spain prompted the *Caudillo* to insist on the differences between Franco's regime and those of fascist Italy and Nazi Germany. In a speech to his pseudo-parliament, the *Cortes*, on 14 May 1946, he declared that the absence of racism and religious persecutions in Francoist Spain was one of the features that distinguished it from the fascist and Nazi regimes.[1]

The propaganda campaign failed to convince the General Assembly, which excluded Spain from all of its dependent bodies and called on its member nations to withdraw their ambassadors in December 1946.[2] In May 1949 the Spanish issue was again discussed by the General Assembly following a Latin American proposal to restore diplomatic relations. Among the fourteen delegates who raised their hands to oppose the cancellation of the diplomatic ban on Francoist Spain was Abba Eban, Israel's newly appointed representative at the UN. Eban made a statement to explain that Israel's decision was due to the fact that the Franco regime "had been an active and sympathetic ally" of Nazi Germany.[3]

Piqued by Eban's remarks and convinced that the attitude of the Israeli delegate had a decisive effect on the general voting on the question of Spain, the Spanish Ministry of Foreign Affairs published a booklet entitled *Spain and the Jews* to reveal "the countless benefits that Jews have been afforded through Spain's protection and assistance".[4] The booklet claimed that during the war Spanish representatives in Nazi-occupied countries had used their influence to save the lives of thousands of Sephardic Jews while the Spanish government had provided shelter to Jews who had escaped into Spain. Spanish protection of the Jews during the war, it asserted, was not motivated by political reasons but by "a cordial and general impulse of sympathy and friendliness towards a persecuted race, to which Spaniards feel themselves attached by traditional ties of blood and culture".[5]

Years later, the pamphlet largely inspired *España y los judíos en la Segunda Guerra Mundial* (Spain and the Jews during the Second World War) and *Franco, Spain, the Jews and the Holocaust*, which Federico Ysart and Chaim Lipschitz published respectively in 1973 and in 1984. Both books echo the Ministry of Foreign Affairs' assertion that Spain had provided unconditional help to Jewish refugees throughout the Holocaust. Aware that the Franco regime could have saved more Jews, Ysart and Lipschitz assert that Spain's rescuing activities were limited by the country's severe economic crisis and by the Allies' unwillingness to take in more refugees from Spain. According to them, the regime was powerless to deal with the flow of Jews as refugee policy was dictated from outside Spanish borders.

Spain, the Jews and Franco (1982) by Haim Avni and *España y los judíos en el siglo XX* (Spain and the Jews in the Twentieth Century) (1987) by Antonio Marquina and Gloria Inés Ospina called into question the notion that the Franco regime did everything in its power to save the Jews. Both books identify two phases in Spain's Jewish policy during the Holocaust. From 1939 to the end of 1942, the Spanish government did not discriminate against Jewish refugees but it also did not allow them to settle in the country, even when they held Spanish passports. Jews who reached Spain illegally during the first years of the war and those whose onward transit arrangements failed were imprisoned in the concentration camp of Miranda de Ebro or even on few occasions turned back at the frontier. Spain changed its policy from November 1942 onwards, leaving its border with France open and allowing representatives of welfare organizations to work within its territory. Avni, Marquina and Ospina stressed the opportunist nature of Spanish refugee policy, noting that the change after 1942 was largely a response to the developments in the war and the Allies' increasing pressure on Franco's government.

Building on the works of Avni, Marquina and Ospina, Bernd Rother has published *Spanien und der Holocaust* (2001), translated into Spanish as *Franco y el Holocausto* (Spain and the Holocaust) (2005), which presents a balance sheet of Spain's rescue activities during World War II. According to Rother, the Franco regime allowed between 20,000 and 35,000 Jews to transit through Spain and provided protection for about 5,000 Jews in German-occupied territories during the war. Like Marquina and Ospina, Rother makes it clear that the Franco regime could have done more to save Jews, particularly those who possessed Spanish citizenship. Rother demonstrates that while Madrid displayed reluctance to evacuate its 4,500 Jewish nationals from occupied Europe, it was eager to control their assets. In the face of international pressure Spain eventually agreed to repatriate the Spanish Jews. However, they were admitted to Spain only in dribs and drabs and on the condition that they would soon be evacuated to another destination.

As useful and seminal as Avni's, Marquina's and Ospina's and Rother's works are, they focus on the international context and tend to divorce Spain's refugee policies from its political culture. As a result they never really explain why the Franco regime was so vehemently opposed to permitting Jewish refugees to settle in the peninsula. In order to understand Franco's stand on the matter it is necessary to understand the place that Jews occupied in the political mythology of the Spanish radical right.

Scholars have recently begun to realize the importance of political myths in creating collective identities within states. Anthony Smith writes that political myths, like all myths, bring together elements of historical fact and legendary elaboration to create an overriding commitment to the community.[6] In addition, as George Sorel points out, political myths enable members of a community to "picture their coming action as a battle in which their cause is certain to triumph".[7] Thus, myths provide not only a vision of the past but also of the future.

According to Raoul Girardet there are four political myths in modern societies: the myth of a Golden Age, the myth of conspiracy, the myth of the saviour and the myth of unity.[8] All four myths were embedded in the political culture of the Spanish radical right, which heralded the Reconquest of the peninsula from the Moors – the *Reconquista* – as Spain's Golden Age, blamed the decline of the country on a Judeo-Masonic-Bolshevik conspiracy and called for an "iron surgeon" to restore Spain's unity, threatened by centrifugal forces. The Jews featured prominently in two of these myths: the myth of the *Reconquista* and that of the Judeo-Masonic-Bolshevik conspiracy.

Myth theorists have noted that political myths are often elaborated in time of political chaos. The myth of the *Reconquista* was no exception; it was developed in the nineteenth century as Spanish intellectuals, traumatized by the loss of Spain's American colonies, pondered their national identity and history. Traditionalist thinkers found a response in the idea that there existed an eternal Catholic-Spanish essence, *Hispanidad*, born in the Visigoth time and resurrected during the centuries-long fight to recapture Spain from the Moors, the *Reconquista*. In this version of history, the fall of the last Moorish kingdom of Granada and the ensuing Decree of Expulsion of the Jews from Spain ushered in the Golden Age during which the Spanish Kings stood as the world's standard-bearers of Catholicism. According to ultra-conservative intellectuals, Spain's downfall was due to the reformism of the Bourbon monarchs and the Napoleonic invasion, which introduced non-Spanish liberal ideas in the peninsula.[9]

The myth of the *Reconquista* was supplemented by another myth in the late nineteenth century: that of the Judeo-Masonic conspiracy, drawn from the French clerical right and encapsulated in the *Protocols of the Elders of Zion*. Reactionary thinkers depicted liberalism and socialism as the elements of a Jewish-Masonic plot which sought to annihilate Catholic Spain. Blending the myth of the *Reconquista* and that of the Jewish conspiracy, they argued that liberals and socialists were *conversos*, descendants of converted Jews, who schemed to corrupt and bring down Spain. The ultra-radical right used the interwoven *Reconquista* and Judeo-Masonic-Bolshevik imagery to justify everything from the repression of the Asturias uprising in 1934 to the Civil War. The insurgents portrayed the Civil War as a new reconquest to regenerate Spain, and Franco as the saviour who would destroy the Judeo-Masonic-Bolshevik conspiracy and reunify Spain.

The persecution of the Jews in Nazi Germany was also interpreted through the patchwork of the *Reconquista* and conspiracy myths. Reactionary thinkers drew a parallel between Germany's situation in the early 1930s and that of fifteenth century Spain. They suggested that the influence the Jews exercised in Weimar Germany was similar to the one they had possessed in medieval Spain and that like Isabella and Ferdinand, the Catholic Kings who had expelled the Jews from Spain in the 15th century, Hitler had to protect his country from Jewish scheming.

A primary aim of this book is to demonstrate that the intertwined myths of the *Reconquista* and the Jewish conspiracy were an integral part of the political culture of the Spanish radical right. These concepts, which were pervasive in the discourse of ultra-conservative propagandists from the late 19th century onwards, came to shape the belief system of the Franco regime. The attitude of high-level Francoist officials towards the Jews was infused with notions of a Jewish conspiracy; indeed dispatches from Spanish ministers and diplomats were frequently filled with references to the centuries-old struggle between Christianity and Judaism and to the alliance of Jews with Freemasons and Bolsheviks.

Was the Spanish radical right antisemitic? The central importance of the Church in Francoist ideology and the fact that the dictatorship adopted the period when the Inquisition was established, the reign of the Catholic Kings, as its Golden Age, has led a number of scholars to argue that the regime's anti-Jewish rhetoric reflected a cultural prejudice based on Christian tradition rather than on racial discrimination. Thus its pronouncements against the Jews should be considered anti-Judaic rather than antisemitic.[10] Such interpretation, which echoes the dictatorship's postwar claim that its Christian spirit inoculated it against racism, ignores the prevalence of eugenic discourse in the rhetoric of Catholic thinkers. Influenced by the turn of the century Regenerationist movement, which saw Spain as a decaying body, and impregnated with notions such as the degeneration of the Spanish race and the Jewish infection, the clerical right blamed the decay of Spain on the racial fusion between Old Christians and *conversos*. The discourse was not innovative: after the expulsion of the Jews from Spain a series of laws, the *estatutos de limpiezas* (statutes of blood purity), had been enacted to prevent anyone with Jewish blood from occupying high offices. The statutes served as a model for the Spanish Church, which excluded descendants of Jews from occupying Church offices.

To assess the nature of the Spanish radical right's anti-Jewish bias the term antisemitism should be defined. Noting that antisemitism has flourished in places and periods without Jews, Gavin Langmuir has defined it as "irrational beliefs that attribute to all those symbolized as 'Jews' menacing characteristics or conduct that no Jews have been observed to possess or engage in".[11] According to this definition, the Spanish radical right's assertions that the Jews were part of a conspiracy to annihilate Spain constituted chimerical beliefs and thus antisemitism.

The omnipresence of Jews in the imagery of the Spanish radical right has been explored by Álvarez Gonzalo Chillida in his standard work on Spanish antisemitism, *El antisemitismo en España: La imagen del judío 1812–2002* (Antisemitism in Spain: the image of the Jews 1812–2002) (2002). Chillida's monograph, however, is primarily a study of literary antisemitism and as such it ignores the dynamic relationship between the image of the Jews and Spain's geopolitical interests and colonial ideology. Scant attention has been paid to the interplay between Spanish imperialism and anti-semitism, or to the attitude of the Spanish authorities towards the Jewish communities during the period of the Moroccan protectorate. Even the recent scholarship on Spanish colonial rule in Morocco, which has focused on the racial perceptions of the Spanish radical right and on the construc-tion of the Moroccan Other, has not addressed the place of Jews in Spain's colonial discourse.[12] The intent here is to fill some of this lacuna.

The current debate on the relationship of Orientalism to the Jews has demonstrated that Europeans' perceptions of the Jews was linked to impe-rialist ideology. Ivan Davidson Kalmar and Derek J. Penslar have noted that "the modern versions of antisemitism and imperialism were both born at the same time, in the second half of the nineteenth century".[13] Spanish anti-semitism and colonial expansion in Morocco did indeed emerge concurrently in the wake of the Disaster of 1898, which destroyed the remnants of the Spanish American empire and prompted the realization that Spain was a secondary power that needed to be regenerated.

Like antisemitism, colonial expansion in Morocco relied heavily on the myth of the *Reconquista*. By the end of the fifteenth century, the *Reconquista* had spread into Northern Africa and Isabella the Catholic had encouraged her successors to continue the struggle against the Muslims. Hence, Spanish colonialists tried to legitimize the expansion in Morocco by presenting it as the fulfilment of Isabella's will.[14] The fact that the conquest of the last Moorish kingdom of Granada and the expulsion of the Jews had gone hand in hand meant that the discourses on Jews and Muslims were often related. As the archetypal "Others" to the Catholic Spaniards, Jews and Moors were described as primitive as well as debauched; Spanish Marxism was blamed on the racial fusion of Jews and Moors with Spaniards. Other standard accu-sations of right-wing intellectuals were that the Jews had aided the Moors against Catholic Spain in the Middle Ages and that the Moroccan Jews had financed the Moroccan nationalist leader Abd el-Krim during the Rif War.

At the same time, parts of the colonial discourse acknowledged the special historical relationship between Spain and Morocco, stressing the shared past of Muslims and Spaniards to legitimize Spanish expansion in the region.[15] The complicities between Moroccan and Spanish cultures were emphasized when useful, sometimes to the detriment of the Jews. Hence during the Spanish Civil War as they mobilized native troops and Moroccan mercenaries to fight the Republicans, the Nationalists and their German allies drew on antagonisms between the Muslims and the Jews by portraying the latter as the ally of the Republicans. They warned the Muslims that in the event of a Republican victory Jews and communists would rule Morocco and that they would become the underdogs.

Yet there also existed an opposite rhetoric, which insisted on Spain's Jewish past. Known as philosephardism (*filosephardismo*), that discourse upheld that Spain's decay was due to the Inquisition and that reconciliation with the Spanish-speaking Sephardim, whose ancestors had been expelled, would help Spain recover some of its former glory. The movement was originally composed of Liberal politicians, journalists and intellectuals who strove to promote commercial and cultural ties with the Sephardic Diasporas spread across the Mediterranean. It eventually became a tool in the hands of a neo-colonial lobby which argued that peaceful commercial penetration of Morocco would pave the way to colonial expansion there and help regenerate the Spanish economy. Persuaded that the Jewish elites of North Africa had promoted France's imperial expansion, Spanish colonial lobbyists argued that Spain had to imitate its rival and set up Hispano-Jewish associations and schools, moulded on the Paris-based *Alliance Israélite Universelle*, which provided educational facilities to Jewish children throughout the Mediterranean.

The imperialist drive of the Franco regime made it receptive to philosephardic ideas. High-ranking officers, such as Colonel Tomás García Figueras, who had built their career in Morocco, were keen to foster ties with the Jewish elites of the protectorate and Tangier in the hope that the move would advance Spain's colonial interests in the region at the expense of its archrival France. Hence, at the same time as the regime used *Reconquista* imagery to justify the Civil War, certain Spanish officials in the protectorate lauded the harmony of the three religions of medieval Spain to foster Spanish interests in Morocco. The consequent balancing act reveals the manipulative use of the past by the dictatorship.[16]

In an attempt to rationalize these ideological contradictions the regime revived the distinction between the Ashkenazi Jews of German and Northern European origin and the Sephardic Jews. It pinned all ills on the former, arguing that the latter had been "cleansed" during their stay in Spain. The opportunism of Spain's philosephardic policy was demonstrated in its attitude towards Spanish Jews living in France and the Balkans who found themselves the victims of antisemitic persecution during World War II. Proposals from Spanish diplomats serving in France, Greece and Romania to transfer to Spain the Spanish Jews, whose lives were in danger, were opposed by the Ministry of Interior. Senior officials dreaded the entry into Spain of refugees who, even though there were Sephardic, were after all Jewish.

The third major focus of this book is the complex interaction between the Spanish radical right's conception of the Jews and Spain's external relations. A first step is to investigate the overlooked link between Spanish anti-Gallicism and antisemitism. France's leading role in the emancipation of the West European Jews combined with the French rivalry with Spain in Morocco, stimulated among antisemites – as well as philosephardites – the myth that France had established its supremacy thanks to Jewish power. The Spanish radical right claimed that the French were allied to the Jews and the Freemasons, and it attacked the *Alliance Israélite Universelle* as the epitome of this partnership. Belief in the French-Jewish-Masonic-Bolshevik conspiracy reached a peak during the Civil War as France's Jewish Premier, Léon Blum, who sympathized with the Republicans, was denounced as "Spain's worst enemy".[17]

The French government was not alone in being linked to the nefarious Jewish conspiracy. Spanish antisemitism was constantly evolving with the geopolitical situation. During the Spanish Civil War, the Nationalists accused the Soviet Union of being in Jewish hands. During World War II, the Franco regime used antisemitism as a canopy to express its hostility not only towards the Soviet Union but also towards the Western Allies. The Jews were accused of being both Bolsheviks and unscrupulous capitalists. The "Anglo-Saxon-Soviet front" was denounced as "the front of Jewish power". Yet it was this neurotic belief that the Jews manipulated the politics and the economy of the United States and Great Britain that encouraged improved treatment of the Jews after 1942. Imbued with belief in Jewish power, the dictatorship hoped that its rescue activities would convince the "international Jewish conspiracy" to put its resources at the disposal of Spain and help improve Spain's image in the Western democracies. The Franco regime's policy towards the Jews might have changed after 1943, but the myths it adhered to did not; they were only reformulated in a different light.

The book is organized chronologically into five chapters. The first two chapters trace the developments of ideas about Jews in Spain between 1898 and 1936. Chapter 1 deals with the concurrent emergence of philosephardism and the *Reconquista* and Judeo-Masonic myths in the wake of the 1898 Disaster and Chapter 2 examines the spread of the Judeo-Masonic-Bolshevik conspiracy theory among the Spanish right during the Second Republic. The rest of the book explores the dynamic between these myths and Spain's geopolitical interests: how the Spanish Civil War, World War II and the Holocaust were interpreted through the prism of ideas about Jews and how, in turn, developments on the international scene shaped Spanish views and attitudes towards the Jews. Chapter 3 analyzes the outbreak of antisemitism during the Civil War and the formulation of the conflict as a re-enactment of the *Reconquista* not only among propagandists but also among high-level officials and diplomatic representatives on the

Nationalist side. Chapter 4 deals with the attitude of the Franco regime towards the Jews during the first half of World War II. It strives to demonstrate that while the Franco regime's identification to the fifteenth century Catholic Kings and the influence of Nazi Germany called for a continuation of the antisemitic rhetoric, the dictatorship's colonial ambitions in North Africa prompted it to promote a rapprochement with the Spanish Jews of Morocco. Chapter 5 investigates the Spanish government's reluctance to repatriate its Jewish nationals from occupied Europe. It also shows that after Operation Torch, the Spanish government pursued self-interested rescue activities in order to improve its image in Western Allies while continuing to promote antisemitism. The conclusion addresses the similarities between Spain's policy towards the Jews during the Holocaust and that of other countries – Brazil, Japan and Italy.

I
Degeneration, Regeneration and the Jews
1898–1931

Spaniards' perceptions of the Jews were deeply affected by the Disaster of 1898, which saw Spain lose the remains of its old empire, Cuba, Puerto Rico and the Philippines, following a humiliating defeat at the hands of the United States. The once great empire became a second-rank nation, a change of status that plunged the country into a mood of pessimism and introspection. While intellectuals, politicians and army officers were united by the idea that Spain was a country in decline that needed to be regenerated, they disagreed on the causes of and the remedies for the decline. Some, like the philosopher José Ortega y Gasset, believed that Spain had to open itself to European influences and modernize itself, whereas others, like the historian Marcelino Menéndez y Pelayo, argued that Spain had been poisoned by the liberal philosophy spawned by the Enlightenment and had to find its true Catholic self. In addition, the defeat of 1898 forced Spain to re-focus its foreign policy on the Mediterranean, particularly on North Africa, which prompted a number of intellectuals and politicians to argue that expansion of Spain's colonial rule in Morocco would help restore its international status.

This chapter explores how Spain's identity crisis, the search for the essence of its nationhood, the widespread acceptance of the need for regeneration, the renewed interest in the Mediterranean basin as well as the colonial rivalry with France, affected Spanish conceptions of the Jews. The first section presents the background to the Jewish question in Spain and deals with the emergence of philosephardism (*filosephardismo*) – a movement whose proponents, concerned about "the degeneration of the Spanish race", asserted that reconciliation with the Spanish-speaking Sephardic Jews would help Spain recover some of its former glory. The second and third sections, which investigate the government's response to philosephardism, show the impact that Spain's colonial and commercial rivalry with France had on the Spanish attitude towards the Jews of Morocco and the Balkans.

The final section sets out how Spanish antisemitism, like philosephardism, was built around the twin concepts of degeneration and regeneration, and was related to the hostility towards France. It demonstrates that Spanish antisemites blended traditional Catholic hostility towards the Jews with the ideas in vogue in other European countries, particularly in France.

Exile, Conversion, Reencounter

On 31 March 1492, the Catholic Kings Isabella and Ferdinand issued the Edict of Expulsion, giving Jews four months either to accept baptism or to leave the Kingdoms of Castile and Aragon. While some went into exile to neighbouring Christian lands, mainly to Italy and Portugal, a great many Jews chose to convert.[1] For centuries to come these *conversos* or "New Christians" were considered to be essentially different from the rest of the population and the Inquisition brought a number of them to trial for "judaizing". The *conversos* were also called opprobrious names such as *Marranos* (pigs) and were subjects of popular satire. Between the fifteenth and seventeenth century, the *Estatutos de Limpieza de Sangre* (the "Blood Purity Statutes") were introduced, denying the new converts and their descendants entrance into universities, religious orders and government.[2]

Yet at the same time some Spanish officials considered the expulsion of Jews to be wrong. As Spain entered into economic recession, these critics became convinced that a loss of wealth was the main consequence of the 1492 measures. They also believed that while Spain was in economic straits, commercial powers, such as Holland and England benefited from the financial acumen of the Jews. In the 1630s the Count Duke of Olivares, Prime Minister of Philip IV, was reported to have opened negotiations with descendants of some exiled Jews, urging them to return to Spain, in the hope that they would help restore the fortunes of the monarchy. This radical policy fell short and might have contributed to Olivares's dismissal.[3] In the late eighteenth century, however, Charles IV's Finance Minister, Pedro Varela, revived the plan. He advocated letting prominent Jewish merchants of Holland return to Spain where they could establish branches of their commercial houses. But Charles IV rejected this proposal and issued a decree upholding all previous laws and regulations relating to the treatment of Jews.[4]

By the nineteenth century, Liberals blamed the Inquisition for the "decline" of Spain. In 1813, in the wake of the war of independence against France, the *Cortes* of Cadiz, which represented the Liberals, abolished the Inquisition. In 1814, upon resuming the throne, Ferdinand VII reinstated the Inquisition's authority throughout Spain. In 1816, he issued another decree renewing all the prohibitions against the admission of Jews into Spain and reiterating the Edict of Expulsion. In 1834, Queen Isabella II finally abolished the Inquisition but did not rescind the 1492 Edict.

By the middle of the nineteenth century there was a handful of Jewish residents in Spain. Among them were some affluent businessmen such as Ignacio Bauer and Daniel Weisweiller who acted as the Rothschilds' agents in Spain and lent the Spanish government 400 million reals in 1868.[5] While the Rothschilds also financed one of Spain's new railway businesses, the Madrid to Zaragoza & Alicante Company, their co-religionists and rivals, the Péreire brothers, were involved with the *Compañía de los Ferrocarriles del Norte de España* (Northern Railway of Spain).[6] But the future of this burgeoning Jewish community was uncertain, as Catholicism remained the only religion permitted in Spain.

Spain's campaign in Morocco in 1859–1860 brought the Jewish question into the limelight. While the official pretext of the war was the defence of the garrison towns of Melilla and Ceuta from the raids of Moroccan tribesmen, the government of Marshall Leopoldo O'Donnell also viewed the war as a crusade against the infidel Moors.[7] Upon capturing Tetuán in February 1860, the Spanish troops discovered that the 6,000 Jews living there were descendants of the exiles of 1492 and spoke a Judeo-Spanish dialect known as Haketia, which incorporated Hebrew and Arabic words. Muslim pillagers had entered the Jewish quarter and sacked all the houses upon the approach of the Spanish troops. Travelling with the Spanish troops, the London *Times* correspondent, Frederick Hardman, wrote:

> *The Jews who, as I afterwards learned, had shown signs of terror, and had for the most part hidden themselves on the entrance of the first Spanish troops, and had taken courage on perceiving that these were orderly and well behaved and did no one harm, and now they began to come out into the streets and even to welcome the soldiers with cries of "Bien Venidos!" "Viva la Renya!" (sic) and the like. They had evidently suffered much. Many of them were nearly naked, others had their garments torn off as if from rough treatment. Like all African and Turkish Jews, they spoke Spanish, and they were voluble in their description of what they had undergone.*[8]

The situation of the Jews improved considerably under Spanish occupation. Marshall O'Donnell and General Juan Prim showed a great deal of compassion for the Jewish community. Relief funds, food and clothing were distributed to the destitute Jews. Thanks to their linguistic skills, Jewish traders played a prominent role in provisioning the Spanish army and the Spanish occupation brought an economic boom to the Jewish community.[9]

After the withdrawal of Spanish troops, the situation of the Jews of Tetuán became once again precarious as their cooperation with the Spaniards made them vulnerable to the reprisals of fanatical Moors.[10] When the Spanish troops withdrew, many Jews fled to Gibraltar, Oran and Tangier. In 1864, the Spanish government instructed its consuls to protect the Jews of Morocco against the injustice of the local Moroccan authorities. In London, the *Jewish Chronicle* declared that the directive was "the finest manifestation of sympathy with the sorely tried Jewish race exhibited by Spain for the last five centuries" and "a striking proof of the extraordinary advance made by Spain on the path of liberalism".[11] The re-encounter between Spain and the Jews of Morocco gave birth to a movement known as "philosephardism", whose aim was to promote cultural ties between the two communities.

In the wake of the 1859–1860 war, the conditions seemed favourable for the readmission of Jews to Spain. The spread of antisemitism in Europe prompted Jewish leaders in Germany, France and England to petition Spain's government for religious equality so that their co-religionists, who were victims of persecutions, could settle there. At first, their pleas fell on deaf ears.[12] In March 1868, Haim Guedalla, a nephew of Sir Moise Montefiore and a prominent member of the Anglo-Jewish community, obtained the assurance of the liberal General Prim, that should he be again in power, he would revoke the Edict of 1492. Seven months later, Prim led the "September Revolution", which overthrew the Bourbon monarchy. In a letter of congratulation, Guedalla reminded him his promise.[13] The Edict of 1492 was not revoked but the 1869 Constitution assured the right to practice any form of worship both publicly and privately. In a famous speech in the Spanish parliament, on 12 April 1869, during the debate on the Constitution, Emilio Castelar, the president of the First Republic declared: "There have been two ideas which never succeeded in the world – one religion for all and one nation for all".[14] Rallying to the slogan "Catholic unity", the clergy staunchly opposed the new Constitution.

The restoration of the monarchy in 1875 led to the promulgation of a new Constitution, which declared Catholicism to be the state religion and that no religious ceremonies or manifestations other than those of the state religion would be permitted in public. The Edict of Expulsion remained in effect. This meant that freedom of worship was only tolerated; legally it was not yet recognized. Under these circumstances, the erection of a synagogue remained unthinkable.[15] The question of religious freedom remained a thorny issue and the forces that had opposed the 1869 Constitution remained hostile to a rapprochement with the Jews.[16]

In 1881, the persecution of Jews in Tsarist Russia prompted the Spanish

Ambassador in Constantinople, Juan Antonio Rascón, to propose to the Spanish Minister of State that Spain open its doors to the persecuted Jews. The Spanish government, under the leadership of Prime Minister Práxedes Mateo Sagasta, agreed to permit the Jews to enter Spain and to settle there. Newspapers all over Europe printed the news of Spain's offer, sparking much enthusiasm. The Spanish government, however, did not intend to help the Russian refugees with transportation to Spain and the project failed to materialize. Five years later a Spanish lawyer, Isidoro López Lapuya, established the *Centro Español de Inmigración Israelita* (Spanish Centre for Jewish Immigration), whose principal aim was to attract Jewish immigrants to Spain – but his efforts had no effect either.[17]

Regenerationism and Philosephardism

In the late nineteenth century there emerged in Spain a reform movement known as Regenerationism, which advocated a number of reforms to cure Spain's ills. Although widely regarded as a consequence of the military Disaster, "Regenerationist" thought existed before Spain's defeat of 1898. Two important works – Miguel de Unamuno's *En torno al casticismo* and Ángel Ganivet's *Idearium español* – which criticized the Restoration system and probed into the reasons of Spain's decadence, had been published in 1895 and 1896 respectively. Although both writers shared the belief that Spain was undergoing a spiritual and mental crisis, they gave different interpretations to the causes of national disintegration. Whereas Unamuno blamed the decline of Spain on the Inquisition, which had closed the country to foreign contacts, Ganivet pointed an accusatory finger on Spain's policy of world involvement, which had squandered its native energies. Correspondingly, they advocated different solutions to the nation's crisis. Unamuno argued that Spain had to open its frontiers to contacts from abroad and Europeanize itself. Ganivet, on the other hand, placed emphasis on the national spirit of independence, advocating a minimum of foreign contacts.[18]

The underlying link between the work of Unamuno, Ganivet and other Regenerationists, however, was their drawing on natural sciences and social Darwinism, which proclaimed that only the "fittest" nations would survive. The so-called Generation of 1898 used biological terms such as "degeneration" and "disease" to describe Spain's crisis. They drew no distinction between biology, sociology and history and viewed Spain's past as a source of evidence by which to interpret its present state and from which to find remedies to its decline.[19] Influenced by the Regenerationist movement,

Spain's early eugenicists espoused the belief that Spain was a declining nation. They blamed the *débâcle* of 1898 on the degeneration of the Spanish race. César Juarrós, a famous racial hygienist and future Deputy of the *Cortes* spoke about the "funeral of the race".[20] Racial enhancement, it was believed, was necessary for the regeneration of Spain.

It was in the context of this debate about Spain's cultural and racial regenerationism that philosephardism unfolded. The movement's most prominent champion, Ángel Pulido y Fernández was a Spanish Senator, closely identified with the Liberal Party and a friend of Emilio Castelar, the republican leader who had ardently defended the clause in the 1869 Constitution granting religious freedom. In the first decades of his professional life, Pulido had been a physician and an anthropologist, particularly interested in the study of the relationship between physical structures and biological function. He was one of the first formulators of racial ideas in Spain, and, as Joshua Goode argues, his interest in the Sephardic Jews must be understood not only through his political ideas but also through his racial ones.[21]

Pulido's initial contact with the Sephardim came during a cruise he took along the Danube in 1880. There he met three Sephardic businessmen who spoke the Judeo-Spanish dialect known as Ladino. But it was his second journey to the Balkans more than twenty years later, in August 1903, which inspired him to strengthen the relationship between Spain and the Sephardic communities. During that trip, he met Enrique Bejarano, the director of a Sephardic school in Bucharest, who informed him that there were over two million Sephardic Jews spread around the world, from the Mediterranean littoral to the Americas, still preserving Ladino after four hundred years of exile. Upon his return to Spain, Pulido began a campaign to promote ties with the Sephardic communities. He wrote a number of articles for Spanish and Latin American newspapers and made speeches in the Senate, all of which he published in 1904 in a book, *Los israelitas españoles y el idioma castellano* (Spanish Israelites and the Castillian language).

The following year saw the publication of his most famous book, *Españoles sin patria y la raza sefardí* (Spaniards without a homeland and the Sephardic race) based on a questionnaire he had sent to Sephardic communities around the world. In this study, Pulido argued that the degeneration of Spain was the direct result of the decree of 1492. Using medical terms, he asserted that the expulsion of the Jews had caused a "bloody amputation" and a "long and painful haemorrhage" to the body of Spain.[22] He asserted that during their stay in the Iberian Peninsula the Spanish Jews had mixed with the Spaniards and that the two peoples had racially improved each other as a result. Their racial affinities could be seen in their similar forms of behavior and dress and in their shared physical characteristics. Writing about the Sephardim he noted that: "nothing in their comportment, dress and personal aspect indicates that they are from a different race than the Spaniards".[23] As a result of their racial fusion with the Spaniards the Sephardic Jews were the most beautiful of all Jewish peoples.[24] Pulido did not approve all racial mixtures and declared that the Ashkenazi Jews of German and Northern European origin were "degenerate because of their mixtures".[25]

Pulido was not the only one to idealise the Sephardic Jews and tout the myth of their superiority. In the late nineteenth century a number of Jewish physical anthropologists of Ashkenazi descent accepted the myth of Sephardic superiority, attributing the noblest physical and moral qualities to the Sephardic Jews while denigrating Ashkenazi culture and pathology.[26] The originality of Pulido's argument lay in his assertion that the repatriation of a number of Sephardic Jews to Spain and their fusion with the Spaniards would revive the Spanish race and remedy Spain's decay. The return of the Jews would promote the "reconstitution of the Spanish race and improvement of the fatherland".[27] The Sephardic Jews, he asserted, would also benefit from returning to Spain because they had not established roots in the places in which they had settled after the expulsion.[28] He recommended that 20,000 to 25,000 Sephardim be repatriated to Spain on the grounds that their immigration would not only regenerate the Spanish race but also give a boost to the country's flagging economy.[29]

Pulido assumed that the expulsion of the Jews had not only caused Spain's racial decay but also its economic decline. On the basis that Spain had owed its "preponderance" to the "financial acumen and laboriousness" of the Sephardic Jews and that their departure had crippled Spain's industry and commerce, Pulido argued that reconciliation with the Sephardim would promote the nation's economic regeneration. *Españoles sin patria y la raza sefardí* revealed that the largest Sephardic communities were found in the Balkans where they exerted much economic and political influence. There were 250,000 Sephardim in the Ottoman Empire, 75,000 of whom lived in Salonica and 50,000 in Constantinople. Outside of the Ottoman Empire, there were about 1,600 Sephardic Jews in Bucharest, 700 in Sarajevo as well as 1,000 families in Vienna.[30] A rapprochement with them, Pulido asserted, would open new markets to Spain and help it get over the loss of Cuba and the Philippines.[31]

Belief in the economic force of the Sephardim was by no means unique to Pulido. According to Benjamin Braude, the "myth of the Sefardi economic superman" dates back to the sixteenth century, when European travellers exaggerated and distorted the role of Sephardic refugees in

Ottoman society. Unwilling to recognize the competence of the Turks, Christian observers attributed the economic wealth of the Ottoman Empire to the Sephardim. In addition, because of their knowledge of Spanish and other European languages, the Jews often played the role of intermediaries between the European visitors and the Ottoman authorities; their indispensability might have permitted the misrepresentation of their situation. The perception of the Sephardim as powerful and influential entrepreneurs prompted Italian city-states as well as Holland and England to reopen their gates to Jewish settlement.[32]

At the time of the publication of *Españoles sin patria y la raza sefardí*, Spain already had a competitor in the Balkans: France, which had been extending its cultural influence among the Sephardic Jews for the past three decades. The schools of the *Alliance Israélite Universelle* (AIU) were France's primary tool for French cultural expansion among Jews living in Muslim countries. The AIU was set up in Paris in 1860 by some of France's most influential Jews, including Adolphe Crémieux, a republican lawyer mostly known for his efforts to obtain French citizenship for Algerian Jews. The aim of the AIU was to defend the rights of and liberate the Jews living in the East by disseminating French secular education. It represented the efforts of French Jewry to remake their coreligionists in the East in their own emancipated image.[33] The first AIU school was established in Tetuán, Morocco in 1862 and by the outset of World War I the *Alliance* had over 188 schools and 48,000 students enrolled in them from Morocco to Iran.[34] The *Alliance* schools taught reading skills, mathematics and basic Jewish studies. The fact that the language of instruction was French and that the AIU teachers used French methods led graduates to identify culturally with France.

The *Alliance* had a considerable influence on the Sephardic communities of the Balkans. In 1912, every community of around 1,000 souls had at least one AIU School.[35] The pupils of the *Alliance* became fully francophone and while they continued to speak Ladino at home, they adopted French for their cultural life and their business dealings. Pulido believed that the AIU schools promoted France's commercial expansion in the region. He considered that by disseminating the French language throughout the Mediterranean basin, these schools were bringing French spirit, sovereignty and products to the area.[36] How could Spain win back the hearts of the Sephardic Jews? Pulido's answer was simple: the Spanish government had to imitate the work of its rival by setting up some schools on the model of the *Alliance Israélite Universelle*, by subsidising the teaching of Spanish in the *Alliance*'s schools and by distributing Spanish books and periodicals to the Jewish cultural centres of the Balkans. Pulido also told the Senate that the government should grant Spanish citizenship to a limited number of Sephardim who would defend Spanish interests in the Mediterranean basin.[37]

Unsurprisingly, while many Jews around Europe welcomed philosephardism, Jacques Bigart, the secretary of the *Alliance Israélite Universelle*, viewed Pulido's campaign with scepticism. In November 1904 he wrote in the *Alliance*'s organ, *l'Univers Israélite*, that Spain was an antisemitic country where Jews were still regarded as the murderers of Jesus Christ. He also pointed out that the Sephardic Jews of the Ottoman Empire were devoted to the Turkish Sultan and had no desire to live in Spain. Although their knowledge of Spanish could promote trade between Turkey and Spain, it was useless since both countries produced the same agricultural goods and raw materials.[38] In his reply to Bigart, Pulido seized the opportunity to attack France's treatment of the Jews. He argued that it was unfair to blame Spain for having expelled the Jews given that France had done the same in 1096, 1250, and again in 1602. He contrasted Spain, where religious tolerance was guaranteed by article XI of the Constitution, to France, where, "that combination of infamy and lies known as the *Affaire Dreyfus*" had taken place. He noted that the "disease called antisemitism" was unknown in Spain because the Spaniards did not "envy or distrust Jewish monopolies, money-lending or predominance".[39]

Pulido's campaign began to bear fruit in 1910 when the Hispano-Hebrew Alliance (*Alianza Hispano-Hebrea*) was established at the initiative of the writer Carmen de Burgos Seguí. In 1913 the Spanish government invited a Jewish scholar of Spanish descent, Abraham Shalom Yahuda, to give a series of lectures on Jewish contribution to Spanish culture. Yahuda's lectures aroused so much public interest that he was invited to occupy a special Chair for Hebrew Literature and the History of the Jews in Spain in the Middle Ages at the University of Madrid. On several occasions, King Alfonso XIII received Yahuda and expressed his sympathy for the philosephardic movement.[40] During World War I, Yahuda convinced the Spanish government to intervene on behalf of the Sephardic Jews with Turkish citizenship who lived in Italy and France, where they were threatened because they were considered enemy aliens. In November 1917, he persuaded King Alfonso XIII to send a telegram to the German Kaiser Wilhelm II to prevent the Turks from deporting thousands of Jews of Palestine to Asia Minor where they would have shared the fate of the Armenians.[41] That same year, the Spanish government also granted 20,000 francs to the Spanish Jews of Salonica, who found themselves destitute after a fire had ravaged that town.[42]

Philosephardism and Spanish Expansion in Morocco

Philosephardism soon became a tool in the hands of a neo-colonial lobby, which argued that peaceful commercial penetration of Morocco would pave the way to colonial expansion there and help regenerate the Spanish economy. Pulido himself stressed the primacy of the Jews of Morocco. In *Españoles sin patria*, he wrote: "No other nation can or should interest Spain as much as Morocco and of all the Sephardic congregations scattered throughout the world, none should attract our attention or should deserve our solicitude as much as the large one that lives in this decomposed Empire".[43]

In fact, Spain had become increasingly involved in Northern Morocco after 1898. Intervention in Morocco was motivated by concerns for Spain's strategic security. Spanish leaders such as the Liberal leader Eugenio Montero Ríos feared that if Morocco became a French protectorate, "Spain would be reduced to seeing itself besieged perpetually in the North and South by the same power".[44] Colonial expansion in Morocco was also a compensation for the loss of Cuba and the Philippines. In an era when a nation's prestige depended on its colonial possessions, Spanish politicians felt that Morocco was essential to Spain's international status.

In its eagerness to get new allies to strengthen its position *vis-à-vis* Britain, France, at first, seemed willing to recognize Spain's sphere of influence in Morocco. In 1902, during some secret negotiations, the French Foreign Minister, Théophile Delcassé, had promised Spain a zone that was to include northern Morocco down to the Sebou and Muluya Rivers and a piece of territory south of Agadir. The Spanish leaders, who feared the British government's objection to a Franco-Spanish alliance, rejected the offer.[45] In the aftermath of the Franco-British Entente Cordiale of 1904, France reduced the area it had proposed to Spain by almost 50 per cent. Under the treaty of Fez of 30 March 1912, the international community agreed to the transformation of the French and Spanish zones of influence into protectorates. Spain was left with a coastal strip of 20,000 square kilometres, representing one-fifth of Morocco. Not only was the mountainous terrain given to Spain not propitious to military conquest it was also inhabited by Berber tribes who had the reputation of being uncontrollable. France, on the other hand, had bestowed itself the most fertile and peaceful area of Morocco.[46]

Adding to Spanish resentment was the fact that Spanish Morocco did not include Tangier, the largest and most important city in northwest Morocco, which had a natural relationship with the other regions of the

Spanish protectorate. An international conference, which met in 1923, internationalized the city port of Tangier, giving it an administration modelled on that of Shanghai. Tangier's executive organ was the Control Commission, whose chairmanship was supposed to rotate between the different nationals who were members of the Commission. In practice, a French official headed the Commission for fifteen years – a development which reflected France's supremacy in Morocco.[47] The Spanish government was suffused with rancour towards France and suspicious. Yet, the desire to imitate the French model determined both Spain's policy in Morocco and philosephardism for the next two decades.

A neo-colonial lobby, composed of businessmen, journalists and politicians and including well-known figures such as the Regenerationist social thinker, Joaquín Costa, and the Premier, Álvaro de Figueroa y Torres, Conde de Romanones, campaigned for the "peaceful penetration" of Spanish capitalism in Morocco. At times this group found itself at odds with army officers who believed that the military penetration of Morocco should precede commercial expansion.[48] Among the different groups making up the neo-colonial lobby were the philosephardites, who hoped that the promotion of commercial and cultural ties with the Moroccan Jews would facilitate Spain's colonial penetration of Morocco.

By 1921, there were about 12,000 Jews in Spanish Morocco; 7,000 of these lived in Tetuán, 3,000 in Larache and 500 in Arzila.[49] The philosephardites were interested in the mercantile elite of these Jewish communities. Thanks to their linguistic skills – many of them were bilingual or trilingual – the wealthier Jews of Morocco played the role of intermediaries between the Muslims and the outside world. They had the monopoly over the textile trade and over the production and distribution of jewellery.[50] Most of the affluent Jews were either foreign Jews or *protégés* of the European consulates. The *protégé* system, which became widespread after the Franco-Moroccan treaty of 1767, exempted a privileged elite of Jews – and Muslims – from military duty as well as from the Moroccan judicial authority and from the payment of certain taxes. Jews who were *protégés* or foreign nationals often served in European consulates and legations as advisors, interpreters or vice consuls. They also tended to cater to the interests of their European employers.[51]

In his first book, *Notas marruecas de un soldado* (Moroccan notes of a soldier), a recording of his experiences as a young conscript in Morocco, the famous litterateur Ernesto Giménez Caballero reminisced his visit to the home of a Jewish banker from Tetuán who belonged to this coterie. The Jewish notable, Giménez Caballero wrote, was "dressed impeccably, in a European way. He had a strong figure [. . .] the face of a businessman, a man of substance. He treated us with an urbanity and a worldliness that came as a shock in this spot of Morocco". Upon leaving, Giménez Caballero was "delighted" and convinced that it was necessary to use the Jews of Morocco "skilfully and tactfully" to promote Spain's interests in North Africa.[52]

The philosephardites believed that the Jews of Morocco, who were obliged to Spain for having delivered them from "the shackles" of Muslim fanaticism during the 1860 war, ought to serve Spanish interests in the region. In the book *Los hebreos en Marruecos* (The Jews in Morocco), the editor of the philosephardic organ *La Revista de la Raza* and collaborator of Pulido, Manuel Ortega, stressed the Moroccan Jews' indebtedness to Spain.[53] Ortega lamented the fact that the Spaniards, "eternal Quixote", had failed to take advantage of their "redeeming work". They had let France reap the fruits that Spain "had sowed in the blood of soldiers", allowing it to become Morocco's first trading partner.[54] After decades of education in the schools of the *Alliance Israélite Universelle*, the Moroccan Jews looked up to France rather than to Spain: "France has occupied the place of Spain with the Sephardic Jews. The Jews view France as the redemptive nation of the Moroccan Israelites. With its schools and its protections, France is a reality. Spain is a romantic ideal [. . .] whose benevolent influence remains too limited".[55]

Ortega, like Pulido, believed that Spain could improve its situation in Morocco if it implemented a policy similar to that of France. Inspired by the Crémieux Decree, which had given the French citizenship to the Algerian Jews, Ortega suggested that Spain grant Spanish nationality to the Moroccan Jews. He also recommended that the Spanish authorities of Northern Morocco set up Spanish schools and oblige the schools of the *Alliance Israélite Universelle* to teach in Spanish rather than in French. Another suggestion was that Spain establish registry offices for the Sephardic Jews in the main cities of the protectorate: Tetuán, Larache, Elksar, Xauen and Arzila. Finally, Ortega believed that the Spanish government should promote its trading relations by having Spanish businessmen visit Morocco and having Jewish businessmen come to Spain.[56]

Among the army officers who administered the protectorate, there was a wide range of response to philosephardism, which reflected the existence of competing schools of thought within Spain's Army of Africa.[57] Influenced by nineteenth-century liberal views, some officers thought of themselves as "enlightened colonialists" and sought to instil European civilization in Morocco. They aimed to subordinate military action to civil initiatives and were receptive to the ideas of the philosephardites. Chief among them were the two High Commissioners in Morocco between 1915 and 1918, General José Marina Vega and General Francisco Gómez Jordana, father of Franco's future Foreign Minister. Both men believed in the importance of winning over the Moroccans by peaceful means and saw Spain's mission in Morocco as a civilizing one. As High Commissioner, Marina prohibited the harassment of the Jews that traditionally took place on Easter Day.[58] His disciple, Jordana, who became High Commissioner in 1915, also showed a great deal of interest in the Moroccan Jews. He began writing the prologue to the second edition of Ortega's *Los Hebreos en Marruecos* but died before he could complete it. In the prologue, he asserted that the Spaniards had to renounce their "narrow-minded prejudices" and promote ties with the Jews of Morocco who were "bound to Spain through ancestry and tradition". The motivation for the rapprochement with the Moroccan Jews was to "advance Spain's legitimate control over the Maghreb".[59]

In contrast to Jordana, his successor, General Damaso Berenguer, pursued an aggressive policy towards the Jews. His hostility was first revealed in October 1913, when he was still commandant of Arzila. At the time, the Jewish community of Tangier informed both the British legation and High Commissioner General Marina that the Jews of Arzila suffered harsh treatment in Berenguer's hands. After assuring them that "the material and moral well-being of the Jews in the zone" was "the object of his constant intention", Marina pledged to order a full enquiry and adopt adequate measures.[60] The only result of his intervention, however, was that Berenguer summoned the notables of Arzila's Jewish community, and berated them for having dared complain. Calling them "thieves", "liars", and "criminals", he flung on the floor before them the sum of five hundred pesetas, which they had previously given to him for wounded Spanish soldiers. Without allowing them to speak he threatened them with severe punishment.

Meanwhile, the Hispano-Jewish Association of Tetuán also intervened with Manuel González Hontoria, the Under-Secretary of the Spanish Ministry of Foreign Affairs, who assured them that King Alfonso XIII himself took a great interest in the welfare of the Jews and would issue instructions in that sense.[61] But this intervention was to no avail maybe because Berenguer who had been Minister of War in the past was a favourite of King Alfonso XIII.[62]

The Spanish colonialists viewed education as an instrument for imperial conquest and one unofficial goal of the Hispano-Jewish association was to campaign against the AIU. The philosephardites hoped to replace the AIU network with Hispano-Jewish schools.[63] In Larache, the leader of the Hispano-Jewish association, Jacob Levy, began campaigning against the AIU schools in the newspaper *Kol Israel*, which he published. The anti-

French tone of the publication prompted France's diplomatic agent in Larache to recommend its banning in the French zone.[64] Spain's efforts to lure the Jews of Morocco and the pro-Madrid manifestations of some Sephardim also irritated the French Résident-Géneral in Morocco, Marshal Hubert Lyautey. In a meeting with Albert Saguès, the director of the AIU school in Casablanca, he accused different Jewish groups in the French protectorate of serving Spanish interests. He denounced the attempt of some Casablancan Jews to obtain Spanish citizenship and asked Saguès if the Jews wished "to undermine French influence in Morocco".[65]

In fact, the AIU was equally concerned about Spanish schemes to limit French ascendancy. Its delegates in Morocco feared that the opening of tuition-free Hispano-Jewish schools in Tetuán, Larache, Arzila and Elksar, presaged the closing of the AIU network in the Spanish zone. They were aware that the philosephardites wished to replace French schools with Spanish ones to eliminate French influence on the Jewish communities.[66] The Spanish consul in Elksar, Señor Clara, was particularly hostile to the AIU. Alarmed by Clara's attitude, the Director of the AIU school in Elksar, Alberto Benaroya, wrote in October 1913:

> The Spanish consul will not rest until he sees the doors of our schools close forever. This gentleman is convinced that our schools, established at a time of strained Franco-Spanish relationship, are working to disseminate French propaganda and he makes it his duty to inconvenience us.[67]

Already in February 1912 Clara had ordered the Jewish notables who were Spanish *protégés* to remove their children from the AIU School. In the face of their refusal, a consulate staff member, Hugo Angerer, had threatened to take their consular protection away. "You are Spanish," he told the *protégés*, "you must work for the Spanish school, go to Fez if you want your children to learn French."[68] The AIU was financially dependent on the local Jewish communities and Clara had the Moroccan authorities burden the Jews of Elksar with taxation in order to limit the school's funds.[69] Clara also had Spanish troops occupy the AIU premises under the pretext that the heightened tension with rebel Muslim Moroccans made such an occupation necessary for the security of the town.[70] Distressed by Clara's animosity, Benaroya asked the French consular agent in Elksar, Monsieur Boisset, to give protection to the Jewish parents whose children attended the AIU.[71] The Jewish Community of Elksar also appealed to the AIU's president, writing to him about their members' deteriorating condition under Spanish rule:

> We would like to attract your attention to the trials and tribulations that the

community is suffering in the hands of the Spaniards. When we lived under Arab rule we enjoyed perfect tranquillity. Unfortunately we have been persecuted since the arrival of the Spaniards.[72]

In the end, Clara's campaign against the AIU came to nothing. The few Jewish notables who removed their children from the AIU at the start of the 1913 academic year reversed their decision within a few months. At the same time, a number of Spanish Catholic parents began sending their children to the AIU. Ironically, Angerer's niece was among the *Alliance*'s new Catholic pupils.[73] The Hispano-Jewish school of Tangier did not encounter great success either. In 1917 twenty pupils were enrolled there, while over 1000 children went to the AIU. Aware that the Hispano-Jewish network would not succeed in replacing the AIU, other Spanish officers tried to "hispanicize" the AIU schools. In Larache, for instance, the Spanish consul convinced the protectorate authorities to grant the AIU an annual subsidy of 2000 francs and to provide a plot of land where the school could build new premises. In exchange, the AIU had to hire teachers of Spanish language and devote more hours to the study of that subject. "All of these actions," wrote Yomtov David Sémach, the AIU delegate in Morocco, "show the desire, the continuous and sustained effort to realize one aim: the transformation of our schools into Spanish institutions."[74]

As High Commissioner, Berenguer tried to bring the AIU under his control as he had done with the Hispano-Jewish associations. In August 1920 he met with the Director of the AIU school in Tetuán, Moise Levy. Impressed by Levy's fluency in Spanish, Berenguer expressed his hope that the AIU would promote the teaching of that language. He assured Levy of his friendship and promised him his support.[75] By then Berenguer was waging war against rebel tribes and had probably realized that it would be wiser not to alienate the Jewish communities as well.

The Spaniards also attempted to subdue the councils of the Jewish communities, known as the *Juntas*. Elected by the community, the role of the *Juntas* was to act as the community's spokesbody, to administer its budget, to help the impoverished and to pay the obligatory taxes. Its members belonged to the Jewish upper class. They were merchants or bankers and very often *protégés* of foreign powers.[76] In several instances the Spanish authorities manoeuvred to have pro-Spanish notables appointed to the council. In 1918, De La Guardia campaigned against the Tetuán council's president Abraham Israel because he was a French *protégé*.[77]

More importantly, the Spaniards tried to woo the Tangier *Junta*, in order to increase Spain's role in the administration of the city. The Statute of Tangier, ratified in May 1924, provided the international city with an executive and a legislative organ: the Control Commission and the Legislative Assembly. At the head of the commission sat an Administrator who was responsible for controlling the bureaucracy, the police and the budget. As mentioned, a French official had occupied the office of Administrator for sixteen years, a fact which reflected France's effective control of Tangier's political life and which inflamed Spanish colonial frustration.[78] The Legislative Assembly was made up of twenty-six indigenous and foreign nationals who lived in Tangier. Spain and France had four delegates, Britain three, Italy two and the USA, Belgium, Netherlands and Portugal one each. Six Moslems and three Jewish delegates represented the native population. The *Mendoub*, who represented the Sultan, selected the three Jewish representatives from a list of nine candidates suggested by the *Junta*.[79] The Spaniards needed the vote of the Jews to counteract the French influence over the Moroccan Muslims who were appointed by the pro-French *Mendoub*.[80]

The Spaniards realized that to ensure that the three Jewish delegates seating at the Assembly were pro-Spanish, they had to win over the Tangier's *Junta*. A few weeks before the June 1924 election of the *Junta*, the founder and president of Tangier's Hispano-Jewish association, Dr Samuel Guitta, declared that the community council needed a Spanish majority at all costs. A French diplomat reported that the Spanish candidates distributed money to the poorest voters and that some ballot papers were fraudulently filled the night before the election. The election resulted in a victory of the Spanish candidates. Out of the fifteen members that composed the council five were Spanish nationals, while three were French.[81] The Spanish daily *ABC* called the election results "a sweeping victory for Spain over the question of Tangier".[82]

Promoting Ties with the Balkans

In 1920 the *Casa Universal de los Sefardis* (Universal House of the Sephardim) was established in Madrid. Its goal was to promote trade with Sephardic Jews, to carry out a census of the Sephardim, to regulate their political and economic problems, to edit Spanish books and newspapers and to set up Spanish cultural institutions in the Mediterranean basin. Members of the *Casa* came from the whole political spectrum and included not only Liberals and Republicans like Niceto Alcalá Zamora and Alejandro Lerroux, but also Conservatives like Antonio Maura and Antonio Goicochea. The writer Manuel Ortega was the organization's secretary while Pulido was its honorary president.[83] Ignacio Bauer, the grandson of the representative of the House of Rothschild in Spain and the head of the Jewish community in Spain, represented the *Casa Universal* at the conference of the International Federation of League of Nations Societies that convened in Brussels in 1920.[84] Bauer also financed the immensely influential, and liberal, publishing house, CIAP (*Compañia Ibero-Americana de Publicaciones*), which published the periodical of the *Casa Universal*, *La Revista de la Raza*, the platform of philosephardism, edited by Manuel Ortega.[85]

In 1921, a new initiative for the expansion of Spanish culture, which came from the philologist Américo Castro and the State Minister Manuel González Hontario, led to the establishment of the *Oficina de Relaciones Culturales Españoles* (ORCE), the Office of Spanish Cultural Relations. The aim of the new organization was to promote the knowledge of Spanish culture and the teaching of the Spanish language abroad.[86] In January 1922 the ORCE sent to the Spanish legations and embassies a questionnaire designed to obtain information about Spanish-speaking communities abroad. According to the responses received, there were 80,000 Spanish speakers in Salonica, 24,000 in Belgrade, 50,000 in Sofia, 30,000 in Bucharest, 10,000 in Cairo, 1,200 in Alexandria and 250 in Port-Said; most of them were Sephardic Jews who continued to speak Ladino and felt drawn to Spain. Yet in none of these countries was there a Spanish cultural institution and Spanish-speaking children were educated in Jewish, French or Italian schools.[87]

In the responses they sent to the Office of Cultural Relations, some Spanish diplomats expressed their concern about France's influence on the Sephardic communities. The envoy in Bucharest, the Duke of Amalfi, noted that it would be very difficult to disseminate Spanish in a country where "the language of Rabelais" dominated and where there was a "firmly rooted tendency to imitate" all that in France was "pleasant or corrupted". He believed that before promoting its language and culture, Spain had to set up a Spanish bank in Bucharest and a shipping line that would link the Iberian Peninsula to the Romanian ports of the Danube and the Black Sea. Drawing on antisemitic stereotypes he asserted that commercial initiatives had to precede cultural propaganda in Romania because "only the lure of money" would make "the Jew's heart [. . .] flutter".[88] The Duke of Amalfi's recommendation to his government was to attract the Sephardim and to use them to obtain new markets for Spain's industry but not to grant them Spanish nationality.[89] The ORCE paid scant attention to the Duke of Amalfi's suggestions and remained eager to expand Spain's cultural influence among the Sephardim.

The philosephardites' campaign culminated in the Royal Decree of 1924, which granted Spanish nationality to a number of Sephardic Jews.

The decree was prompted by the abolition of the system of capitulations in the aftermath of World War I. That system had allowed some residents in the Ottoman Empire to enjoy extraterritorial rights and protection by a foreign power. Among the people affected by its abolition were a number of Sephardic Jews who had been *protégés* of the Spanish delegations in the Ottoman Empire. They found themselves without legal status or protection in countries that were prey to nationalist policies.[90] The military dictatorship of General Primo de Rivera seized the opportunity to expand Spain's influence on the Sephardic Jews. On 20 December 1924, a Royal Decree was promulgated which granted full citizenship to "individuals of Spanish origin who had enjoyed the protection of Spain's diplomatic agents as if they were Spanish citizens and were under the false impression that they already were Spanish citizens". Applications to obtain full civil and political rights had to be filled before 31 December 1931.[91] The Spanish government's reluctance to repatriate the Sephardic Jews was explicit. To forestall a mass emigration of the Sephardim to Spain, the decree added that "when filling the application, the petitioner should assert that he will not settle in Spain and explain the circumstances that will prevent him from coming to Spain to get his naturalization papers".[92]

On 29 December 1924, a circular directed the Spanish delegations to give the maximum publicity to the decree. Many Sephardim, however, who were convinced that they were already Spaniards, missed the opportunity to obtain the full citizenship. In some Balkan countries, like Greece, protection by a foreign power was no longer accepted and the Sephardim, who previously had been Spanish *protégés*, were automatically considered Spanish subjects by the governments, while for the Spanish envoys they were foreigners. In fact, they were stateless. Others who lived in countries where nationalism raged, such as Turkey or Greece, feared that by demonstrating their attachment to a foreign power, they might provoke some animosity.[93] Finally, many Sephardic Jews did not benefit from the decree because the Spanish government required many documents that they did not always possess and because the procedure was quite arduous.[94] This negligence was to have dramatic consequences during World War II.

In 1925 the diplomat José Antonio de Sangróniz, who was in charge of the ORCE, published *La expansion cultural de España* (Spain's cultural expansion), a blueprint for the institution. He devoted a chapter on the Sephardic Jews, in which he claimed that the Sephardim formed a "true aristocracy among the Jews" and that they considered Spain to be the "venerable Holy Land of their elders". Even if his interest in the Sephardic Jews lay in the cultural arena, he nonetheless pointed out their "extraordinary commercial influence".[95] Wary of the influence of other European countries on the

Sephardic Jews, Sangróniz declared that through the *Alliance Israélite Universelle* and the Zionist Association, France and England "had established a protectorate over the Jewish communities of the world".[96] He noted that since the end of the World War I, Italy had also been striving to extend its influence on the Sephardim and had inaugurated a school in Salonica as a first step towards achieving that goal.[97] Sangróniz believed that Spain had to follow suit and open a primary school in Salonica where there existed a Sephardic community of 80,000.[98]

In 1929, the ORCE sent the famous litterateur Ernesto Giménez Caballero to Yugoslavia, Bulgaria, Greece, Turkey and Romania to report on the most effective means to promote Spain's cultural expansion in these countries. The ORCE's choice of emissary might seem incongruous given that Giménez Caballero was set to become the ideologue of the Spanish fascist programme. But at the time of his trip to the Balkans, the *Gécé*, as he was called, was an ardent philosephardite. He had become interested in the Sephardic Jews as a young conscript in Morocco in 1921. While visiting the city of Xauen he recorded the folk tales known by an old Jewish lady, which he forwarded to the linguists Menéndez Pidal and Américo Castro in Madrid.[99] In *Notas marruecas de un soldado* he praised the Moroccan Jews' "adaptability" and "intellectual curiosity", noting that even middle-class girls spoke French. He contrasted the cosmopolitanism of the Jews to the parochialism of the Spaniards living in Morocco. "With these Jews," he wrote, "one can have worldly discussions, which is impossible with the Spanish settlers."[100]

In 1927 Giménez Caballero founded *La Gaceta Literaria* (The Literary Journal) in collaboration with Guillermo de Torre. Considered the main organ of Vanguardism, the journal's contributors included illustrious figures such as the poet Federico García Lorca, the writer Pió Baroja, the historian Américo Castro and the painter Salvador Dalí.[101] In addition to reporting on new trends in the arts, the *Gaceta* aimed to "pass through that historical corner occupied by the Sephardic Jews".[102] Américo Castro set the tone in the essay "*Judíos*" (Jews), published in the first issue, in which he lamented the "brutal extradition" of the Jews from Spain during the Inquisition. In later issues, the *Gaceta* devoted a special section to the Sephardic Jews featuring poems and articles by Sephardic writers.

The review supported Pulido's philosephardic campaign, which Giménez Caballero viewed as "admirable and romantic". In the issue of 1 October 1929 Rodolfo Gil Benumeya wrote a piece, which echoed Pulido's theory on the "racial fusion" between Sephardic Jews and Spaniards. He noted how this racial mixture had made the Sephardic Jews superior to their brethren:

*Spain is the only country where the Jews { . . . } have mixed with the indige-
nous population. Only in Spain did the Jews abandon their race, their language
their religion { . . . }. The Jew and the Spaniard fused together, the Spaniard
adopted the Jewish mentality and the Jew acquired in Spain what he was lack-
ing: aristocracy, gesture and pomp. The Sephardic Jew stands out from the other
Jews because of his appearance { . . . }. Compared to the other Jews, the
Sephardim represent an aristocracy. They are first-class Jews, more ancient and
more pure.*[103]

While the *Gaceta* courted Sephardic Jews, offensive comments about the
Jews from Eastern Europe, the Ashkenazim, were not rare even from the
pen of some of the review's Sephardic collaborators. Sam Levy, for instance,
who was a Paris-based collaborator, wrote that the Ashkenazim were not
"true" Jews, but descendants from the Khazars who not only carried
"Semitic blood" but "Slavic and Tartar blood".[104]

Giménez Caballero's trip to the Sephardic communities of the Balkans
was announced in the 1 September 1929 issue of the *Gaceta*. He declared in
an interview that the aim of his trip was to prepare a proposal on the means
to expand Spain's cultural ties with the Sephardic Jews.[105] It was in Salonica
that the *Gécé* realized the extent of France's influence on the Sephardim. In
his report to the ORCE, he wrote that "all the Sephardim but especially
those of Salonica speak French and they do it with the pride of having been
saved by a superior culture".[106] For Giménez Caballero, the French had
established their cultural predominance through the work of the *Alliance
Israélite* and other French schools and through the subvention of French-
speaking papers. He suggested that Spain emulate the work of its archrival
by setting up Spanish institutes throughout the regions, subsidizing
lecturers in Spanish and Spanish-speaking periodicals, and setting up a
Spanish school in Salonica. He also recommended that Spain establish a
shipping line, which would link it to Greece and Turkey.

Concern about France's ascendancy over the Sephardim incited Giménez
Caballero to go to Paris in 1930 to inquire into the subject. Upon his return
he wrote that "the Sephardic forces are at this moment in time under the
control of France" and that France's "pro-Sephardite campaign was another
aspect of its colonialism in the Mediterranean and Morocco". The *Gécé*
suggested that to counteract France's influence and gain the sympathy of
the Sephardim, Spain had to repeal the 1492 decree of banishment, facilitate the naturalization of the Spanish-speaking Jews and allow a select
minority to immigrate to Spain. Finally the Spanish government had to
organize a Sephardic congress and launch a propaganda campaign in Paris.
As a result of Giménez Caballero's trip, five universities of the Balkans set

up chairs of Spanish language, a ship line between Spain and Yugoslavia was established, and in 1931 the exhibition of Spanish books took place in Bucharest and Salonica.[107]

According to Herbert Rutledge Southworth, Giménez Caballero never really cared for the Sephardim. His main preoccupation was Spain's imperial expansion and in the years of Primo de Rivera's dictatorship that meant backing philosephardism.[108] An essay published in the *Gaceta* in July 1931 under the pen of the Conde de Foxá seems to corroborate Southworth's view. It recounted an imaginary encounter between Giménez Caballero and the spirits of Isabella and Ferdinand, the Catholic Kings who had expelled the Jews from Spain. When the monarchs alleged that that he was undoing one of their achievements – the expulsion of the Jews from Spain – Giménez Caballero retorted that in fact he was completing the *Reconquista*, the fifteenth century reconquest of Spain from the Moors, because the Sephardic Jews were Spain's "last unrecovered province".[109]

Giménez Caballero was not the only one who had specific ambitions for the Sephardim. In March 1930, upon his return from an official trip to the Balkans, the oddly-titled Spanish commercial agent to Europe, José María Doussinague, wrote an official report on the Sephardim, entitled "Economic Sefardism". Doussinague's aim was to "take the Sephardic problem away from the nebulous zone of judicial, philological and sentimental observations [...] and to consider it in concrete and precise terms". "Outside of the strictly commercial field," he wrote, "Sefardism was of no interest for Spain." [110]

Between Dr. Pulido's trip in the Balkans and that of Doussinague, the cultural life and the socio-economic status of the Sephardim had hardly changed. Spanish-speaking Jews continued to exert much influence on the commercial and political life of their countries. They remained under the aegis of France and Italy, which had protected them in difficult times and had established schools throughout the region. They spoke Spanish only as a vernacular. They could not write or read it since they did not know Spanish grammatical rules and the Ladino press used Hebrew script rather than Latin script. Contrary to Pulido, Doussinague did not think that the Sephardim were "particularly loyal to Spain" or that they felt "linked to it by moral ties". Projecting his own opportunism onto the Sephardim, he claimed that the latter felt closest to the nations that "offered them the best business opportunities".[111]

He believed, however, that the Sephardim "constituted an arm for [Spain's] commercial penetration in the region"[112] and that they could help Spain resolve its main problem in the Balkans: the absence of Spanish banks in the area. Spain's exports in the region were limited because the Spanish government could not provide credit to those who bought its products, a problem that was all the more acute because the Balkans were hit by inflation and there was a lack of liquid assets in the region. France and Italy, on the other hand, had several banks in the region such as the *Banque Franco-Belge et Balcanique*, the *Banque de Salonique* and the *Banca Commerciale*, which had many Jewish employees.

Doussinague's plan was to set up Spanish Chambers of Commerce, which would act as substitute for the banks. They would be composed of Sephardim because of the latter's commercial knowledge, extensive network of connections and the fact that many of them worked in the banks of the region, where they could get some data and information on the commerce of the Balkans. Doussinague was convinced that the Sephardim would not refuse to serve Spain's interests because they realized that Spain could retaliate by denying them its protection on which they depended.

Doussinague made a number of recommendations to the Spanish government. First of all, the "Sephardic problem", which was vital to Spain's trade in the Near and Middle East, should be under the authority of the Department of Exterior Trade in the Ministry of Economy. Second, Spain had to speed up the naturalizations, with the minimum of formalities, of all the elements whose "position, commercial credit or financial power" were considered "useful to Spain's commercial expansion". All Spanish delegations had to follow the example of the Consulate in Istanbul, which had succeeded in gathering a group of three hundred Sephardic families, "selected among the richest, the most respected, the most cultivated, so that those who are acquiring our nationality are distinguishable from those who have the French or Italian one". Spain's consuls in Belgrade, Sofia and Bucharest had to devote their time to the naturalization of the Sephardim. They were to "attract the Sephardim" but, at the same time, they were to be careful not to treat them as Spaniards and to prevent them from settling in Spain where they would no longer be useful to Spain's commercial expansion. In addition, the Chambers of Commerce had to offer free Spanish classes to Jewish children and adults. Doussinague's final advice was that Spain should set up a bank in the region in the near future.

Despite his claim to be solely interested in the economic ramifications of philosephardism, Doussinague's report was saturated with Darwinist references, which revealed that some Spanish diplomats were also imbued with scientific racism. Doussinague discussed the "racial" differences between the Sephardim and the Ashkenazim, arguing that there had been a racial fusion between the former and the Spaniards. He argued that the "Sephardic race" stood as an intermediary between "the pure Israelite and the Castilian". "The pure Jew", who could be found in "the Jewry of

Warsaw" "would be out of place in any Spanish city" because he had "extremely harsh features" and "the physical and psychological profile that literature and satire had attributed to him on many occasions". In contrast, it would be difficult to distinguish the Sephardim from the Spaniards because they had mixed themselves with the Spanish population during their long stay in Spain and "had improved their race in a perceptible way". According to Doussinague, there were also some moral differences between the Sephardim and the Ashkenazim. He vilified the Jews of Eastern Europe by declaring that, "the classical miser, completely dominated by covetousness, exploiter of the Christian and without any scruple" was found in Poland.[113] The Sephardim, on the other hand, possessed virtues such as dignity and generosity, of which the other Jews were devoid.

Antisemitism

Parallel to the growing interest in the Sephardim, there survived in Spain a strong undercurrent of antisemitism. A large portion of the Spanish clergy and the Carlists, who wanted to replace the liberal monarchy of Alfonso XIII with a traditionalist Catholic monarchy, remained hostile to a rapprochement with the Jews whom they viewed as the murderers of Christ and the allies of Liberals and Freemasons. The Carlists and the clergy interpreted Spain's history since the eighteenth century as a deviation from an authentic tradition symbolized by the Catholic monarchs and they blamed liberal ideas, imported from France for the Disaster of 1898. Like antisemites throughout Europe, they equated the Jews with liberalism, Freemasonry, capitalism and socialism.

Traditionalist thinkers shared the philosephardites' concern about the "degeneration of the Spanish race" and were influenced equally by social Darwinism. While the philosephardites stressed Jewish contribution to Spanish history, conservative ideologues emphasized the Reconquest of Spain from the Moors and the establishment of the Inquisition in the formation of Spanish civilization. Ménendez y Pelayo, for instance, declared that the Inquisition was "inevitable" because "the danger of Jewish infection was great and very real".[114] He explained that the prosperity of the Jews had provoked the ire of the Catholics and that the Spanish Kings had had no choice but to promulgate the Edict of Expulsion to protect the Jews from popular wrath.[115]

The argument that Spain's decay was due to the racial mixing between the Jews and the Spaniards was further elaborated by César Peiró Menéndez. Using pathological language, he declared that "the ulcer that corrodes

Spain, the gangrene that rots it and the cancer that kills it is Jewish".[116] He asserted that descendants of the converted Jews, "the Jews by blood", suffered from "racial bastardisation" and were responsible for the degeneration of Spain.[117] Borrowing heavily from the contemporary scientific discourse on the Jews as a race, he listed the physiological characteristics that distinguished these New Christians from the other Spaniards; which included an oval face, a large forehead, ears that stick out, thick nostrils and a bad smell. They were the bearers of all kind of diseases, ranging from hysteria and neurasthenia to syphilis and leprosy.[118] Peiró Menéndez accused the New Christians, of having exploited Cuba and provoked the separatist revolt. The converted Jews, he declared, had ruined Cuba and were now ruining Spain.[119] "These invaders" he wrote, "rule us despotically, persecute us, impoverish us and vilely prevent any regenerative and redemptive action." The exclusion of the New Christians from politics and public administration was a prerequisite for the regeneration of Spain.

During the years of the Dreyfus Affair, the Catholic hostility towards the Jews took a new dimension as the works of French antisemites such as Edouard Drumont were propagated in Spain.[120] In their coverage of the Dreyfus Affair, Spanish antisemites echoed their French counterparts and accused the Jews of taking over France. The Carlist newspaper *El Siglo Futuro*, for instance, declared that France was "suffering from the Jewish cancer" and recommended conversion to Christian faith as an antidote and expulsion of the Jews from France as a protective measure.[121] Like their French counterparts, the Spanish antisemites blended traditional Christian anti-Judaism with economic antisemitism, accusing the Jews of being capitalist exploiters. In 1891, Peregín Casabó y Pagés produced a Spanish equivalent to Drumont's *La France Juive* (Jewish France), entitled *La España Judia* (Jewish Spain), in which he denounced the economic dominance of the Jews in modern Spain. He called for the re-establishment of the Inquisition to halt the Jewish conquest of Spain.[122] Drumont's influence also manifested itself in the frequent diatribes that Spanish antisemites directed against the Rothschilds. In a speech to the parliament on 19 August 1896, the Carlist ideologue, Juan Vázquez de Mella y Fanjul, denounced the Spanish government's attempt to finance the war against Cuba by getting a loan from the Rothschild Bank and mortgaging the mines of Almadén. He declared that the "Jewish bank" was "guilty of double dealing"; he accused it of financing the Cuban insurrection through the Morgan House in the United States, while trying to "take out the last remains of Spain's wealth".[123]

In Spain, like in France, the idea of a Jewish-Masonic conspiracy was gaining ground, particularly among the Carlists. In 1912, the Carlist writer

José Ignacio de Urbina founded the *Liga nacional antimasonica y antisemita para la protección de los intereses catolicos* (The antisemitic and antimasonic national League for the protection of Catholic interests). This organization, whose motto was "The money of the Catholics for the Catholics", called for the boycott of the economic activities of the Jews in Spain. Its mouthpiece *El Previsor* recommended that its readers did not acquire shares in any new company without having previously checked through the intermediary of the *Liga* that it was not a new business introduced by the Jews and Freemasons in Spain.[124]

Another firm believer in the Judeo-Masonic conspiracy theory was Dr Joaquín Girón y Arcas, Professor of Canonical Law at the University of Salamanca, who stood at the forefront of the campaign against Dr Pulido. In 1906 he published *La cuestión judáica en la España actual* (The Jewish question in present-day Spain) replete with quotations from both Drumont's *La France Juive* and Isidore Bertrand's *La franc-maçonnerie secte juive* (Freemasonry a Jewish sect). Like the French antisemites, Girón y Arcas identified the Jews with the Freemasons, claiming that "the ultimate work of the Jews is the Freemasonry". He designated the *Alliance Israélite Universelle* as the fruit of their cooperation, revealing that the AIU president Crémieux was the grand master of one of the branches of the Freemasonry, the Scottish rite.[125] He dismissed Pulido's proposition to grant a subvention to the AIU on the grounds that it would burden the Spanish treasury and would be a waste of money.

According to Girón y Arcas, Sephardic Jews did not have much sympathy for Spain and were much more interested in Zionism than in returning to Spain.[126] They spoke Ladino not out of affection for Spain but because they could use it as "a secret language", which the people among whom they lived did not understand. "If the Sephardic Jews came to Spain," he warned, "they would probably use Turkish, Hebrew, Arabic or any other language other than Spanish among themselves."[127] Girón y Arcas also prophesised that the reintegration of the Sephardim into national life would lead to the expropriation of houses and Churches as the Jews would try to recover the properties that their forefathers had left behind when they were expelled in 1492.[128]

Another opponent to the philosephardic campaign was the Carlist parliamentary leader and ideologue Juan Vázquez de Mella y Fanjul. In 1920, while Pulido campaigned for the Hispano-Jewish association, Vázquez de Mella wrote that the senator had "the fervour of a Jew, who had been left behind in the Peninsula but whose cause failed to win supporters".[129] One of Vázquez de Mella's arguments against the philosephardism was that a rapprochement with the Jews of Morocco would alienate the Muslim Moroccans. On the grounds that Muslims and Jews hated each other, he warned that "to ally oneself with the Jews, is to separate oneself from the Moors". Ironically, he shared the philosephardites' belief that the *Alliance Israélite Universelle* was the "instrument of foreign colonialism".[130]

The *Alliance* was also the target of a Franciscan Father known by the pseudonym Africano Fernández, who lived in Tetuán. In *España en África y el peligro judío* (Spain in Africa and the Jewish peril), published in 1918, Fernández called Pulido his "enemy" and expressed his staunch opposition to the repatriation of Jews to Spain.[131] He asserted that the expulsion of the Jews in 1492 was a "providential act", which "was absolutely necessary" because the Jews were guilty of proselytizing, of exploiting the Christians through usury, of betraying the nations which sheltered them and of committing "atrocious crimes". Using traditional Catholic arguments, Fernández accused the Jews of murdering Christian children and using their blood for the Passover ritual. To justify his allegations he gathered evidence from the past, including the 1840 Damascus blood libel.[132]

Fernández discredited philosephardism as the hobbyhorse of Freemasons whose ultimate goal was to destroy Catholicism. Hence, Sagasta, who had offered to repatriate Sephardic Jews to Spain, was "the great Master of the Orient Lodge in Spain". Pulido, Fernández asserted, was misled in his belief that the Sephardic Jews loved Spain. On the contrary, what the Jews felt towards that country was "rancour, hatred, and a repressed thirst for revenge".[133] The only tie they had to Spain was the Spanish language, which they tried to replace with French.

At the centre of Fernández's attacks was the *Alliance Israélite Universelle*. "In harmony with its origins," he asserted, "this Franco-Jewish institution is anti-Catholic and anti-Spanish."[134] He accused the schools of the AIU of neglecting Spanish history and geography and of "oppressing the consciousness" of its Catholic students and teachers by forcing them to attend school on Sundays and on Catholic holidays.[135] Echoing Girón y Arcas, he criticized the Spanish government's subvention to the AIU. "To support the *Alliance*," he declared, is "anti-patriotic and a heinous act of apostasy."[136]

Another victim of Fernández's indictments was Professor Yahuda. Fernández accused the newly appointed Chair of Hebrew Literature of being "a herald of Freemasonry and calculating Judaism" who "propagated Jewish dogmatism" and convinced his disciples of getting a circumcision.[137] The campaign by Fernández and the likes prompted Yahuda to resign in 1922. No other Jewish professor replaced him.[138]

World War I and the success of the Bolshevik revolution in Russia engendered new myths about the Jews, which found enthusiastic propagators in Spain. In Germany ultra-nationalists grew convinced that Jews had helped the Entente powers. Javier Bueno, who was the Berlin correspondent of the monarchist organ *ABC* between 1918 and 1919, reiterated the legend of the Jewish treachery against Germany. Under the pseudonym of "Antonio Azpeitua", Bueno wrote that the Jews had betrayed Germany by serving the interests of the Entente. Stressing the French influence on the Jew, Bueno wrote that the German Jews had set up cabarets in Berlin on the model of Parisian ones. "The Jews," he wrote "are admirers of the French; moral degeneration brings them closer to the French race."[139]

The triumph of the Bolshevik revolution, in which Jews seemed to predominate among the leaders, was seen as further evidence of Jewish global power. As the success of the Bolsheviks in Russia triggered off revolutions in Hungary and Germany, which were also led by Jews – Béla Kun in Hungary, Kurt Eisner, Gustav Landauer and Rosa Luxemburg in Germany – European antisemites became convinced that the Jews were dangerous revolutionaries, striving to take over the rest of the world.[140] The myth became transformed into the Jewish-Masonic-Bolshevik conspiracy theory, which cropped up in the writings of Spanish ultraconservative thinkers. Oblivious to their own contradictions, they portrayed the Jews as Bolshevik revolutionaries and capitalist exploiters. Hence in February 1920, Vázquez de Mella wrote in *El Pensamiento Español*:

> *The main driving force and leader of the universal revolution { . . . } is Judaism. Not only the socialist movement, from Karl Marx to Fernand Lasalle, but also Communist anarchism { . . . } is Jewish. And the Israelite capitalist movement in its most oppressive form is also Jewish.*[141]

Adding weight to the myth of a Jewish world conspiracy was the publication of the first Spanish edition of *The Protocols of the Elders of Zion* in 1927.[142] The source of the *Protocols* was a pamphlet written by a Frenchman Maurice Joly against Napoleon III in 1864, which was unrelated to the Jews. In the 1890s agents of the Russian secret police, the *Okhrana*, forged Joly's political essay into the *Protocols*. The pamphlet purported to be minutes of a congress in which members of a secret Jewish organization – the Learned Elders of Zion – plot to achieve world domination. To this end the Elders conspired to spread liberalism and socialism, to provoke a financial crisis and to deprive the Gentiles of all faith in God.[143]

In the wake of the Russian revolution, "White" Russian officers spread the *Protocols* throughout the world from Western Europe to Japan. The Spanish translation came from a French version, which had been edited by Father Ernest Jouin, an ecclesiastic who took credit for coining the term "Judeo-Masonic". In 1912 he founded the *Revue internationale des sociétés secrètes* (International review of secret societies), which had a decisive influence on the Carlists.[144] A second Spanish translation of the *Protocols* was published in Leipzig, Germany, in 1930. In Spain, like elsewhere, the book was set to become the bible of the antisemites, who took its central thesis to heart and used it in their struggle against progressive forces.

Paradoxically, the parallel developments of antisemitism and philosephardism were due to common factors: the spread of social Darwinism in Spain and the Disaster of 1898, which destroyed the remnants of the Spanish empire, prompted the realization that Spain was a secondary power and exacerbated Spanish rancour towards France. The philosephardites argued that reconciliation with the Sephardic Jews would help Spain regenerate. Envious of France's ascendancy over the Jews, which promoted French colonial expansion, they suggested that Spain emulate its rival by setting up language schools and chambers of commerce, and naturalize some of the Sephardim. The Carlists and the clergy were also aware of Spain's decay and wanted to strengthen their country. But they held the Jews responsible for Spain's degeneration. They considered that along with the French and the Freemasons, the converted Jews had provoked the demise of the empire. Now the Jews were plotting to take over Spain. For them, it was not France which was exploiting the Jews to promote its colonial expansion but the Jews who had made themselves the masters of France. In the 1930s the abolition of the monarchy in Spain, the establishment of the Second Republic, the declaration of religious freedom and the attacks against the privileges of the Church were to inflame this hostility against the Jews.

II
Anti-Republican Antisemitism
1931–1936

Historians have noted that the Second Spanish Republic, which was proclaimed on 14 April 1931, modelled itself on the French Third Republic (1870–1940).[1] Both regimes aimed to reform the army, separate Church and State and introduce some sort of social equality through labor legislation. In the process, they alienated the Catholic right and a number of military officers. Another similarity between the French Third Republic and the Spanish Second Republic, largely overlooked by scholars, is the extent to which the anti-Republican right in both countries adopted conspiracy theories.[2] Inspired by its French counterpart, the Spanish reactionary right disseminated pamphlets largely derived from the *Protocols of the Elders of Zion*, which described centuries-old plots and provided simplistic explanations for the complex set of events that took place in Spain in the early 1930s.

The Judeo-Masonic-Bolshevik conspiracy theory fulfilled a double function in the Second Republic: it enabled the various right-wing groups to focus their attention on a group of imaginary enemies and served as the unifying agent that held them together.[3] The heterogeneous Spanish radical right did need a binding agent. Its forces included Alfonsine monarchists, who strove for a restoration of Alfonso XIII, Carlists who followed an alternative pretender to the throne, the CEDA (*Confederación Española de Derechas Autónomas*), which favoured a Catholic corporatist state and the fascist Falange, which wanted the establishment of a modern state in which the privilege of wealth would be abolished. Their shared hatred of Republicans, socialists, Freemasons and Jews was more than sufficient to overcome the divisions of these different rightist groups.

While drawing heavily on French anti-Republican literature, the conspiracy theories that emerged during the Second Republic also built on and responded to Spain's own myths and issues. Moulded by the history of the *Reconquista*, the colonial rivalry with France and the war in Morocco, the radical right portrayed the Jew not only as the ally of the Freemason and the Bolshevik but also as the accomplice of the French and the Moor. Radical right-wing intellectuals upheld that the Jews, who had aided the Moors against Catholic Spain in the medieval period, had also financed the Moroccan nationalist leader Abd el-Krim during the Rif War (1919–1926). Also included in the catalogue of co-conspirators of the Jews were Catalan nationalists, whose project to establish a Catalan state within the Federal Spanish Republic was unacceptable to the Spanish radical right. The influx of a small number of German Jewish refugees into Barcelona in the early 1930s added weight to the belief that the Jews were scheming with Catalan nationalists to attack Spain's territorial integrity.

In the same vein international developments, particularly the persecution of Jews in Germany, were interpreted through the patchwork of Spain's national myths and conspiracy theories in vogue at the time. Hence, ultra-conservative intellectuals drew a parallel between Weimar Germany and medieval Spain, claiming that both were in the hands of Jews. According to this analysis, Hitler had had no choice but to emulate the Catholic Kings, Isabella and Ferdinand, and to expel the Jews. This portrayal of the Spanish monarchs as Hitler's precursors was not only part of the general antisemitic campaign but also answered the long-term worries of the Spanish right about Spain's backwardness.

Although it was built on chimerical beliefs, the Judeo-Masonic-Bolshevik conspiracy theory drew on and distorted Spain's political reality, namely the rapprochement between the Republic and the Jews.[4] The first section of this chapter examines how Jews throughout the world welcomed the establishment of the Republic and the limited overtures that the left-wing government made towards them between 1931 and 1933. This enthusiasm was seriously dampened by the economic crisis and the rise of right-wing antisemitism. The second section recounts how the radical right invoked the twin myths of the *Reconquista* and the Judeo-Masonic conspiracy to explain some of the key events of the Republic such as the uprising of the Asturian miners in October 1934. The last section investigates the reaction of the anti-Republican right to the persecution of Jews in Germany and its hostility towards the handful of refugees who had emigrated to Spain.

The Second Republic

Spanish antisemitism reared its head during the campaign for the municipal elections of April 1931, in which monarchist candidates opposed those of the Republican-Socialist alliance. Under the leadership of Indalecio Prieto, the Spanish Socialists had come to accept that reforms would be achieved only through the victory of a broad democratic front. They had joined "the Pact of San Sebastián", a coalition of democratic forces forged in the Basque resort in August 1930, whose main aim was to establish a republic and to establish a broad system of regional autonomy for Catalonia. During the electoral campaign, monarchists attacked the newly formed alliance and warned that a Republic would inevitably lead to social revolution. They predicted that in the new regime "Bolshevik Jews will dominate our beloved Spain, spreading terror and misery, corrupting and ultimately destroying our traditional home life".[5]

The monarchists were dealt a severe blow in the elections, winning 42.2 percent of all seats overall and only 27 percent of the seats in provincial capitals.[6] As a result of the defeat, King Alfonso XIII left the country. The provisional government, which came into office on 14 April, represented a broad alliance. Its members ranged from the Prime Minister, the former monarchist Niceto Alcalá Zamora, via liberal Republicans such as the Minister of War, Manuel Azaña, to the Socialist Minister of Finance, Indalecio Prieto and the Minister of Labor, Francisco Largo Caballero. The coalition was divided over which issues should be given priority: the Republicans were concerned with institutional reform such as the separation of Church and state, and the streamlining of the army, the Socialists were more committed to agrarian reform and protective labour legislation. Nevertheless, the coalition was united in desiring rapprochement with the Jews. Back in 1916, the future Minister of War Manuel Azaña, the Minister of the Interior, Miguel Maura, and the Foreign Minister, Alejandro Lerroux, had lent their names to a letter to the French government, pleading that Sephardic expatriates from Turkey living in France be spared the indignities imposed on citizens of enemy nations.

Sensing that the new regime would be well disposed towards them, Jewish communities around the world welcomed the establishment of the Republic. Among the first congratulatory telegrams received by the Provisional Government, was one from the largely Sephardic community of Bayonne, whose Chief Rabbi wished "long life and prosperity" to the new Republic.[7] In late April, the Republican newspaper *La Libertad* reciprocated the gesture by encouraging the Provisional Government to revoke the Edict of Expulsion of 1492.[8]

The government was quick to respond to the appeal. On 29 April 1931 it issued a decree, which granted special concessions to the citizens of Latin America, Portugal and the Spanish protectorate of Morocco. The time of residence on Spanish territory for those who wished to be naturalized was reduced from ten to two years. The order was set to facilitate the naturalization of the Jews living in Spanish Morocco.[9] Conciliatory words accompanied the gesture. In May 1931, Maura made a speech in Bilbao condemning the religious intolerance towards the *Marranos* that had hitherto existed in Spain. He gave his assurance that these "secret Jews" would no longer be molested. That same month, the Minister of Finance, Indalecio Prieto, informed Ignacio Bauer, the President of the Jewish community of Madrid, that the government would take steps to facilitate the naturalization of Spanish-speaking Jews.[10] In an interview with the *Jewish Telegraphic Agency*, Bauer noted that for the first time since 1492 a synagogue had been consecrated in Madrid. The government also granted the community a plot of land to establish a Jewish cemetery.[11]

Two interrelated issues emerged almost immediately: the rescinding of the Edict of Expulsion and the repatriation of Sephardic Jews to Spain. In late May 1931, the Foreign Minister, Alejandro Lerroux, told a representative of the *Jewish Telegraphic Agency* that there was in Spain a feeling of sympathy towards all Spanish-speaking people, and above all towards the Sephardic Jews who had retained the Spanish language for centuries. Lerroux declared that the Spanish government was considering the question of naturalization of the Sephardic Jews of Morocco and that the Edict of Expulsion issued by the Catholic Kings in 1492 was no longer valid.[12] In July, the Prime Minister, Niceto Alcalá Zamora, received Paul Goodman, the Secretary of the Spanish and Portuguese congregation in Great Britain, and expressed to him his pleasure at the warm sentiments of Sephardic Jewry towards Spain.[13]

The philosemitic stance of Republican Spain reverberated throughout the Jewish world. In June 1931, Jewish newspapers buzzed with the news that Spain had just witnessed the first public celebration of a Jewish marriage since the Expulsion.[14] Menahem Coriat, a Jewish rabbi from Ceuta, had traveled to Spain specially to perform the wedding. As rumours abounded that the Spanish government was preparing a decree for the purpose of abolishing the Edict of 1492, Coriat placed himself at the head of a movement to obtain the abrogation of the Edict.[15] Similarly, the Chief Sephardic rabbi of Romania, Sabatay Djaen, wrote a Letter to Lerroux exhorting the Republican government to rescind the 1492 promulgation.[16] The Spanish representative in Cairo urged the government to make an official announcement recalling that the *Cortes* of Cadiz had abolished the decree in 1812.[17] Finally, in July 1932, the Minister of Education and Fine Arts, Fernando de los Ríos declared that a new enactment was unnecessary because the laws of the new Constitution nullified the Decree of Expulsion.[18]

A number of papers also announced that the provisional government had called for the resettlement of all Sephardim to Spain. In June 1931, *American*

Hebrew reported that the Prime Minister Alcalá Zamora had declared that all republican political parties accepted the reintegration of the Sephardic Jews into the Spanish nation and that Spanish consuls would receive instructions to facilitate their reintegration into Spain.[19] The Carlist organ *El Siglo Futuro* began an immediate campaign against the return of the Sephardim. Grossly exaggerating the figure, it claimed that two million Sephardim were hoping to come to Spain.[20] *El Siglo Futuro* was adamant in opposing their immigration on the grounds that it would introduce in Spain "the racial problem" that other nations were experiencing and that it would cause "severe disturbances", which Spain had until then been spared, thanks to the Decree of Expulsion.[21]

Meanwhile the government denied that it had invited the Sephardic Jews to return to Spain. In June, the mouthpiece of the Sephardic community of Smyrna, *Le Levant*, claimed that the Spanish government had decided to open its doors to the Jews who had been expelled in the past. The article prompted the Spanish consul, Federico Gabaldón Navarro, to write a letter to the editor, in which he declared that the Spanish government had adopted no measure to facilitate the immigration of the Sephardim, whose entrance and stay in Spain were subject to the same conditions as those of other foreigners. "Statements about a presumed invitation from the Spanish government to the Jews of the Near and Middle East to return to Spain", Gabaldón concluded "have no foundation."[22] Gabaldón Navarro's statement did not defer from Spain's official position. In August 1931, the government wrote to its ambassador in Washington that it had not invited Jewish immigration to Spain and that Jews could enter the Spanish territory according to the entry conditions applicable to foreign nationals.[23]

This stance was confirmed a year later by Manuel Azaña, Prime Minister since October 1931, who told a correspondent of the *Jewish Telegraphic Agency*: "There can be no question of a repatriation of the Sephardic Jews to Spain, such as some romantically-minded Spaniards have dreamt of. The question has not come up even once at any meeting of the Cabinet."[24]

Among the obstacles that stood in the way of the repatriation of the Sephardic Jews was the backwardness of the Spanish economy. If the depression had been milder in Spain than in northern Europe and the United States, it was largely due to Spain's limited industrialization. Furthermore, in the 1930s, Spain, which was traditionally a country of emigrants, became saddled with an increase in immigration, due mostly to the repatriation of migrant workers from Latin America.[25] Their return to Spain had exacerbated levels of unemployment and many feared that an influx of Jews to Spain would further aggravate Spain's economic difficulties. In 1932, a

Jewish organization, whose purpose was to help immigrants, conducted an extensive study of Spain's economic and financial conditions. It came to the conclusion that there was no possibility for the establishment of a nuclei of Jewish immigrants in Spain; the majority of Jewish candidates for immigration to Spain were mechanics, employees and small merchants and one could find already a large number of people in such professions in Spain.[26]

Among those who opposed Jewish immigration to Spain was Ignacio Bauer, who told the *Jewish Telegraphic Agency* that given the severe economic crisis facing Spain, the government should not encourage the immigration of Jews.[27] Words of caution were also heard from Professor Yahuda, who had formerly occupied the Chair for Hebrew Literature and the History of the Jews in Spain in the Middle Ages at the University of Madrid.[28] Asked about his views on the reintegration of the Sephardim in Spain, he declared that the mass return to Spain of the Sephardic Jews "would be for the country a burden rather than a benefit".[29] What Spain needed, according to Yahuda, were Jewish capitalists of an enterprising nature. Yahuda failed to realize that in the early 1930s the Jews who had attained this standing still saw no need for abandoning their respective countries.[30]

Some Jewish observers also feared that the repatriation of Sephardim to Spain could provoke the ire of the increasingly nationalistic Balkan states, where most Sephardic Jews lived. The Sephardic paper *La Vara,* published in New York, reported that in 1930 the exclusivist Turkish ruler, Mustafa Kemal, had accused his Jewish subjects, without any foundation, of having sent a message of fidelity to the King of Spain, Alfonso XIII. In the Kemalist period, nationalist policy forbade independent activity with a foreign association. "One can easily imagine," *La Vara* stated, "the provocative effects which a Jewish immigration to Spain could have, even if it be in small numbers. And what fate would await those Jews, who [. . .] would have to remain in Turkey."[31]

While hesitant to encourage the emigration of Sephardic Jews to Spain, the Republican-Socialist government made several goodwill gestures towards the Jews. A number of these conciliatory moves came from Fernando de los Ríos. Born in Andalusia – where Christian, Jewish and Muslim cultures had long coexisted – Fernando de los Ríos served as Professor of Law at the University of Granada and as a Socialist Deputy, before being appointed Minister of Justice in the first cabinet of the Second Republic. In the autumn of 1931, he seized the opportunity provided by a debate in the Constituent *Cortes* on the vexed question of the separation of Church and state to express his friendly sentiments towards the Jews. He declared:

The history of Spain shows a tendency towards decline since the year 1492, when Spain expelled the Jews, to whom I wish now, at the first opportunity while the Chamber is debating the question of religion, to pay a tribute of respect, and to express our esteem and our gratitude.[32]

The new Constitution, which was approved on 9 December, embodied the Republic's goodwill towards the Jews. Two of its articles affected the Jews directly by granting them rights equal to the Catholics. Article 3 stated that "the Spanish state has no official religion" and Article 27 declared that freedom of conscience and the right to worship and practice freely any religion were guaranteed on Spanish territory, provided public morals were safeguarded.[33] Furthermore, Article 23 promised a special law which would lay down procedures that would ease the acquisition of Spanish citizenship to persons of Spanish origin living abroad. Although that law was never promulgated, this promise hinted that all the Sephardim and not just the former *protégés* of the Spanish delegations could benefit from the 1924 Nationality Decree.[34]

A trip to Spanish Morocco in December 1931 presented de los Ríos with another opportunity to express his goodwill towards the Jews. "Israelites", he told a gathering at the Jewish Casino of Tetuán, "I have the pleasure of feeling at home with you".[35] He spoke of the grave injury done to the Jews by the Edict of Expulsion of 1492 and of the joy he felt that the new Republic had wiped out this "ignominy". "Israelites of Tetuán," he concluded, "don't think of the past. Think of the present, of enlightened Spain to whose development Jewish and Arabic cultures have contributed so much."[36] Shortly after his visit, de los Ríos decided to comply with the request of the Jewish leaders in Spanish Morocco and to invite teachers from Palestine to teach Hebrew in the Jewish schools of the protectorate.[37]

These friendly words made Fernando de los Ríos a prime target of anti-semitic attacks. Along with Maura and Alcalá Zamora, he was accused of being Jewish.[38] He was called a "heretic" after declaring that he felt at home with the Jews of Tetuán in December 1931.[39] In December 1932, the Spanish right attacked his proposal, as Minister of Education, to grant a subsidy of 57,000 pesetas to the *Alliance Israélite Universelle* and the rabbinical schools of Tangier. The subsidizing of Jewish schools, at a time when the government was building a secular system of state education and trying to eliminate Catholic schools in the long run, was particularly unpalatable to the Spanish conservatives. *El Debate*, the organ of the umbrella party of the Catholic right, the CEDA, campaigned against the proposal on the grounds that by subsidizing Spanish teachers in Jewish schools the government was "putting the Jews before the Spaniards".[40]

To the Carlist deputy from Burgos, Ricardo Gómez Rojí, who had expressed his outrage at the government's proposal in the *Cortes*, Fernando de los Ríos retorted that the subsidy should be approved for political reasons. He asserted that Spain remained anxious to increase its political influence in Tangier and that more than any other Spanish institution the Jewish schools perpetuated Spanish traditions in Tangier.[41]

In February 1932 de los Ríos announced that a cultural and commercial delegation would be sent to the colonies of Sephardic Jews in the Orient and the Mediterranean countries. Heading the mission was the writer Agustín de Foxá, formerly a contributor of the philosephardic *Gaceta Literaria*. Upon his return to Spain, Foxá wrote a report on the Sephardic communities, which echoed the one Giménez Caballero had drafted a few years earlier.[42] Like the Gécé, Foxá feared that because they were educated in either the schools of the *Alliance Israélite Universelle* or in Italian schools, the Sephardic children of the Balkans would eventually stop speaking Spanish. "Hence", he wrote, "the [Spanish] language, which has remained miraculously untouched for four hundred years, is now beginning to disappear and be forgotten."[43] He urged the government to found a network of schools and kindergartens in the Balkans, modelled on the *Alliance Israélite Universelle*, and he recommended that the Jews who held Spanish passports be forced to send their children to these Spanish schools. In the commercial realm, Foxá suggested that Spain set up chambers of commerce which would put Spanish exporters in touch with Sephardic merchants and which would organize trade shows of Spanish products. He also reiterated Giménez Caballero's request that a shipping line be established to link Spanish ports to the Black Sea.

In his report, Foxá also noted the growth of Zionist activity in the Balkans, especially among Sephardic intellectuals. The organization of the first Zionist Congress in Basel in 1897 and the weakening of the Ottoman Empire encouraged the outburst of Jewish nationalism in the region. Zionism was particularly powerful in Bulgaria, where Jewish national consciousness was inspired by the success of Bulgarian nationalism against the Ottomans. Foxá noted with much interest the antagonism between Zionist leaders and supporters of the *Alliance Israélite Universelle*, known as the "Alliancists". Indeed both groups competed to secure local predominance and Zionists accused the *Alliance* of sacrificing Jewish interests in favor of those of France.[44]

Ironically, many Zionist leaders were *Alliance* graduates and hence knew intrinsically the positions they were striving to undermine. Eventually the Zionists succeeded in winning over the Jewish intellectual elites of the Balkans. In Bulgaria, the schools of the *Alliance* were ousted and the Grand

Rabbi, a known Alliancist, was expelled from Sofia.[45] Drawing a lesson from the feud, Foxá wrote: "It is necessary to reach an agreement with the leaders of the Zionist movement, if we do not want to suffer the same blow as the *Alliance*."[46] He wanted Spain to convey the message that philosephardism was a cultural and spiritual movement, which would "complete" Zionism.[47]

In fact, de los Ríos, Prieto and Maura had expressed their support for the Zionist Movement to the *Jewish Telegraphic Agency* as early as May 1931. In October 1932, Fernando de los Ríos received Chaim Weizmann, the leader of the Jewish Agency, who would later become Israel's first President.[48] The Republic also tolerated Zionist activities in the Spanish protectorate of Morocco and permitted the creation of a local federation.[49] In 1933, an American journalist estimated that the Zionist organization of Tetuán had 5,000 members.[50] Noteworthy among the Zionist militants was Augustine Anshel Perl, who was active in Spanish Morocco, Algeciras and Tangier. He was inspector of education of the Spanish zone and published a Zionist paper subsidized by the Spanish authorities, *El renacimiento de Israel*.[51]

The Catholic right attacked the Republic's tolerance of Zionist activities in Spanish Morocco. The Catholic daily, *El Debate*, contrasted the leniency of the Republicans to the attitude of the French authorities, which cracked down on Zionism on the grounds that it constituted a threat to French influence in Morocco. *El Debate* had three objections to Zionist propaganda in Spanish Morocco. First, it was not beneficial to Spanish interests; second it was hindering a possible Sephardic policy; last but not least it provoked the ire of the Muslims of the zone. "Zionist propaganda in a Muslim country," wrote the journalist Santos Fernández, "will inflame Arab nationalism. The main target of pan-Islamic attacks is the Zionist enterprise." "In Spanish Morocco", he stated "there used to be neither a nationalist nor a Zionist problem. Now both exist."[52]

The Socialist-Republican government also adopted a more cooperative attitude towards the *Alliance Israélite Universelle* in Spanish Morocco. The *Alliance*, which under the monarchy had been perceived as the primary tool of the expansion of French influence in Morocco and had sometimes elicited hostility, now received expressions of friendship from Spanish officials. The fact that the new Inspector General of Education for the protectorate, Señor Alvero, was a graduate from the AIU school of Tangier might have contributed to that change. More importantly, however, the reduction of the education budget meant that Spanish officials had to forgo their plans to build Hispano-Jewish schools and cooperate with the *Alliance* instead. Moise Levy, the director of the AIU in Tetuán noted the Spaniards' change of heart. In July 1932 he wrote to the AIU president in Paris that the

Spanish authorities were now treating the personnel of the *Alliance* as their "true collaborators".[53]

The goodwill of the Republic towards the Jews of Morocco reached its apogee during the trip of President Alcalá Zamora to the protectorate in November 1933. Accompanied by the High-Comissioner, Alcalá Zamora visited a synagogue in Tetuán, where he was acclaimed. In his welcome speech, the Chief Rabbi of Tetuán, Judah Halfon, asserted the loyalty of the Moroccan Jews to Spain:

> *This is a moment of intense joy and emotion for our Jewish community. We view your visit as an expression of friendship and we feel highly honored { . . . }. Our community, which feels a deep filial love for Spain, is particularly happy to welcome the President of Spain as the first foreign head of state to visit a Jewish place of worship in this country. Our tie to Spain is indestructible.*[54]

Alluding to the coexistence of Jews, Muslims and Christians in the protectorate, Alcalá Zamora replied that he was delighted to note "that the perfect union of the three races ensured the good fortune of Spanish Morocco".[55]

By the time of Alcalá Zamora's trip to Morocco, the Socialist-Republican government was faced with a new problem: the possible immigration of German Jews into Spain. In April 1933, three months after he became chancellor of Germany, Hitler implemented the first stage of his long-standing obsession: the elimination of Jews from Germany's political, economic, intellectual and social life. The Nazi party organized a four-day boycott against Jewish businesses, Jewish doctors and Jewish lawyers. On 7 April, the Nazis passed the Law for the Reconstruction of the Professional Civil Service, which excluded Jews from public services. Quotas were imposed on the number of Jewish students in universities and public schools.[56]

These antisemitic legislative measures fostered the first wave of Jewish emigration. About fifty thousand Jews left Germany between the beginning of 1933 and the spring of 1934. While France emerged as the principal haven, followed by Holland and Czechoslovakia, a small number of refugees considered immigrating to Spain. In April 1933 the Spanish Consul General in Copenhagen, Ginés Vidal, reported that Jews from Germany had expressed the wish to move to Spain. Vidal noted that the existing Spanish laws and regulations did not allow the government to put a limit on the number of German subjects who could immigrate to Spain. He asserted alarmingly that these prospective immigrants would compete in the job market with the Spaniards, which would exacerbate Spanish unemployment. Vidal wrote in conclusion, "I do not know to what extent the emigration of these elements, who are so difficult to integrate, is worth our while".[57]

As a result of Vidal's dispatch the government decided to impose visa requirements on German Jews who wished to come to Spain. Prospective immigrants also had to report their income.[58] In his reply to Ginés Vidal, the sub-secretary to the Foreign Ministry, Justo Gómez Ocerín, expressed his hope that the new measure "would suffice to limit the possible flux of undesirable foreigners and particularly of people who could contribute to the unemployment".[59] A few years later Ignacio Bauer noted that Spain had been among the first countries to impose visa requirements on German Jews.[60]

The distinguished diplomat and intellectual, Salvador de Madariaga, who was at once Spain's representative in the Council of the League of Nations and Ambassador to France, also opposed the immigration *en masse* of German Jews. In late April 1933 when the German-Jewish journalist Georg Benhard inquired about possible immigration of Jews to Spain, Madariaga responded that although there was no antisemitic prejudice in Spain, there was some economic protectionism, which was not specifically directed against the Jews but against all foreigners. He noted that the coming of a large number of Jews could fuel antisemitism especially among the monarchists. Madariaga came to the conclusion that "it would be advisable to avoid at all cost any official or public action, which would direct a substantial part of the German-Jewish emigration towards Spain".[61]

Although it was unwilling to see Spain receive a large contingent of refugees, the Spanish government did not hesitate to voice its sympathy for the persecuted Jews. In May 1933, the Minister of Foreign Affairs, Luis de Zulueta, supported the complaints registered by the Jews of Upper Silesia against Germany in the League of Nations, arguing that the system for the protection of minorities should be applied integrally.[62] Despite his rebuff of Benhard, Madariaga, whose idealism had earned him the nickname of "the conscience of the League of Nations",[63] was equally moved by the plight of the German Jews. He expressed his solidarity with them in a debate in the League in the fall 1933, during which he acknowledged Spain's indebtedness to the "great Jewish race".[64]

In the summer of 1933 the Spanish committee to help the victims of Hitlerian fascism was set up. Presided by the Professor of Law and Socialist Deputy Luis Jiménez de Asúa, it included luminaries such as the former civil governor of Barcelona, Ángel Ossorio y Gallardo, the historian Américo Castro and the deputy leader of the Radical Party, Diego Martínez Barrio. But Spain's gestures remained limited, and in October 1933 Spain refused to appoint a representative to the League of Nations High Commission for Refugees. The Spanish government told the Secretary General of the League that Jewish refugees proceeding from Germany should settle in German-speaking countries or in countries close to Germany. Spain then asked to be excluded from the list of nations willing to receive the refugees on the ground that the country was going through a serious economic crisis.

There were, however, a number of emigrants that the Republic was eager to admit. Albert Einstein was one of them. His work was well known in Spain and his trip to Barcelona, Madrid and Zaragoza in the spring of 1923 had created a sensation.[65] In the spring of 1933, the Spanish consul in England, Rámon Pérez de Ayala, got in touch with Abraham Yahuda to negotiate the immigration of the famous physicist. Fernando de los Ríos, who was also involved in the project, announced Einstein's acceptance of a chair at Madrid University on 10 April 1933. The news caused immediate uproar among the clerical right. Alluding to the supposedly Jewish origins of de los Ríos, *El Debate* contrasted the Republic's offer to Einstein to its hostility towards the Catholic Church:

> *Socialism only bestows this kind of protection upon its coreligionists, particularly if they are Jewish. If Einstein were a Jesuit, he would not be able to come to Spain despite his scientific knowledge, his reputation and the prevailing climate of understanding and fraternity.*[66]

Einstein, who had initially accepted the offer, declined it, opting instead to stay in the United States.[67]

Between Catholic Antisemitism and Biological Racism

The deteriorating political situation in Spain might have played a part in Einstein's decision to refuse the offer. By the end of 1931, the more radical Socialists had become increasingly frustrated with the government's failure to secure social reforms and did not want to maintain the coalition with the Republicans. The situation was embittered in the South, where local officials colluded to prevent the implementation of the new labor legislation. Hence in the village of Castilblanco in the province of Badajoz in the southwest, a peaceful demonstration on December 31 degenerated after four Civil Guardsmen intervened to break up the crowd. They opened fire, killing one worker and wounding two others. The infuriated workers hacked the guards to death with stones and knives.[68] The episode of Castilblanco dealt a severe blow to the Republican-Socialist coalition, as the Socialists' enthusiasm for continued governmental participation showed signs of abating. In the

political debate that ensued the Socialist deputy for Badajoz, Margarita
Nelken, who was of German-Jewish origin, was subjected to vicious sexist
and antisemitic abuse for interpreting the events of Castilblanco in terms
of the long history of hunger and Civil Guard's brutality in the province.
The Director-General of the Civil Guard, José Sanjurjo, who blamed
Nelken for the episode, claimed that she was "not even a Spanish citizen",
an accusation that was to be repeated continually afterwards.[69]

Throughout 1931, the radical right was busy reorganizing itself.
Already in July 1931, those hostile to the Republic founded a new group,
Acción Española, whose ideas and doctrines would have considerable influence on the Franco regime.[70] *Acción Española* drew much of its inspiration
from the anti-Dreyfusard Charles Maurras, who led the *Action Française* and
strove for a return to the France of the *Ancien Régime*.[71] Financed by
members of the Basque financial and industrial elite, such as José-Félix de
Lequerica, who was later to become Spain's Ambassador to Vichy France,
the aim of *Acción Española* was to propagate integrist-monarchists ideas.[72]
The base of *Acción Española* was very broad. In addition to the Carlist and
to the Alfonsine monarchists – who laboured for the return of the exiled
King Alfonso XIII – the group included some army officers such as General
Luis Orgaz. The three leaders of Spanish fascism – José Antonio Primo de
Rivera, Ramiro Ledesma Ramos and Onésimo Redondo Ortega – were also
involved in the venture.[73] The future *Caudillo*, Francisco Franco
Bahamonde, was a subscriber of the review since its first issue in December
1931.[74] The doctrine of *Acción Española* reflected the heterogeneity of its
members, blending Carlist Traditionalism with the ideas of *Action Française*
and other foreign sources.[75]

The *Protocols of the Elders of Zion* were widely promoted by *Acción
Española*. In 1932 Pablo Montesinos y Espartero, Duque de la Victoria, a
cavalry officer and Germanophile, published a new edition of the *Protocols*.
Although he acknowledged that a number of articles had revealed that the
Protocols were a forgery, Montesinos nonetheless considered them to be
"prophetic". In the epilogue he concluded that while the World War I and
the Bolshevik Revolution were the first steps in the Jewish drive for world
domination, the proclamation of the Second Republic demonstrated that
Jews were now intent on obtaining dominion over Spain.[76] Between
February and July 1932, Onésimo Redondo Ortega, one of the founders of
Spain's first fascist political organization, the *Juntas de Ofensiva Nacional
Sindicalista* (JONS), serialized the *Protocols* in the weekly paper *La Libertad*,
which he had founded.[77] An indefatigable propagandist of the myth of the
Jewish world conspiracy, Redondo gave a lecture on the historical impor-
tance of the *Protocols* in Valladolid in March 1932. Blaming Spain's decay

on Jewish influence, Redondo asserted that Juan Álvarez y Mendizábal, the Liberal leader who had confiscated most of the landed property of the Church in 1835, was Jewish. He also asserted that in Spain, like in Russia, Jews were trying to dominate the country by taking over the control of the media, finance and political parties. According to Redondo, the ultimate aim of the Jewish plot was the destruction of the Christian civilization.[78]

In May 1932 the ultra-Catholic Marqués de la Eliseda reviewed the *Protocols* in the journal of *Acción Española*. The unmasking of the *Protocols* as a forgery by Lucien Wolf in 1920 did not make a difference to Eliseda, who argued that other historical texts, such as the *Letter of the Jews of Arles*, were confirmatory evidence that a Jewish conspiracy was at work.[79] According to Eliseda, not only were the *Protocols* helpful in understanding Jewish mentality they also provided arguments against "false democratic principles". The Jews had invented the concept of political freedom as a mean "to convert the masses into a disorganized and barbarous mob, capable of all crimes". This, he argued, was illustrated the "bloody episodes" of the French and Russian revolutions and by the murder of Civil Guards by landless peasants in the village of Castilblanco. In short, Eliseda suggested that because they had brought about the "liberal and democratic venom", the Jews were responsible for the exacerbation of class hatred in Southern Spain.[80]

The greatest propagator of the *Protocols* during the Second Republic was probably the Catalan priest Juan Tusquets. A *protégé* of the bishop of Barcelona Manuel Irurita, Tusquets belonged to a Jesuit secret society, linked to the International Anti-Masonic League.[81] His source of inspiration was the work of Monseigneur Ernest Jouin, the French prelate who had devoted his life to alerting Catholics to the Jewish-Masonic threat. Jouin had published a series entitled *Le péril Judéo-maçonnique* (The Judeo-Masonic peril) in which he compared the German, Russian and Polish versions of the *Protocols of the Elders of Zion*. His work had received papal blessing.[82]

In an effort to emulate Jouin, Tusquets had begun his own exhaustive series *La biblioteca de las sectas* (The library of the sects), whose principal targets were Jews and Freemasons. The first book of the series, *Orígenes de la revolución española* (Origins of the Spanish revolution), was published in 1932. It quoted Jouin abundantly. That book, according to José Luis Rodriguez Jimenez, had the distinction of being the first one that used the *Protocols* to account for the different episodes of Spanish history.[83]

According to Tusquets, Jewish machinations against Catholic Spain predated the forming of the Judeo-Masonic coalition. He disclosed that it was the treachery of the Jews that had brought about the Inquisition. He explained how during the fifteenth century *Reconquista*, the Jews had loaned money to both sides at "usurious rates of interest", always "helping the weaker side in order to prolong the war". He noted, however, "that in the decisive moments they [the Jews] favoured the victory of the Mahometans".[84] Tusquets praised the decision of the Catholic Kings Isabella and Ferdinand to promulgate the Edict of Expulsion. Using the pathological language so in vogue at the time, he wrote that after the *Reconquista*, Spain had "felt sufficiently strong to cast out the microbes that were poisoning it".[85] Tusquets believed that the Jews in Morocco remained disloyal. "Nowadays", he wrote "like in the fifteenth century they combat on the side of the Moors, they devote themselves to spying, and they corrupt the [Spanish] army". The solution, he advocated, was to expel them from Morocco.[86]

The allegation that there was an alliance between the Jews and the Moors was not unique to Tusquets. After Moroccan rebels, led by Abd el- Krim, crushed a large Spanish force in Anual in 1921, the colonial army adopted more brutal methods against the Muslim Moroccans, such as the use of chemical weapons. Accompanying this process of brutalization was the construction of the image of Muslim Moroccans as the enemy. Racist diatribes became prevalent in the press; the Moors were described as barbaric, deceitful and avaricious.[87] The Jews were naturally associated to them. The leader of the ultra-rightist *Partido Nacional Española* (PNE), Dr José María Albiñana, stated that the Jews of Morocco were partly responsible for the Disaster of Anual. In the mouthpiece of his party, *Legión*, he claimed that: "Jewish money had subsidized Abd el-Krim" and that "the Jews and Masons were responsible for the arms smuggling in Morocco".[88] Drawing on the tales of Jewish lust for human blood, Andrés Flores wrote in the Carlist daily *El Siglo Futuro* that during the Rif War, the Jews of Morocco were real "vampires who fed themselves the blood of Spain to amass money".[89]

In addition to financing the Muslims rebels in Morocco, the Jews were accused of inspiring and funding Spain's new enemy: the Socialist movement. According to Tuquets, while "the Jew Karl Marx" had founded the First International, "the German Jewish bankers Jacob Schiff and Marx Warburg bankrolled the Third International".[90] Similarly during the 1933 election campaign, one of the CEDA electoral manifestos described the Republican-Socialist coalition as "lunatics" who were "paid by" and "served the interests of the Jews".[91]

The radical right depicted the Jews as false revolutionaries whose ultimate aim was to increase their own power. In May 1934, José Antonio Primo de Rivera, son of the late dictator and founder of the fascist party the Falange, declared that Marx himself was a Jew, who was in the service of

Jewish international capital and considered that the workers "were only rabble".[92]

Nurtured with the works of French antisemites such as Drumont and Maurras, elements of the Spanish radical right specifically accused French Jews of financing the Spanish Republican-Socialist coalition. A promoter of this idea was Albiñana, who declared that the aim of "the Jews of Paris who had paid the revolution" was to provoke the dismemberment of country and the triumph of communism.[93] Similarly *El Siglo Futuro* attacked the leader of the French Socialist party, Léon Blum, "the grandson of Israel", for his alleged interference in Spanish politics. His ultimate aim, according to the Carlist daily, was to foment a revolution in Spain.[94]

The Catalan question was also interpreted through the Judeo-Masonic conspiracy theory. The Catalan nationalist movement, which had emerged in the middle of the nineteenth century, strove for regional autonomy rather than separation from Spain. The confederation of left Catalan groups *Esquerra Republicana de Catalunya* (Republican Left of Catalonia) had joined the Pact of San Sebastián. Shortly after the proclamation of the Republic, an autonomous executive power, the *Generalitat*, was established in Barcelona to prepare the terms of the promised Catalan autonomy statute and to oversee the region's education, finance, health and public works.[95] Catalan autonomy was received with hostility by the Spanish radical right. Albiñana called the autonomy statute an "absolute disgrace" and declared that it was "another episode of the Freemasons and Jews' merciless struggle against Spain". According to Albiñana from the end of the eighteenth century, Jews had tried to weaken Spain "not only by fomenting internal disorders but also by encouraging territorial fragmentation".[96]

While responding to national issues, such as Catalan separatism, the antisemitism of the Spanish radical right also drew on the Darwinist theories in vogue at the time. A number of right-wing intellectuals crossed the thin line that separated traditional Catholic antisemitism and biological racism even though it contradicted Church teachings on the oneness of humankind and imperiled the sacraments of baptism. Their use of racial terminology was ambiguous. While at times they used the term "race" to describe a nation, without any biological connotation, they increasingly used it to categorize the Jews, to emphasize their otherness and to tie them closer to the Moors. The fortnightly Jesuit magazine, *La Estrella del Mar*, for instance, announced that there were 14,600,000 Jews in the world and that the "Jewish soul" abhorred those of other races and wanted to dominate them.[97]

Ramiro de Maeztu, who was one of the most influential writers of the Generation of '98 and the editor of *Acción Española*, made a similar argument. In 1934 he published *Defensa de la Hispanidad* (Defense of the Spanish mission), in which he blended traditional Christian antisemitism with racial discrimination against the Jews. Among his claims was that that the Jews formed "the purest race in the world" and that their conversion to Catholicism could not be considered valid because "Jews come back to their religion as soon as they have the opportunity".[98]

According to Maeztu, it was in opposition to the fatalism of the Moors and the intolerance of the Jews that the Spaniards had built their missionary empire in the sixteenth century. "It is against the Jews who are the most exclusive people on earth", he wrote, "that our feeling of catholicity, of universality was formed."[99] Maeztu believed that Spain would recover this traditional sense of Catholic mission (*Hispanidad*), but that first a crusade against the forces of the Antichrist – the Jews, the Freemasons and the left – would have to take place.[100]

In terms identical to Maeztu, Giménez Caballero, the former philosephardic intellectual turned fascist propagandist, also accused the Jews of being "fundamentally racist" in their claim to a pretended superiority. He drew a parallel between the supposed intolerance of the Jews and that of the Germans and wrote that the Jews were the "Hitlerians of the Orient".[101]

The reference of the Jews as "oriental" was not unique to Giménez Caballero. In a description of Marx, Maeztu wrote: "He was a Jew, and oriental, and as such [. . .] an enemy of our civilization".[102] Spanish anti-semites, like their French *confrères*, frequently repeated that it was from the East that the wandering Jews came.[103] By emphasizing the Semitic origin of the Jews, they tied them closer to the Moors and implied that they could not integrate into European civilization. Like the Moors, the Jews were characterized as primitive, violent, irrational and debauched. Hence, the journalist Luis Astrana Marín wrote in *Informaciones* that the Jews were "vengeful", "distrustful", "fickle", and "ostentatious". He also asserted that Jews were "involved in all kind of dirty businesses: white slave trade, brothels, alcohol, cabarets, drugs, usury and war".[104] Conservative intellectuals argued that through their subversive devices the Jews had enslaved the Spanish working class. One consequence of this subjugation was that the Spanish workers themselves came to possess "orientalist attributes". The Spanish radical right began to see the working class as imbued with Jewish and Muslim fatalism, treachery and barbarism.

For Spanish antisemites, as for Spanish orientalists in general, the "Orient" was in fact in the South, Morocco more precisely. An article which the ultra-Catholic Onésimo Redondo, wrote in the fascist monthly *JONS* in May 1933, reflected this reading:

Historically, we are a friction zone between civilized element and African element, between Aryan element and Semitic element { . . . }. Faced with attacks from the South the many generations who built our fatherland took up arms and never put them down { . . . }. Isn't there a risk of a new domination of the African element? { . . . }. We ask this important question with dispassion and we will answer it right away by pointing out the danger of the new Africanisation: "Marxism". While Marxism symbolizes the Jewish – Semitic – conspiracy against Western civilization in the whole world, it is in Spain that it has the most direct affinities with the Semitic element, the African element.[105]

By asserting that Marxism was derived from Jewish or African stock, Redondo tried to tie Spain's archetypal "others", the Jew and the Moor to Spain's new enemy: the left. His argument was convoluted but his message could still be understood: a new *Reconquista* was needed to prevent Spain from falling to the hands of the modern foes.

The identification of the Jew as the Oriental other and its association with the Moors was reflected in the CEDA's propaganda during the *Cortes* election campaign of November 1933. One of the party's posters depicted the four sinister forces that were encroaching the country: a Bolshevik, a Separatist, a Freemason and a Jew. The Jew was identified by a tarboosh, a brimless cap, which is traditionally worn by Muslim men.[106]

Along with anti-Bolshevism, antisemitism was a recurring theme of the CEDA's electoral campaign. In a speech given on 15 October in the Monumental Cinema of Madrid, Gil Robles declared that Spain had to be "reconquested" and "purged" of "judaizing Freemasons."[107] The party's General Secretary declared in an interview: "Jewry as an international power is the principal enemy of the Catholic Church and thus of our party, whose programme is based on the principles of Catholicism. In this general sense Gil Robles is an antisemite".[108] Jewish communities around the world were concerned that the CEDA might become the largest single parliamentary group in the November 1933 election. *The Jewish Chronicle* declared that the party presented "a grave menace to Jewry", "not only in Spain but the world over".[109]

Profiting from the divisions of the left and middle-class fears about the anticlericalism of the Republic, the CEDA did emerge with the largest parliamentary delegation. The formation of a center-right government, and the CEDA's insistence on dismantling the newly enacted labor legislation, led to a radicalization of the Socialist leadership. The climax of social tension was reached in October 1934 when the entry of three CEDA ministers into the government provoked a general strike in Madrid, Barcelona and all Socialist strongholds.

The real drama of the uprising, however, took place in Asturias, where twenty to thirty thousand miners rebelled against the new right-wing government, setting up the first revolutionary commune in Western Europe since Paris in 1871.[110] The insurgence, which was brutally smashed by the Army of Africa, provided the clerical right with another excuse to express its xenophobia and antisemitism. The bishop of Oviedo wrote in a pastoral letter in November 1934: "The revolutionary and criminal strike has been organized by the Jews and Freemasons."[111]

Ironically, while the colonial troops included Moroccan volunteers, known as *Regulares*, the radical right-wing press portrayed the Asturian uprisers as aliens.[112] The transposition of the Moorish enemy, the Jewish enemy and the leftist enemy was flagrant when the Catholic daily *Informaciones* declared that the insurgents were "a pleiad of eunuchs and slaves in the service of international Judaism".[113]

Given the interest that some antisemitic intellectuals had in the concept of race, it was only natural that they would closely watch Adolf Hitler's rise to power and his onslaught against the Jews. The Führer drew much admiration from the Spanish radical right. César González Ruano established a parallel between Hitler and the Catholic Kings, Isabella and Ferdinand. He considered Hitler a "Natural King", a "Gothic King", a "new Siegfried" who "grasps the mysterious swastika cross with the same fervour that the Catholic Kings Isabella and Ferdinand grasped the Catholic cross, under which the Jews were expelled".[114] "Aren't Isabella and Ferdinand by any chance the precursors of Spanish fascism?" asked González Ruano, who reminded his readers that like the Spanish monarchs, Hitler strove to accomplish the national unity of Germany.

The argument echoed in the work of ultra-clerical intellectuals, such as Maeztu, another of Hitler's Spanish admirers, who had expressed his wish to see a similar movement in Spain under the leadership of Albiñana.[115] In an article entitled *Hitler, los judios e Isabella la Catolica* (Hitler, the Jews and Isabella the Catholic), Maeztu drew a comparison between the situation of Germany in the early 1930s and that of Spain in the fifteenth century. He asserted that while Isabella had had to defend Christianity against the Jews, Hitler had to defend "German nationalism" against them. According to Maeztu, the influence that the Jews exercised in Germany after the World War I was similar to the one they had possessed in medieval Spain under Enrique IV and Juan II. Like Isabella the Catholic, Hitler had "to protect himself from the Jews", who were "plotting with their coreligionists in other countries to facilitate an invasion of Germany".[116]

The Jews, it was felt, deserved to be persecuted because they had caused havoc in Germany as they had in Spain. In March 1933, Antonio Bermúdez de Cañete, the Berlin correspondent of *El Debate*, justified the outburst of German antisemitism by drawing a parallel between the Treaty of Versailles, which humiliated Germany, and the Pact of San Sebastián, which ushered in the Second Republic. He prophesized that Jews who had wanted "to destroy the Christian civilization" would "be defeated by it".[117]

In *Acción Española* the monarchist army officer, Jorge Vigón, later a minister of the Franco, regime portrayed the Nazis as the victims of the Jewish conspiracy. In March 1933, he lamented the Jewish press campaign against Germany, asserting that the antisemitic actions of the Nazis, which included the boycott of Jewish businesses, had not "shed much blood".[118] In May 1933 he declared the burning of books by the Nazis to be "just" and "well-deserved", denouncing the targeted Jewish authors as "undesirable".[119]

Wenceslao González Oliveros, who was later to become the president of the tribunal of the repression of Freemasonry and communism under Franco, praised German racism and justified it in the German context, although he acknowledged that its methods were not necessary applicable to the Hispanic world.[120] Similarly, Dr Francisco Murillo Palacios argued in *Acción Española* that the German race had declined because the "inferior" Jewish race had "infiltrated it slowly through crossbreed".[121] He defended Germany's policy of forced sterilization of "undesirable people" on the grounds that it would put an end to the "decline" of "German and Nordic races".[122]

Even those who had some reservations about the Führer's pure race concept and neo-paganism felt much sympathy for his struggle against "International Judaism". The Catalan Carlist René Llanias de Niubó, whose book *El Judaismo* was published in Tusquets series of *Las Sectas*, wrote:

> We do not pretend to defend Hitler. We hate his tough policies, his dangerous nationalism, his animosity towards Catholicism, and the attempt by some of his ministers to revive the mindless cult of some old Pagan Gods of Germany. With regards to his radical antisemitic campaign, however, he acts with reason.[123]

Germany sponsored this antisemitic campaign in Spain. The German Embassy in Madrid began distributing hate material shortly after Hitler's accession to power. It also provided financial assistance to a number of ultra-conservative journalists, including César González Ruano, and Vicente Gay, the author of *Qué es socialismo. Qué es el marxismo. Qué es el fascismo* (What is socialism. What is Marxism. What is fascism). The Nazis also subsidized *Informaciones*, whose editor Juan Pujol was a CEDA deputy for Madrid from 1933 to 1935 and for the Balearic Islands after the 1936 elections.[124]

Antisemitic propaganda emanating from Germany also reached the shores of Spanish Morocco, at the request of some local Spaniards who resented the Jewish economic activity in the zone. In June and November 1935, for instance, Juan Pérez Martín, a resident of Melilla, sent letters to the *Deutschlander Reichsender* and to the *Reichs-Rundfunk Gesellschaft*, asking for some hate material. He wrote that he wanted to campaign against the Jewish race, who "through their despicable and shameful methods" had "taken over the commerce and industry" of the Spanish protectorate.[125]

Uneasy Asylum

Meanwhile despite the government's reluctance, a number of German Jews managed to settle in Spain between 1933 and 1935. By March 1934 about 3,000 Jews had taken up residence in Barcelona, which was the main commercial and industrial centre in the country. The regional administration, the *Generalitat*, was well disposed towards them. Its president and the dominant political figure of Catalonia, Francesc Macià, had authorized the opening of a new synagogue in Barcelona at the beginning of 1933.[126] A new Jewish quarter grew near the Calle Muntaner, with some German restaurants and cafés.[127]

In April 1935, the liberal daily *El Sol* published an article on the life of the German Jewish refugees in Barcelona. The correspondent estimated that out of 56 people queuing in front of the movie theatre on a Saturday evening, 18 were German. He wrote that German could be heard everywhere "in the theatre, in the cinema, in bullfights, at the soccer game, in restaurants [. . .] in the underground, in the train" and pondered whether a "Jewish invasion" was taking place.[128]

The great majority of refugees were affected by the economic crisis and by legal restrictions concerning the work of foreigners. Back in September 1932, the Labor Minister Francisco Largo Caballero issued a decree, which required all alien workers, including those who were already established in Spain, to obtain a work permit. A clause banned employers from discharging Spanish workers to replace them with foreign workers.[129] More than half of the Jews were penniless and in need of relief. *El Sol* noted that they added to "the number of unemployed" and that those who did not find any work begged in the streets, sold newspapers or drifted around.[130]

Welfare to the émigrés was provided by the foremost international Jewish emigration organization, HICEM,[131] which opened a branch office named "Ezrah" (relief) in Barcelona. Even the most affluent members of the Jewish community, such as Ignacio Bauer, the distinguished President of the Jewish community of Madrid were affected by the deepening of the economic crisis. The collapse of Bauer's banking firm, Bauer & Co, was caused by the bankruptcy of his gigantic publishing house the CIAP whose publications had included the mouthpiece of philosephardism, *La Revista de la Raza*, and Giménez Caballero's *La Gaceta Literaria*.[132] The crash of his bank was a severe blow for the rebuilding of Judaism in Spain.

The radical right-wing press deemed the Jewish refugees to be "undesirable". *El Siglo Futuro* provided an explanation to the epithet: "They are wandering people with no homeland, and for that very reason they are undesirable in the homelands of others".[133] Emphasizing the Oriental origins of the German Jews, *Informaciones* proclaimed that they had transformed Spain into the international centre of Semitic boycott against Hitler's Germany which had saved Europe "from the Red Asian hordes".[134] Inspired by the traditional antisemitic belief that Jews engage in ritual murder and well poisoning, *El Siglo Futuro* charged that the Jewish refugee doctors threatened the lives of their Spanish patients and that Jews were responsible for the death of the former dictator, Primo de Rivera.[135]

Wary of the rise of antisemitism, Jewish refugees in Barcelona held aloof from the synagogue. In an article on the life of the refugees in Spain, the *Jewish Chronicle* reported that a Catholic priest, who was visiting a school, had exclaimed upon learning that a young pupil was a Jewish refugee: "This is impossible. Where are your horns and tails?"[136]

As the depression deepened due to the loss of export markets and to increased labour costs, Jewish refugees became easy scapegoats. The CEDA Labor Minister, Federico Salmón Amorín, who gave priority to reducing unemployment,[137] pushed a series of decrees which made it more difficult for aliens to obtain work permits. The new legislation also prohibited alien peddling and petty trading from which most of the poorer refugees were making their living.[138] In the face of the difficult economic environment, the majority of the Jewish refugees planned to emigrate overseas to Palestine or South America. They hung about the doors of foreign consulates in the hope of obtaining visas.[139]

El Debate asserted that the refugees' unethical methods were "ruining small Spanish businesses".[140] Antisemitic attacks centered on the Jewish-owned SEPU department stores, which were opened in Barcelona and Madrid in 1934. Llanias de Niubo wrote that they symbolized the "Jewish invasion".[141] In December 1934, the *Jewish Chronicle* reported that a Catholic bishop had issued a confidential circular among his aristocratic followers exhorting them to withhold their patronage of the store. The attempt to engineer a boycott, however, was a failure. While the Spanish aristocrats who received the circular did not shop at SEPU, they did not have any feelings of guilt about sending their maids there.[142] The campaign against the store took a new turn in March 1935 when the SEPU in Madrid

was the victim of vandalism. Armed with truncheons, a group of men penetrated the store. After dividing themselves up throughout the building,
they knocked down the shop windows and counters. The police force, which
intervened, managed to restore order but failed to arrest anyone. The entire
group of vandals had disappeared.[143]

The treatment of the Jewish refugees in Catholic publications revealed
the radical right's obsession with issues of purity and "moral hygiene".
Hostile to the "permissive" trends of the Second Republic, which had
granted women the right to vote and legalized divorce and civil marriage,
orthodox Catholics expressed their sexual anxiety in antisemitic terms.
Drawing on the traditional Catholic notion that Judaism was a religion of
no morality and that Jewish sexuality, beginning with the ritual circumcision, was deviant, Spanish antisemites associated prostitution and
pornography with the Jewish refugees. In an article entitled "the undesirable foreigners", *El Debate* claimed that the Jewish immigrants brought in
"pornographic publications" and "immoral entertainment", which had a
"corrosive" effect on Spain. The Catholic daily contrasted the "trafficking"
and the "machinations" of the refugees to the "naivety and kindness of the
Spaniards", whose morality the Jews were trying "to undermine". The
authorities were accused of encouraging the "subversive activities" of the
Jews and of protecting them. *El Debate* advocated that the refugees be put
under surveillance.[144]

Spanish antisemites also railed against the rapid naturalization of the
Jewish refugees, alleging that in exchange for bribery payments, officials
provided refugees with the Spanish nationality. In August 1935, *El Debate*
denounced a number of people – "some of them well known in politics",
who had made "profitable gains" naturalizing into Spaniards "this bunch
of foreigners" who had been expelled from their own country and who "did
not like Spain, its language and culture".[145]

The theme of Jewish political corruption gained prominence during the
Straperlo scandal, which broke out in October 1935. The *Straperlo* was a new
electronic type of gambling machine, which resembled a roulette table but
with twelve numbers instead of thirty-six besides the zero.[146] Its promoter,
the businessman Daniel Strauss, tried to legalize it by negotiating with
politicians from the Radical Party. He reportedly gave various gifts to
obtain authorization from the government. As legalization did not take
place a disheartened Strauss got in touch with Indalecio Prieto and Manuel
Azaña who encouraged him to write to the President of the Republic Alcalá
Zamora, which he did. Alcalá Zamora turned the matter to the government.

On 19 October the council of ministers announced that it had received
a complaint from a foreign source pointing to fraudulence by a number of

Spanish officials. A parliamentary commission was appointed, which reported that Strauss had reached an agreement with the Catalan radical leader José Pich y Pon and with Aurelio Lerroux, the adopted son of the Radical party's leader and former Prime Minister, Alejandro Lerroux. Pich y Pon and Aurelio Lerroux reportedly persuaded Strauss to form a new company and to give them 50 per cent of the stock in return for governmental permission. After obtaining the license, Strauss gave both Alejandro Lerroux and the Minister of the Interior, Rafael Salazar Alonso, expensive gold watches.

Strauss opened a table at the Casino of San Sebastian on 12 September 1934 but the Casino was closed within three hours. Aurelio Lerroux then convinced Strauss to open in the Balearic island of Formentara a casino, which the police also closed within eight days. While there was no material evidence that bribes had been paid, the *"Straperlo* commission" recommended that all those suspected of corruption including Aurelio Lerroux, Pich y Pon and Salazar Alonso resign their positions.[147] The scandal caused a political sensation in Spain. It discredited the Radical Party and led to the resignation of the two leading Radicals in the government, Alejandro Lerroux as Foreign Minister and Juan José Rocha as Minister of the Navy.

The *Straperlo* Affair was compared to the Stavisky Affair, a corruption scandal involving French radical politicians, which provoked one of the most important domestic political crises in France during the 1930s.[148] The Jewish origin of Stavisky and Strauss enhanced the climate of antisemitism in France and in Spain. According to the Spanish press, Strauss was a Polish Jew who had been brought up by his uncle, a rabbi. He had lived "a troubled life" in Germany, Mexico, the United States and Holland. It was reported that he had owned an inn in Texas where "the contraband of alcohol, gun powder, dynamite" took place and had smuggled prostitutes from Guatemala and Cuba.[149] The radical right-wing press in Spain referred to him as "the Jew Strauss", or as "the Jewish adventurer". For *El Debate*, Strauss was "one of those many undesirable foreigners who live at ease and flourished in Barcelona under the protection of some mysterious guardians".[150]

Declaring that the scandal "was a Jewish maneuver", the monarchist daily *La Nacion* insinuated that the Strauss affair was linked to the alleged Jewish-Masonic-Catalan conspiracy against Spain. *La Nacion* claimed that Strauss retained a French Jew, Henry Torrès, as his lawyer. Torrès had become famous in 1928 as the lawyer of Samuel Schwartzbard, who two years earlier had murdered Simon Petlyura, the former president of Ukraine and the man responsible for the 1919 pogroms against the Jews of the

Ukraine.[151] More importantly for the Spanish radical right, Torrès had had close contact with anarcho-syndicalists and Catalan nationalists. He had supported Francesc Ferrer i Guàrdia, the independent anarchist who was considered the instigator of the tragic week of 1909. That event which began with a general strike to protest against the sending of three contingents of Barcelona conscripts to Morocco had then turned into an insurrection in which religious schools, convents and monasteries were destroyed.

Not only did Torrès take part in the campaign waged all over Europe against the trial and execution of Ferrer i Guàrdia, he had also been the lawyer of Francesc Macià. In 1925 Macià, who was in exile in France, had planned a separatist insurrection in Catalonia. But the French stopped the expeditionary force before it crossed the border. The trial of Macià in Paris in 1927 had attracted international attention. In his pleading, Torrès had declared that it was an honour to defend "the most honourable, the most moving, the most noble of men", his "friend" Colonel Macià".[152] When the Catalan regional administration, the *Generalitat*, was proclaimed under the Second Republic, Torrès became its representative in France, even though he was not Catalan. To top it all, *La Nacion* revealed that Torrès was the president of the international aid committee for the Asturian miners who had been brutally repressed in October 1934. In the words of *La Nacion*, Torrès, who was "constantly in touch with Spanish revolutionary émigrés", had long been plotting against Spain. "From Ferrer until nowadays," the newspaper asserted, "there has not been in France a movement against Spain in which this Jew and Freemason did not play a prominent role."[153]

Since they interpreted the Strauss scandal as an episode in the Judeo-Masonic-Bolshevik conspiracy, it was only natural that the radical right would claim that the Socialist leader Indalecio Prieto had taken part in it. Prieto had fled to France after caches of arms in possession of the Socialists were discovered in September 1933.[154] According to *La Nacion*, he had subsequently requested a passport from the government to circulate freely in Europe. In the face of the government's refusal, Prieto had conspired with Strauss to bring down the Radicals. Despite the flimsy evidence, *La Nacion* declared that "the intervention of the Spanish revolutionaries in the Strauss affair left no doubt". The wave of antisemitic attacks in the wake of the *Straperlo* affair prompted Ignacio Bauer to complain to the papal Nuncio in Madrid, Monsignor Tedeschini. Tedeschini promised him that he would ask the radical right-wing press to put an end to the campaign.[155]

Another scandal broke in late November 1935, when Lerroux was accused of having made improper payment of state funds while he was Prime Minister. This affair completed the discrediting of the Radicals and created a governmental crisis that ushered the dissolution of parliament and new elections. In the meantime, the trauma of the Asturian uprising and the desire to remove Lerroux and Gil Robles drew the left together. The Socialists, Republicans, Communists and Catalan nationalists formed an alliance known as the Popular Front. The ultraconservative right immediately presented the new coalition as the enemy of Catholicism and the fatherland. The CEDA asked its partisans to work "against the revolution and its accomplices", a veiled reference to the left, the Freemasons and the Jews.[156] *El Siglo Futuro* ominously presaged that if the "Judeo-Masonic-Bolshevik popular front" won the elections Margarita Nelken, along with the French Jews, would be "the new masters of the Socialist Soviet Federal Republic of Iberia".[157] Similarly *ABC* warned its readers against the anti-clerical, "honorary Jew" Fernando de los Ríos.[158] The anti-Republican weekly, *Gracia y Justicia*, begged for the expulsion of all conspiracy members:

International Marxists.
Foreign Marxists.
Stateless Jews.
Why should Spain put up with them?[159]

The Popular Front, which won the elections of February 1936, adopted a more liberal attitude towards the Jewish refugees. In contrast to its center-right predecessor, the new government of Manuel Azaña opposed the deportation of the German Jews.[160] In fact, shortly after the victory of the left, two German Jewish scientists were offered chairs at the University of Barcelona. Their appointment prompted the German consul-General in Barcelona to lodge an unsuccessful protest to the rector of the university.[161] In March 1936 a delegation of Jewish refugees met with Lluis Companys, the provincial governor of Barcelona. They complained about the persecution to which Nazi agents in Barcelona subjected them. They also requested the support of the Catalan government to integrate into the region. Companys promised that he would help them;[162] a pledge that could only add weight to the allegations that the Catalan nationalists were the allies of the Jews.

Spanish ultraconservatives relied on conspiracy theory to interpret the victory of the left in the February elections. According to them, the Popular Front government was in the hands of Jews and Freemasons whose ultimate aim was to deliver Spain to Soviet Communism. *El Siglo Futuro*, for instance, asserted that Spain had become a "laboratory for Judeo-Masonic revolutionary experimentation".[163] Ironically while they argued that the election of the Popular Front was the end-result of the Judeo-Masonic-Bolshevik conspiracy, Spanish ultraconservatives themselves were plotting against the Republic. The assertion that there existed an evil Judeo-Masonic-Bolshevik conspiracy justified the creation of a virtuous counter-conspiracy involving the right, the army and Catholic societies. In a way it was their own machinations that the rightists projected on their political opponents.[164] In fact, the principal aim of *Acción Española* group since its inception had been to legitimize the idea of a rebellion against the Republic and the group made various attempts to overthrow the Republic, the most notable being the abortive revolt of General José Sanjurjo in August 1932. Shortly after the failed uprising the determination to overthrow the Republic prompted the reactionary right to set up a "conspiratorial committee".[165] Its members included the Marqués de la Eliseda and Jorge Vigón, two of the propagators of the *Protocols*, men who equated the Republic with a Jewish-Masonic-Bolshevik conspiracy. Their schemes finally bore fruit on 17 July 1936 when a group of Spanish generals staged an uprising against the Popular Front government, presenting their rebellion as a religious crusade against the Jewish-Masonic-Bolshevik conspiracy to take over Spain.

III
Antisemitism as a Weapon of War
1936–1939

On the evening of 17 July 1936 a group of Spanish generals staged an uprising against the Popular Front government. The rebels quickly established control in Morocco, Andalusia and the Northwestern provinces of Spain but failed in the Southwest, the centre and the Basque country. For the next two and a half years the country was split into two camps fighting a brutal war. Germany and Italy intervened almost immediately on the side of the Nationalists. In consequence, the Soviet Union eventually came to the aid of the Republicans. The insurgents presented the war as a religious crusade against the "Jewish-Masonic-Bolshevik" conspiracy to take over Spain and an extensive array of antisemitic titles was published in the Nationalist zone.

The historiography of the Franco regime's policy towards the Jews has long glossed over the subject of Nationalist antisemitism, devoting instead its full attention to the problems of rescue during the Holocaust years. Recent scholarship has investigated the prevalence of anti-Jewish sentiments among the different Nationalist factions, noting the influence of Nazi and fascist propaganda.[1] However, it has overlooked the other factors that motivated the insurgents' antisemitism. Notable among them was the fact that an important number of Jews outside of Spain supported the Republican government. The large proportion of Jews who fought on the side of the Republicans in the International Brigades and the initial decision of France's Jewish Premier, Léon Blum, to send military aid to the Spanish government seemed to offer proof to the Nationalists that the Republic was backed by a Judeo-Masonic-Bolshevik conspiracy.

Little attention has also been paid to the indigenous roots of Nationalist antisemitism and to the place of Jews in the formulation of the Civil War as a re-enactment of the *Reconquista*. The insurgents, who claimed to be heirs of the Catholic Kings and wanted to restore the true Spain – that is ancestral Castile – identified the Republicans as descendants of the *conversos*.

The latter were accused of practicing the Jewish faith in secret and of hating the "old Christians" for the forced conversion of their ancestors. To take their revenge the Republicans had conspired with their co-religionists abroad as well as with the Freemasons and the Bolsheviks. Hence the Jew was both the external enemy and the enemy within. Blending the ideas of Gobineau with those of Torquemada, the more extreme Nationalists regarded the racial fusion between Old and New Christians as the cause of Spain's decay. They advocated the revival of the Inquisition to promote Spain's regeneration. The myth of the *Reconquista* was not only central to Nationalist thinking, it was also the lens through which it perceived the external world. Thus, Hitler's antisemitic campaign was labeled a crusade to save Christian Europe.

Historians have tended to disparage the antisemitism of the Nationalists as a mere rhetorical device, with little impact on Spain's dwindling Jewish community. According to this interpretation, the Nationalists attacked an abstract image of Jews, but "real" Jews were left unharmed. One of the aims of this chapter is to show that the Nationalists' hostility towards the Jews was not just pure intellectual discourse and that at times their actions towards the Jews living in the peninsula, in Morocco and in the Balkans reflected their hostility. Dispatches from Spanish diplomats in Italy, Germany and Southeastern Europe also demonstrate the wide acceptance of anti-Jewish stereotypes among the Nationalists and their reluctance to provide a safe haven for persecuted Jews even when they held the Spanish nationality or had converted to Catholicism.

The *Africanistas*, the Republic and the Jews

Most of the senior officers who rose against the Republic on 18 July 1936 were veterans of Spain's Moroccan wars and as such were dubbed the *Africanistas*. José Sanjurjo, Francisco Franco, Emilio Mola and Queipo de Llano had earned their stripes in the protectorate where they had faced enormous risks but at the same time had benefited from fast promotions. They shared a political culture characterized by authoritarianism and nationalism, and wanted to restore the "true" Spain – that is the ancestral Castile of the Reconquest from the Moors and the discovery of America.[2]

One of the sources of the *Africanistas*' opposition to the Second Republic was the rise of Catalonian and the Basque nationalisms, which they perceived as a threat to national unity. They were also hostile to working-class activities, as they saw every strike as a Communist-inspired revolution and viewed left-wing workers with the same contempt as the Moors.[3] Hence, in October 1934, the Moroccan army, under the leadership of General Franco, crushed the rising of the Asturian miners with a savagery that it had until then reserved to the tribesmen of the Rif. In the aftermath of that ruthless repression, the left dubbed Franco the "butcher of Asturias".[4]

While the working-class and nationalist movements sparked the *Africanistas'* hostility to Republic, the reforms carried out by the Minister of War, Manuel Azaña, inflamed it. Azaña's aim was to cut down the inflated officer corps and to make the army more efficient. In 1931, he tackled the problem by offering retirement to 8,000 surplus officers on full basic pay. He reduced the number of new entrants in the officer corps by closing the General Military Academy. That decision was resented bitterly by the academy's director, Franco. Even more controversial were Azaña's decrees for the *revisión de ascensos* (review of promotions) whereby some of the promotions on merit awarded during the Moroccan campaigns were to be reconsidered. Many of the senior army officers feared that they would be demoted. Franco himself faced the prospect of going back to the rank of colonel.[5] Conservative newspapers, such as *La Epoca* and *ABC*, encouraged the officers' hostility to the Republic by alleging that Azaña's aim was to crush the army and that the new regime was responsible for the country's economic problems, mob violence and anticlericalism.

The *Africanistas'* abhorrence of the Republic was brought nearer to the surface by the outbreak of violence against the Catholic Church that followed both the establishment of the Republic in April 1931 and the election of the leftist Popular Front in February 1936. In March 1936 when the military governor of Cadiz told General Francisco Franco that "Communists" had set fire to the convent near his barracks, the latter asked him in anger: "Is it possible that the troops of a barracks saw a sacrilegious crime being committed and that you just stood by with your arms folded?"[6]

Like Franco, many of the *Africanistas* were deeply attached to Catholicism. This religious fervour led some of them to espouse a traditional Catholic antisemitism. It was the case of General Emilio Mola, a key figure of the rebellion. In 1922, Mola wrote:

For what rational reasons should the Spaniards be hated by Israel's descendants? There are three fundamental ones: the envy that they {the Jews} resent towards any people who has its own fatherland; our religion towards which they feel undying abhorrence and on which they blame their dispersal throughout the world, their memory of the expulsion which was not due, as some assert, to the whim of a king but to the popular will.[7]

Did Franco share Mola's antisemitism? There has been a lot of specula-
tion about his Jewish origin but it seems to be unfounded. His first reference
to Jews, which can be found in an article that he wrote in 1926 for the
Africanistas' journal, *Revista de Tropas Coloniales*, of which he was the
director, was devoid of antisemitism. The article, entitled *"Xauen la triste"*
("The sad city of Xauen"), describes how in 1924 the Spanish troops were
forced to evacuate the city of Xauen, which they had been occupying for the
past four years. Franco, who lamented the abandonment of the city, thus
described the evacuation of its Jewish inhabitants:

> *This small Hebrew community no longer wants to live in the shameful slavery of
> the past; it is with tears that they abandon their poor homes and their humble
> neighborhood, which were the centre of their lives. Now that they know the advan-
> tages of civilization and of law; they do not want to leave { . . . }. As we abandon
> the neighborhood, we remember the great days of our arrival in this city. { . . . }
> That day, when the wretched, humiliated Israelites were shedding tears of joy
> and, with their typical accent and their old Castillian vocabulary, were cheering
> Queen Isabella, the good queen.*[8]

Written at a time when he was advocating that Spain maintain its colonial presence in Morocco, Franco's description of the Moroccan Jews was
imbued with paternalism. By depicting the Sephardim Jews as victims of
the "barbaric Muslims", nostalgic for Queen Isabella who had expelled
them from Spain, and by describing the Spanish soldiers as their protec-
tors, Franco was making a case against withdrawal from Africa. He wanted
to advance Spain's colonial expansion in Morocco and believed that the
Sephardim, who spoke Spanish and controlled a large portion of the
Moroccan trade, could help the Spanish army in this endeavour.

Years later, in the aftermath of the Civil War, Franco's rhetoric was very
different. In a speech made in Madrid on 19 May 1939 to celebrate the
Nationalists' victory he warned that "the Jewish spirit, which permitted the
alliance of big capital with Marxism and which made so many pacts with
the anti-Spanish revolution, could not be extirpated in a day".[9] What
happened during this thirteen-year interval that led the *Caudillo* to give up
his opportunistic philosemitism? One of the most probable sources of
Franco's later hostility towards the Jews was the radical right journal *Acción
Española* of which he became a subscriber and on whose ideas and doctrines
he based the dictatorship.[10]

Students of the Alliance Israélite Universelle (AIU) School in Tetuan, Spanish Morocco *c.* 1900. The AIU is a French-Jewish organization which operated day schools for Jewish children in Muslim countries. The fact that the language of instruction was French led graduates to identify culturally with France. The AIU schools were denounced by Spanish officials as a tool for French cultural expansion in Spanish Morocco.

The writer and propagandist Ernesto Giménez Caballero. during a meeting of General Franco's single party, the Falange Española Tradicionalista de las JONS (5 June 1939). Giménez Caballero, who had become interested in the Sephardic Jews as a young conscript of Morocco, had been an ardent philosephardite in the 1920s. He espoused fascism in 1929 and during the Spanish Civil War he advocated the re-establishment of traditional forms of religious persecution such as "auto-da-fe" "to purify" Spain from the Jews who had infiltrated the country.

XIII° BRIGADA ·DOMBROWSKI·   VOLUNTARIOS INTERNACIONALES DE LA LIBERTAD   BATALLON ·PALAFOX·

באטווין

אָרגאַן פֿון דער יידישער קאָמפּאַניע אַג. פֿון נאַפּטאַלי באָטווין

קאַטאַלאָניע   נומער 5   3 נאָוועמבער 1938

א געזעגענונג

נישטאָ נעכן מער נאָר נוייל דיר אָנדערוומעו
האָכן פֿאָרשאַמען ס טורען, קעדדי נישמ
צו, ועו ועו איטאַליענישע דיוישעו או
מאָראָקאַנישע שקלאַפן פֿאַרספּויצען שפּאַ־
ניש. מען האָכ נעכאָמעו אלע סאַנדעעע
שמעלונגעו מאָר די פֿאַמאָמ בריועוויקע
פֿו דער פֿרייהיים.

דורך ד־2 יאָר קריג האָכן די אַני־
מערנאַזשאָנאַלע פּיל סאָל הערדירם אַ ועמ
נוויל פֿו קאָמף, או אַנדערע מאַן האָכו
ויי מיסמאַהאַלמעו איו די ראַמעו פֿו זיר
ערע סענדינקיעקיוסם. אָכער שמענקיק ען־
נעו די אַנמערנאַזשאָנאַלע נעוומו נלויך
מו ויִיִיִיער העלדישקייסם או אוכערגענעכ־
ענ קייסם. מאַרקריריו ויונדויק ויינער ליכן
איו דער היונ פֿו דער פֿאָלקספֿרייהייסם.
שפּאַניק איו פֿאָר ויי נעוואָרען ויונער
צוויים פֿאַ מערלאַנד אַו פֿאָר פּיל ראַם
איינציקע פֿאַמערלאַנד. וניל איו ויונער
הויס מאַנד דער העראָם ראַם שיקואָל פֿו
פֿאַשיום. ויונער קראָליע או אונענרעעכ־
קיום או וועלכע צו נעהערן קעו

מימ 2 סעו צוריק האָכ באַרעצי
לאָנע קאַמעדיקע קאַמף האַ אַנינשמייניקע.
אַ סאָליאַק פֿו נאַזעאַנאַליועע. א ייר פֿו
אמשטאַסאָנים. או אַלמבעמער. או איינע אַפֿ־
קעמספּער פֿו די אַנימערנאַזשאָנאַלע ברי־
גאַדעם. נאָם או נעואָמו אופֿ צערום
פֿראַנם. דאָם איו נעווע די אַנימער־נאַז־
דיקינע פֿו די אַנימער־נאַזשאָנאַלע קאָל־
דאָם, די שפּאַניע־שע רעגירונג. די איינגערום
דעמאָקראַמישע רענירונג איו אירעאַם
וועלכע האָם נאָך קיינמאָל נישמ נעפֿרוד
כעו איר צורות. דאָם איו די המקספים מים
איר אַלגעמיוכאַמפֿאָנעו דערקלערונג
איו דעם פֿעלקקערערבונד ווע קואויערדם
פֿו דער קרויזאָאַנע אלע קעמפֿער פֿו די
אַנימערנאַזשאָנאַלע בריגאַדעם, וועמנדיק
אויספֿאָרעו פֿו שפּאַניק ייריריום־אַירצו צו.
דאָם לעכ פֿו אַנינשמיניקען אינ
דאָם לעצמעו. ואָם די אַנימערנאַזשאָנאַלע
קעמספּער האָב נעגעכו פֿאַר דער שפּאַ־
שער אומאָפּהענגענקיום עם וענעו נים
ואָלמעו נעוואָרו־אַמַרייער־דעדעקם. נאָך דעם
אין ג־ין פֿאָרשמיייונג פֿו דער אַרמ־
או פֿו סאָלמ־שע אָרמאַני־ואַרעעע. מייר־
לער קראָאַ בלומעו או קרעניק. דער
ארקעמסמער שמ־לם דעם מרוער־קאַמר.
איו אַרנליך מים אַואַוימע העלדן
נעסאַלעלעם או די כעיא פֿו אַראָאָן. אין
די פֿעלדער פֿו נואַהאַלאַהאַראַ. כי־י־ הי
מורעו פֿו מאַדרידי. אין לעוואַוכע או
אין אַנדאַלוזינ. אין עקספּאַרמאַהוררע או
אין קאַמאַלאָניע. ואָם מאָסקל האַנ־רם או
שמ־יי נאַמעוען אויסערנענואיולעכ לעכ
ואַכע. אלע עעלקמעו האָכ אים אַספֿענעגכו
דעם לעצמעו קאָוורעה. נאָר דר רעגערולוערי
מאַוק־ו. פֿו דער אַרמיי או דעם שפּאַניער
שע פֿאָלק איו נעואַנגעו אַ דעלעגאַזיע

Page from the 'Botwin' the newspaper of the Jewish Botwin unit in the International brigades. The newspaper was published in Yiddish. The first issue stressed that the Jewish Brigadiers had come to Spain to fight not only Spanish Nationalists but also "to defy" the Nazis.

Group portrait of the members of the Jewish Botwin company in the International Brigade fighting in Spain. The unit was named after Naftali Botwin, a Jewish trade-unionist from Lvov, who was arrested and hanged in Poland in 1926. It included Jews from Poland, various European countries, and Palestine, but also a Greek and two Palestinian Arabs in addition to Spaniards. The unit had a Yiddish marching song and newspaper. The first issue stressed that the Jewish Brigadiers had come to Spain to fight not only Spanish Nationalists but also "to defy" the Nazis.

Franco and on the left Ramon Serrano Suñer. Franco had just made a speech to the national council of the Falange in the monastery de las Huelgas (26 September 1939).

✳ ARRIBA ESPAÑA

PRIMER DIARIO DE FALANGE ESPAÑOLA

AÑO II número 158   PAMPLONA martes 2 de Febrero de 1937   Cuartel S. Martínez de Espronceda

El trabajo tendrá una garantía absoluta, evitando su servidumbre al capitalismo".
El Jefe del Estado, Generalísimo FRANCO.

HOY HACE UN AÑO
de Febrero de 1936 pronunció su discurso en el cine Europa, José Antonio Primo de Rivera
¡ARRIBA ESPAÑA!
CESAR

Visado por
la censura

Visado por
la censura

Arriba España
sta es la verdad

Arriba España
Esta es la verdad

A year ago on
2 February 1936, José Antonio Primo de Revera
gave his speech at the Cine Europa.
Onwards Spain!

Onwards Spain. This is the truth

Arriba Espana, 2 February 1937.

International Reaction to the Civil War and the Rise of Antisemitism

The latent antisemitism of the insurgents was exacerbated by international reactions to the outbreak of the war. Throughout the conflict the Nationalist press claimed that Jews from all countries had mobilized their financial resources and their political power in defense of the Republic. Giménez Caballero, the one-time champion of philosephardism, and now one of Franco's chief propagandists, declared that "all Jews and Freemasons" were "on the side of Barcelona" and "the Bolsheviks".[11] Similarly Juan Pujol, the former deputy of the CEDA, who headed the Nationalist press and propaganda department, wrote in *Domingo* that Jews viewed the Spanish Civil War as "their holy war" and that they were "sending volunteers to Spain to plunder".[12]

A large number of Jews did indeed support the Republic. German Jews who had taken refuge in Spain and Jewish participants in the Workers' Olympiad, which was scheduled to take place in Barcelona in July 1936 in protest against the holding of the Olympics in Germany, were among the first to volunteer in the Republican army. Some of these men joined the Thaelmann Centuria in Barcelona, which referred to itself as the "Jewish Thaelmann group" because out of the eighteen volunteers, thirteen were Jewish.[13] Once the International Brigades were formed, a large number of Jewish volunteers joined them. Estimates on the number of Jewish Brigadiers vary between 5,000 and 10,000 out of a total of about 40,000 volunteers. The difficulty in calculating the number is due to the fact that many of these Jewish volunteers did not identify themselves as Jews but as internationalists and anti-fascists. Still, even the lower estimates indicate that at least 12.5 percent of the volunteers were Jewish, a proportion larger than that of any other nationality.[14] Josef Toch, a Jewish Brigader from Austria, claimed that there were about 7,758 Jews in the International Brigades, among whom 2,250 came from Poland, 1,236 from the USA, 1,043 from France, 214 from Great Britain and 267 from Palestine.[15] His figures indicate that about 50 percent of Polish Brigadiers were Jewish. Albert Prago, who fought in the Abraham Lincoln Battalion, estimates that about 30 percent of all American volunteers were Jewish.[16] A large number of the Jewish Brigadiers belonged to the communist party of their respective countries.

Many of these volunteers were of Ashkenazi origin but there were also some Sephardic Jews from Yugoslavia, Bulgaria and Greece. The fact that

some of them spoke Russian as well as Ladino enabled them to serve as intermediaries between the Soviet officers and the Republicans. These linguistic
skills gave them rank within the framework of the International Brigades.
The Bulgarian volunteer Ruben Levi Abramov, for instance, became
Inspector General of the Spanish Republican Army.[17] Other Jewish
Brigadiers also held leading positions. A Hungarian Jew, General Lukacs
(alias for Béla Frankl), commanded the Garibaldi Brigade, an Italian,
Commandant Carlos (Vittorio Vidali), was commissar of the fifth regiment
and a Polish Jew, General Wacław Komar, founded and commanded the
129th Brigade. Both the highest-ranking American officer in the Brigades,
Lieutenant-Colonel John Gates (Sol Regenstreif) and the last commander
of the Lincoln Battalion, Major Milton Wolff, were Jewish.[18]

Jews belonging to the French Communist Party demanded the forma-
tion of a separate Jewish unit, which was established on 12 December 1937.
It was named the Jewish Botwin unit after Naftali Botwin, a young Jewish
Communist who had been executed by the Polish authorities in 1925. The
unit had a Yiddish marching song and newspaper. The first issue stressed
that the Jewish Brigadiers had come to Spain to fight not only Spanish
Nationalists but also "to defy" the Nazis who, as we shall see, were backing
Franco.[19]

Francoist propaganda, which asserted that they were not fighting a legal
Spanish government but a "Jewish-Bolshevik dictatorship", emphasized
the participation of Jews in the International Brigades. Newspapers in the
Nationalist zone published pictures of Brigaders, insisting that they looked
Jewish.[20] In October 1938 *ABC, Sevilla* noted that "thousands of Jews from
all corners of the world have flocked to the defense of the Reds".[21]

The initial reaction of France's Jewish Premier, Léon Blum, added fuel
to the Nationalist antisemitic fervour. At first, as the leader of the French
Popular Front government, Blum wanted to help its sister regime in Spain.
Pressures from the French right, and from Britain, both of which were
opposed to any French involvement in the conflict, forced him to opt for a
policy of Non-intervention.[22] Members of the French government,
however, secretly dispatched seventy aircraft to Spain and sent funds to the
Republic.

While Blum sympathized with the Republicans, the *Action Française*,
which supported Franco, did its best to prevent the French government
from supplying arms to the Spanish Republic. The radical monarchist
group viewed the Spanish conflict as a dress rehearsal for the conflict that
was bound to break out between French Catholics and the "worthless" Third
Republic. Several leaders of the *Action Française*, including Maurras himself,
traveled to Nationalist Spain where the red carpet was rolled out for them.

During his four-day visit in May 1938 Maurras was lavishly welcome as if he was a chief of state meeting both Franco and the latter's brother-in-law and Minister of the Interior, Ramon Serrano Suñer.[23]

The *Action Française* exerted undue influence on the Francoists and its antisemitic diatribes against the French Popular Front resounded in the Spanish press. Like Maurras, Nationalist writers made a distinction between "real France", Catholic and rural, and "legal France", the French Popular Front, which was allegedly in the hands of the "warmongering Jews".[24] Pujol, for instance, wrote an article entitled "France taken by Israel". In it he declared that France had "fallen in the hands of a Judeo-Masonic organization", which "subjugated it, exploited it and used it to achieve the ultimate goals of Zion".[25] Pujol called on the "authentic" France to follow the Spanish example. He concluded his article by asking, ominously, if France would take the decision and "have the will to free itself from these rascals?"[26]

Similarly in *Qué es "lo nuevo"* (What is the new spirit?), one of the most influential books of political doctrine published during the Civil War, which was considered to be the Nationalist equivalent to Hitler's *Mein Kampf*, José Pemartín praised the "extraordinary prophetic vision" of the nineteenth-century antisemitic French polemist Edouard Drumont. Pemartín declared that the Jewish banking dynasties "had little by little taken possession of the French industries, finance, press, turning France into the slave of the repulsive and cowardly Léon Blum and bringing it to the edge of the abyss".[27]

The *Action Française's bête noire*, Léon Blum, found himself at the centre of the Nationalists' attacks. Pujol nicknamed him "Spain's worst enemy".[28] In an article entitled "A Jew", Jesus Pábon, a former member of the Catholic party, the CEDA, linked Blum's administration to a nefarious Jewish conspiracy and accused him of supplying arms to the Republicans, Pábon declared: "the national uprising is bound to be a ruthless war, a heroic crusade against what is going on in France under Mr Léon Blum".[29]

Echoing the *Action Française*, the Francoists accused Blum of making common cause with the Soviet Union. From October 1936 to the summer 1938, the Soviet Union provided the Republicans with aircraft, tanks, cars, artillery pieces and oil. Stalin also sent between 2,000 and 3,000 military advisers to Spain and the Soviets exerted considerable influence upon Republican Spain.[30] The Nationalist press repeated tirelessly that the Soviet Union was "controlled by the Jews". In December 1936 Pujol wrote an article entitled "When Israel Commands," in which he accused the Soviet Ambassador to the Republic, Marcel Rosenberg, whom he called the "Jew Rossemberg" (sic), of being "the real dictator of Spain". Another of Pujol's accusations was that Russian museums, "in the hands of the Jewish Government of Moscow", were stealing the pictures of the Prado.[31] Similarly, in March 1937, Tusquets gave a lecture in Saragossa on "Freemasonry and the working class", in which he declared that the misery of the Russian workers was due to the fact that "more than eighty per cent of the Soviet leaders were Jewish".[32]

The Nationalists alleged that Jews had penetrated the leadership of England and the United States, which jointly with France pursued an official policy of neutrality. Gonzalo Queipo de Llano, Commander of the Army of the South, whose nightly radio broadcasts from Seville were listened to by thousands of Spaniards, accused the British Foreign Minister, Anthony Eden of being a tool in the hands of the "Jewish and Freemasonic masters, who are now joining hands with the Spanish Freemasonic Marxists".[33] At the same time, the influence of the *Protocols* was reflected in the insurgents' claim that the British and American media and banking sectors were under the control of the Jews, and hence hostile to the Nationalists. Pemartín warned England where "Jewish finance controlled the city of London", to be careful not to be dragged into the war's abyss.[34] In the same vein, on 1 May 1938, the rebel newspaper in San Sebastian, *La Voz de España*, carried an article headed the "Jewish-English Bank and the Basque Offensive", which accused "the Jews who monopolize the Bank of Piccadilly" of supporting the Basque nationalists because they had large investments in the mining industries of that region. On 3 April 1938, *Domingo* claimed that Hollywood, "which was ruled by the Jews", had given a million and a half dollars to the Republicans.[35]

Stirring Nationalist antisemitism and hostility towards the Soviet Union and the Western democracies was German propaganda. Shortly after the onset of the conflict, Adolf Hitler agreed to supply the insurgents with rifles, anti-aircraft guns and transport planes. He did so upon the request of the Nazi *Ausland*-Organization's local representatives in Morocco, Adolf Langenheim and Johannes Bernhardt.[36] Hitler's backing of the Nationalists was motivated by his anti-Communism and his fear that the Spanish Popular Front would ally with its French counterpart and stand in the way of the Third Reich's plans for expansion.[37] German propagandists turned Spain into a mirror image of Germany, asserting that "red Jewish henchmen" threatened the peninsula. In a speech at the Nuremberg party rally of 1937, Hitler claimed with reference to Spain that "Jewish Bolshevism has moved via the detour of democracy to open revolution".[38]

It is interesting to note that General Erich Ludendorff was allegedly pressuring Hitler to cease assisting the Spanish rebels on the grounds that Franco himself was Jewish.[39] Turning a deaf ear to Ludendorff's advice,

Hitler maintained his commitment to the Nationalists. In return for aid, Spain became a training ground for the German army and a propaganda forum for the antisemitic material. According to Robert Whealy, the Spanish conflict preyed on the mind of Joseph Goebbels, Hitler's Propaganda Minister. Monitoring carefully the Spanish press, he hoped that Nazi propaganda would strengthen the Falange. It was his belief that a Falangist government would sign a military pact with Germany and Italy.[40]

The Falange was indeed very receptive to Nazi literature. After the outbreak of the Civil War, the fascist group became increasingly hostile towards the Jews. The movement's founder, José Antonio Primo de Rivera, was imprisoned in March 1936 and his successor, the former Carlist Manuel Hedilla, was a fervent Germanophile, who declared in a speech "long live Spain's economy, free from Jewish maneuvers".[41]

One of Hedilla's appointees, Juan Sampelayo, the secretary of the Falange's *Jefatura Nacional de Prensa y Propaganda* (Department of Exchange of the National Leadership of Press and Propaganda) forged alliances with antisemitic propagandists in Germany, introducing their ideas in Spain. He began a correspondence with Ulrich Fleischhauer, who published *Welt-Dienst* (World-Service), an anti-Jewish broadsheet, which translated and summarized articles from antisemitic newspapers throughout Europe. Sampelayo expressed his gratitude for Fleischauer's "work against communism and the Jewish plague". He agreed that he would send issues of the Falangist publication *Vértice* in exchange for the antisemitic and anti-Communists bulletins of the *Welt-Dienst*.[42] Sampelayo also maintained close contacts with Dr Wilhelm Schmitt, who was the Spanish translator for the Nazi paper *Der Stürmer*. On 30 April 1937 Sampelayo wrote a letter to Schmitt praising his denunciations of the "International Jews, the Jewish serpent" and of "that dirty book, the Talmud". He informed Schmitt that the Nationalists would have "to mount a campaign against Judaism and Freemasonry, both mortal enemies of all Western civilization".[43]

This agreement with the Nazis prompted the Falange to step up its anti-semitic campaign. In 1937, the fascist party issued a poster bearing the slogan "Spain Awake", which reproduced two cartoons showing some malevolent-looking Jewish men thrilled about the destruction surrounding them. One of the captions read, "Down with the emblem of Judaism, Red Freemasonry and White Freemasonry united against the Falange". These cartoons, which were supposed to illustrate the attitude of Jews towards the Civil War, had been directly taken from the *Stürmer*.[44]

The Spanish insurgents' attitude towards the Jews was modeled not only on the Germans but also on the Italians. Like the Germans, the Italians supported them with men, arms and credit. Hostility towards the French government was the main motivation behind Mussolini's decision to aid to Nationalists. The *Duce* resented his "Latin neighbour", which was endowed with rich colonies in North Africa and stood in the way of fascist expansion across Europe. He believed that the establishment of a Nationalist government in Spain would tip the balance in favour of the Axis and that in the event of war, Spain would block French colonial troops in North Africa.[45]

Until 1938, the Mussolini regime was largely devoid of antisemitism but Italy's alignment with Germany, which culminated in the signature of the anti-Comintern pact in November 1937, led to a change of policy. In October 1938, the Fascist Grand Council of Italy promulgated a number of racial laws, which forbade the Jews to serve in the armed forces or the state bureaucracy, to teach in state schools or universities and to employ Aryan domestic servants.[46] Franco's representatives in Italy closely followed the antisemitic campaign that was unraveling, sending clippings to the Nationalist Ministry of Foreign Affairs in Burgos. They paid special interest to the Italian press's assertion that Jews from around the world were supporting the Republic and that flocks of them were joining the International Brigades to fight the Nationalists.[47]

"The Crusade"

The Nationalists did not simply rehash foreign hate material but blended it with their own historical myths. They portrayed the conflict as both the continuation and the replication of the process of Reconquest from the Moors, depicting themselves as the representatives of "true" Spain and the Republicans as the "anti-Spain", who had sided with the Jews. The Nationalists posed as defenders of Spain's immutable institutions: the Church, the army, the family, and the fatherland – all of which were attacked by the Jewish-Masonic-Bolshevik conspiracy. Describing the war as a crusade against the "Jewish red hordes" enabled the rebels to avoid dealing with the myriad of social and economic issues that had provoked the conflict.[48]

El Poema de la Bestia y del Ángel (The Poem of the Beast and the Angel), which José María Pemán wrote in 1938, exemplified the Nationalist blending of Spanish myths with German propaganda. Imbued with religious elements, the epic also drew on modern antisemitic writings such as the *Protocols*. For Pemán, the Civil War was part of the titanic struggle between God and the "Jewish Satan".[49] God had entrusted Spain with the defense of the western civilization, threatened by "the Beast", which Pemán called alternatively "the red and Semitic East", "the Synagogue" and "the

Elder of Zion". Although Queen Isabella had expelled the Jews from the peninsula, they had lingered there, usurping all the wealth of Spain. They had murdered Calvo Sotelo because he had resisted the power of the Jewish-controlled oil multinationals Standard Oil and Royal Dutch.[50] Spain's new hero, Francisco Franco, would annihilate "the Beast". In this endeavour, he had received the help of "two eagles" –"one Germanic, the other Roman".[51] Although filled with references to Spanish history, Peman's poem was also reminiscent of Goebbels' speech to the Nazi Party Congress in Nuremberg in September 1937. Goebbels had then described the Spanish conflict as a semi-religious crusade against the wicked plots of Satan. He had declared that the "Bolshevik-Jewish Satan" was behind all the atrocities committed by the Republicans.[52]

In the Nationalist version of the Civil War as a re-enactment of the medieval *Reconquista*, the Republicans were cast as descendants of the Jews who had converted to Christianity but continued to practice Judaism. The Republicans were accused of being "judaizers", "illegitimate children of Israel" or "camouflaged Jews" who hated Spain and plotted against it with their co-religionists abroad. Juan Pujol denounced the "lack of patriotism" and the "tribal instinct" of the "enormous number of Jews", who for many years have been scheming against their fatherland. He revealed that while some Republican leaders, such as the Minister of National Defense, Indalecio Prieto, did not know that they were Jewish, others tried to conceal their true name and religion.[53] Chief among the latter was Fernando de los Ríos, the Republic's Ambassador in Washington, whom the Nationalists called the "Rabbi of Spain". According to *Domingo*, he was a *Marrano* who had been ordained rabbi in Amsterdam in 1926 and had then taken the name of Solomon. His family, which had been forced to convert to Catholicism during the Inquisition, had long wanted "to take revenge on traditional Spain". This explained why as a Minister of Justice in the days of the Republic, de los Rios "had withdrawn the financial aid to the Catholic schools" while giving "a large subsidy to the Jewish schools in Tangier". In the US, where he "intrigued" to have the Senate send arms to the Republicans, he had "the enthusiastic support of his co-religionists".[54]

Catalan nationalists were also denounced as Jews. Pujol revealed that the success of separatism in Catalonia was largely due to the fact that "an enormous portion of the population" there was "of Jewish origin". Some of these Jews "had been there since the Inquisition". These were "converted Jews, scattered among the rest of the inhabitants" who "lived in urban centres" and "ended up concealing the real Catalan population of rural origin". According to Pujol the Jews formed the "nucleus of the bourgeois Catalan movement, the *Lliga Regionalista*". Even though the leaders of this "wicked organization" did not really profess Judaism, they were "of Jewish race".[55] Pujol asserted that Lluis Companys, the leader of the *Generalitat*, was another camouflaged Jew: "Companys," he wrote in *ABC, Seville* in December 1936, "is Jewish, the descendant of converted Jews. One does not need to explore his genealogical tree to realize it, one look at his face is enough."[56] The Nationalists accused the converted Jews of plotting with the "sixteen thousand", "unmasked" Jews, "mostly Germans" who "had fled Nazi Germany and settled in Barcelona in the early 1930s".[57] Basque nationalists were also denounced as "Jews". After the bombing of the Basque market town of Guernica by the German Condor Legion on 26 April 1937, a massacre that caused international outcry, the journalist Víctor de la Serna declared that the Basques themselves had destroyed the city. Using the word "Jew" as a synonym for Basque separatists, he asserted that Guernica had "perished in the Basque altar in the hands of the Jews".[58]

The Nationalists did not content themselves with chasing down converts in Spain. They grew convinced that in France, as in Spain, there were a number of Jews who claimed to be converted but remained Jews at heart. Such was the case of two Catholic intellectuals, Jacques Maritain and George Bernanos, who had dared to condemn the atrocities perpetrated by the Nationalists in the Basque country and in Mallorca respectively. Ramon Serrano Suñer, Franco's all powerful brother-in-law and Minister of the Interior, denounced Maritain as a converted Jew, whose "wisdom was reminiscent of that of the Elders of Israel".[59] In the same vein, Bernanos's "false Catholicism" was excoriated in *Domingo* in June 1938.[60] A few months later that same paper published the family tree of US President Franklin Delano Roosevelt, alleging that his forefathers were Spanish Jews named Rossocampo, who had changed their names after having being expelled from the Peninsula and immigrating to the Netherlands. The paper asserted that the President's lineage explained why there were only Jews in his government.[61]

Influenced by the Regenerationist movement, the Nationalists claimed that Spain's decay was due to the racial mixing between the descendants of the Jews who had converted in the fifteenth century and the Spaniards. The Spanish nation was degenerate because it had been polluted by Jewish blood, which was seen as a carrier of disease and disorder. In October 1938 the monarchist Eduardo Aunós, formerly General Primo de Rivera's Labor Minister, wrote in *ABC, Sevilla* that "the fusion of Jews with Spaniards had led to "the infiltration of Semitic ideas in Spain". All of Spain's decadence was due "to the survival in the larva stage of Jewish stigma".[62]

Doctor Antonio Vallejo-Nágera, the future chair of psychiatry at the

University of Madrid and author of studies on Spanish eugenics, blamed Spanish communism on the racial fusion between Spaniards, Jews and Moors. "The racial stock of the Spanish Marxist," he wrote, "is a mixture of Jewish-Moorish blood."[63] As polluting agents, Jews were identified with diseases, microbes and the lowest of animals. At the outset of the Civil War, General Cabanellas, president of the military *junta,* railed against "Freemasons, Jews and similar parasites".[64] In the same vein the Falangist daily *Amanecer* wrote, "The nations which have been able to get rid of and expel the Jewish leprosy, have become powerful".[65] Related to the characterization of Jews as dirty and polluting agents was the charge that they smelled foully, an accusation that had long been prevalent in Church writings.[66] The Falangist mouthpiece *Arriba España* asserted that the three million Polish Jews "must produce fetid miasmas in the Catholic and military atmosphere of Poland".[67]

For the insurgents, Margarita Nelken, the Socialist deputy whose family was of German Jewish origin, embodied all the negative qualities of the Jews. Her free sexual life – she was the mother of two children born out of wedlock – clashed with the prejudices of the Nationalists.[68] Attacks against her in the Nationalist press reflected both religious anti-Judaism and sexism. She was "cursed" because her forefathers had rejected Christ and were responsible for the Crucifixion. For this crime of deicide, she was to be eternally punished. Nelken was characterized as a witch, a temptress who led a scandalous private life and had frightening sexual power. In *El Poema de la Bestia y del Ángel*, Péman wrote the following about her:

> *Oh, cursed, cursed*
> *You, the Hebrew*
> *You, unmarried mother: Margarita!*
> *Name of a flower and spirit of a hyena!*[69]

The feistiness with which she had defended the rights of the landless labourers as deputy of the Badajoz province during the Second Republic remained intolerable to the Francoists. Thus, the journalist Manuel Sánchez del Arco wrote that "the Jewish Amazon Señora Nelken", "has spread poison among the men of Extremadura, who are in rebellion today because of her Marxist preaching".[70] Similarly in *Domingo* Juan Pujol contrasted Nelken, a "Red Jewess", to the "virtuous" Spanish Catholic women, whose place was at home. According to Pujol as she stood at the opposite pole to Catholic women, Nelken possessed a disturbing sexual nature. She was "a snake with skirts", who had "induced her rural followers" and "used her sexuality to arouse the virile crowds of Extremadura".[71] The idea that Jews used their sexual depravity to delude the Christians was a recurring theme in

Nationalist propaganda. Hence, in September 1936, Queipo de Llano declared that "pornographic literature" was "one of the most powerful weapons" used by "the Freemasons, the Jews and the Marxists".[72]

Since the Jews were agents of pollution and a source of immorality, a "cleansing operation" was required. Calls for their expulsion and for the revival of the Inquisition were common in Nationalist publications. In 1938, the *Correo Español*, another of the Falange's organs, published an article announcing that after their victory the Nationalists would reintroduce the Inquisition and establish an alliance with Portugal and the Moslem countries to combat the Jewish spirit. Using German terminology, the newspaper pledged that Spain would keep its territories *Judenrein* (free of Jews). Nationalists were urged to use the tools of the Inquisitors such as the burning of books. In 1936 the organ of the Falange, *Arriba España*, exhorted its readers "to destroy and burn" the periodicals and books of Jews, Freemasons and separatists.[73]

Giménez Caballero advocated the re-establishment of traditional forms of religious persecution such as "auto-da-fe" "to purify" Spain from the Jews who had infiltrated the country.[74] Similarly Vallejo-Nágera believed that "inquisitorial chromosomes" were in the "paternal and maternal genes" of the Nationalists, and that "nothing would contain their impulse to resurrect the Tribunal of the Holy Inquisition".[75]

Despite the numerous references to the "race", "genes" and the purity of blood, Nationalist writers continued to claim that there were not racist and that their antisemitism was based on Catholic theology. In December 1938, Giménez Caballero asserted in *Domingo* that "the racism of the Jews" gave him "the nausea".[76] In the same vein, Manuel Graña wrote that the Jews could not complain about racism because they had invented these exclusionist practices. According to Graña, Jews "hated all foreigners", they "refused to assimilate" and they "set strict segregation laws".[77] Similarly, Yzugardia Lorca declared that the essence of Catholicism was anti-racist and that it was the Jews themselves who had brought racial theories to Germany and Italy.[78]

The Situation in Mainland Spain

The Nationalists did not always content themselves with antisemitic diatribes directed at the Republican leaders and their external allies. Even though there was no systemic persecution of the Jews, verbal antisemitism was sometimes followed by acts of vandalism in the peninsula. In the Nationalist zone, Queipo de Llano declared in one of his nightly radio broadcasts that every Jew in the world was "subject to a supreme council known as the *Kahal*", to which he gave ten per cent of his earnings. Altogether Queipo declared the *Kahal* had received 4,1181,399,952,000 pesetas. "All this money," he said "the Jews are spending on the promotion of Communism and the preparation of revolutions."[79] The supposed existence of the *Kahal* was used as an excuse to fine the Jewish community of Seville the sum of 138,000 pesetas.[80] In Saragossa, the Nationalists closed a department store that had been founded by Jewish refugees. The firm's entire property was confiscated.[81]

In areas controlled by the Republicans, the breakdown of law and order also caused distress among the Jews. At the outbreak of the conflict a large number of well-to-do Jews, including Ignacio Bauer, fled the Republican zone, out of fear that their property might be confiscated. In Barcelona, German Jews found themselves in a precarious situation as the Republican government treated them as Germans despite their refugee status. Many of them left Spain, some even returned to Germany where they were given the choice between being sent to a concentration camp or leaving the country.[82] A number of German Jews, however, were stranded in Spain as the Republican government refused to grant them immigration visas to leave the country. They lived in a state of anxiety, convinced that in the event of a Nationalist victory they would either be shot or expelled.[83]

An agreement that was reached between the Gestapo and the Nationalists in July 1938 seemed to justify their fears. According to the arrangement, the Gestapo could declare any German citizen living in Spain an enemy of the state and repatriate him or her by force to Germany.[84] It is not known whether German Jews were directly affected by the agreement, but they were aware of the looming presence of Gestapo agents. In Barcelona, where there remained about eight hundred Jews, agents of the Gestapo broke into the synagogue shortly after the Nationalists troops entered the city in January 1939. They committed a number of desecrations, destroying the vestments used in worship and carrying off the silver vessels. A delegation of the Jewish Community, which presented itself at police headquarters to make a formal complaint, was refused a hearing and told that the police were already aware of the matter.[85] In February 1939, several German Jews who had called on the German consulate general were arrested on orders of that consulate-general.[86]

The situation was also delicate for Jewish Brigadiers who had been captured by the Nationalists. Bob Doyle, an Irish volunteer who was arrested in Calaceite on the Aragon front on 31 March 1938, recalled that the Italian fascists ordered the Communists, Socialists and Jews to step forwards. That night, fearing for the life of his full-bearded Jewish comrade, he slipped him his razor and advised him to shave. Later on, during his incarceration in a monastery in San Pedro de Cardeña near Burgos, Gestapo agents came to carry out some oral and written tests as well as measurements of the body, of the head and the length of the jaw. The idea was to prove that they were subnormal. "Anyone who looked Jewish or was a bit abnormal was singled out".[87] Similarly, Garry McCartney, a Scottish volunteer, recalled that in the camp of San Pedro de Cardeña Gestapo agents were constantly asking the prisoners to denounce their Jewish comrades.[88] In accordance with the agreement it had signed with the Nationalists the Gestapo forced a number of German brigadiers to return to Germany.[89] It is highly probable that German Jews were among those repatriated.

The Situation in Morocco

The situation in the Spanish protectorate of Morocco was very different from that of mainland Spain during the Civil War. In contrast to the peninsula, the Nationalists established control over the protectorate at the onset of the conflict and the Jewish community, which numbered 13,000 people, found itself under their rule. The climate in the first days of the rebellion created anxiety and insecurity in the Jewish communities. The local Falangists, who had received weapons from the military conspirators in preparation for the insurrection, were eager to fight.[90] Guns in their hands, they took the streets of Tetuán, Melilla and Ceuta. Shouting "you are a despicable race", they forced their way into the home of Jews, whom they obliged to pay financial contributions to the insurrection. They victimized the Jews by boycotting their businesses and confiscating their properties on the ground that they were sympathetic to the Republican government.[91] In Xauen and Larache they extorted money from members of the Jewish communities by forcing them to swallow castor oil. In Tetuán the Falangists decided on their own authority to establish their headquarters in the house of a Jewish notable, Sicsu, whom they sent to a concentration camp.[92]

The worst excesses, however, took place in Ceuta and Melilla. In Melilla, six leftist Jews were immediately shot by order of a court martial, the hair of several Jews was shaved in the shape of a cross and dozens were imprisoned in forced labour camps.[93] For ten days, the president of the Republican Union Party of Melilla, Benaim, was brought to the local market where he was publicly humiliated and tortured until he was shot.[94] As incarnation of the "Jewish-Masonic-Communist conspiracy", the Jews affiliated to the

Republican parties were tortured and forced to kiss the cross before being shot. About twenty of them were killed in the cities of Melilla and Ceuta.[95] In some cases, the insurgents extorted money from the family of those shot: they asked them for money in exchange for the corpse.[96] The physical punishments imposed on the Jews, as well as on the Republicans, were not simply arbitrary. Behind them stood the Nationalists' yearnings to purify Spain and the memory of Inquisitorial activities. The Francoists hoped that ingesting castor oil would purge communism from the bodies of the Republicans and the Jews. The shaving ritual, as Michael Richards has noted, replaced the penitents' caps worn during the Inquisition.[97] Both the penitential garment and the shaved hair were meant to cast deliberate shame on their wearers. Similarly confiscations and fines were common practices during the Inquisition.[98]

The motivating force behind these acts of violence was the belief that the Jews of Morocco were supporting the Spanish Republic. On 23 September 1936, the Native Office of Tetuán reported that the Jews of Spanish Morocco, as well as those of the French Morocco and Tangier, were scheming to delay the arrival of a freight train to the Spanish protectorate. Their aim was to prevent the supplying of the Nationalists. Word had it that the Republican government had promised the Jews of Tangier full control over the international city in exchange for their assistance.[99] A few days later an informant reported that on the occasion of the Yom Kippur holiday, the Jews of Tangier had prayed for the triumph of the Republic. "This is hardly surprising,"he wrote "for in every Jew there is a propagandist against our cause."[100] Among the accusations levied against the Jews of Morocco was that they had established a fund to finance the enrolment of young Spaniards in the Republican army. In a letter to the Foreign Office, which he wrote in November 1936, Britain's Consul in Tetuán, Monck Mason, noted that there was "a good deal of feeling against the Jews" who were "accused of cordial sympathy" with the Republicans.[101]

Another factor that affected the Jews of Northern Morocco was the Nationalists' reliance on native troops and Moroccan mercenaries to fight the Republicans. To recruit indigenous units the Nationalists used a combination of bribery and propaganda. They tried to get the backing of the Berber tribesmen by offering large subsidies of silver and grain to their chieftains. The attractions of food, money and fighting appealed to the Moroccans and 70,000 of them enlisted in the Nationalist army. Many of these recruits came from the northern portion of the French protectorate.[102] The Nationalists also obtained the support of the rural Moroccan Nationalists by making vague promises of future autonomy and granting some concessions such as freedom of the press, the arabization of indigenous education and limitations on the land that non-Moroccans could purchase. At the same time, the Spanish insurgents tried to channel Moroccan nationalism against the common enemies: the French and the Jews.[103]

The Nationalists' efforts to enlist the support of the Muslim population had an adverse affect on the Jews living in the protectorate. In the spring of 1937, the Spanish authorities promulgated a law which forced the Jews of the zone to lower the rents on their properties by 35 percent. Although the decree's aim was to gain the sympathy of the Muslims, it had, in fact, the opposite effect. The houses belonging to the Arabs or the Spaniards stood empty whereas the Jewish properties, being much cheaper, were let.[104] In the same vein, on the occasion of the Moslem feast of *Korban*, the Jewish community of Tetuán was forced to give 50,000 pesetas to purchase sheep for the enlisted Moors.[105]

At the same time the Nazi community of Spanish Morocco was responsible for disseminating antisemitic propaganda to the Muslims in the Spanish and the French zones as well as in the international city of Tangier. The Germans were aware of the strategic importance of Morocco not only for the Nationalists but also for themselves. By the time Hitler came to power in 1933, the Nazis had set up local sections in Tetuán, Melilla, Ceuta and Larache. They wanted to use the Spanish protectorate as a propaganda and military base in North Africa.[106] A key player in the anti-Jewish agitation in Northern Morocco was Adolf Langenheim, the head of the Tetuán section of the Nazi party.[107] Langenheim had been one of Franco's emissaries to Hitler at the outbreak of the war. Along with Johannes Bernhardt, another German businessman resident in Spanish Morocco, he had been instrumental in convincing Hitler to provide military assistance to the Nationalists.[108] Known as the "German Lawrence" he was rumoured to have translated *Mein Kampf* into Arabic.[109]

The arrival of German steamers in Moroccan harbours was accompanied by the distribution of propaganda material to the Moors. The antisemitic speeches of Hitler and Goebbels were distributed to the Moroccan population. Leaflets printed in Arabic accused both the Jews and the French of being the "representatives of Red Spain". They warned the Muslims that if the communists triumphed, the Mosques would be burnt, the harems would be violated, properties would be destroyed and the Jews along with the Communists would be in command and would treat the Muslims like animals.[110] Pamphlets portrayed the Germans, along with the Spanish rebels, as role models to be emulated by the Muslim Moroccans:

The Jew is devouring you, as vermin devour sheep. France protects him. He is the agent and tool of France. Germany locks him up or drives him out. Germany confiscates the property of the Jews. You could do the same, Moroccans, if you were not the slaves of France.[111]

In the international city of Tangier, the Germans founded the international anti-Jewish League whose members were mostly Spanish Nationalists. They also published and translated the antisemitic broadsheet *Welt-Dienst* as *Servicio Mundial*. The recipients of the sheet included the Spanish Bureau of Press and Propaganda and the Moroccan nationalist leader Abdelkhalak Torres.[112] The antisemitic propaganda seemed to bear fruit. In 1937, Léon Aranias, the Director of the *Alliance Israélite Universelle* school in Larache, noted that Arabs were chanting "death to the Jews" in a demonstration to celebrate the seizure of Malaga by the rebels.[113]

The Nationalists boasted that the Moors fully shared their antisemitism. Pujol wrote in *Domingo* in March 1937 that the Moors had "rallied instinctively" to the side of the Nationalists "in the fight against Jews of the world".[114] In the same vein, Franco recounted to a group of generals that during a visit to the Protectorate he had met a group of Moroccan soldiers who had enrolled in the Nationalist army. They had allegedly told him that they were happy to be allowed to kill Jews.[115]

The propaganda created a climate of fear. In January and February 1937, as the Nationalist troops attempted to capture Madrid, word spread that while Moroccan soldiers were dying at the front, Jews were getting richer.[116] Rumours abounded that definite action against the latter was being prepared.[117] On the evening of 1st of April 1937, two Moroccan mercenaries entered the Jewish Club, the *Circulo Israelita*, in Tetuán. They began insulting and threatening those present with cries of "Down with the Jews", "Death to the Jews", "We will burn the Club down". The two young men destroyed the Portuguese passport of a Jewish man.[118]

Some senior officers frowned upon these acts of arbitrary violence. Colonel Tomás García Figueras, who administered the region of Larache, deplored the antisemitic campaign. In a letter to the office of native affairs in Tetuán, he warned that the "purposeless" campaign could have serious negative consequences for the Nationalists.[119] Despite his calls for moderation, violence continued. In June 1937 the Nationalists' victory in Bilbao gave rise to anti-Jewish and anti-French demonstrations in Tetuán.[120] In August, twenty-three Jews – principally women and children – were wounded during a riot of Moorish soldiers in El Ksar. The Nationalist authorities fined the city's Jewish community 1,800 pesetas a month for "having failed to avoid troubles".[121] In September 1937, the Falange gave instructions that all Jews working for Spaniards be dismissed and replaced by Spaniards and Moors. The High Commissioner rescinded the order.[122]

In October 1937, Saguès wrote that the Jews residing in the Spanish protectorate of Morocco lived "in a climate of definite insecurity and terror".[123]

The Jews of the zone found themselves in a vicious circle, for those who
wanted to leave the protectorate faced a number of impediments. Not only
did they have to ask for a special permission to leave the Spanish zone, but
the Falangists also confiscated the properties of those who did not come
back within the allotted time.[124] A wave of antisemitism swept the protectorate but the Moroccan Jews realized that it was not comparable to that
existing in Nazi Germany. They kept a low profile and hoped that this
hostility would disappear with the end of the Civil War.[125]

Still the precariousness of their situation raised grave concern among
their co-religionists. The Hispano-Jewish association of Barcelona
published pamphlets on Nationalist excesses and distributed them to the
Jewish communities of the Netherlands and Great Britain, urging them to
support the Republican government.[126] In London the *Jewish Chronicle*, the
mouthpiece of the British Jewish community, published reports of the antisemitic acts carried out by the rebels. Anxious to build favourable public
opinion in England, Franco's press officer issued a statement to the newspaper claiming that the Nationalists could not be antisemitic because there
was no Jewish problem in Spain.[127]

Another reason that prompted the Nationalist authorities to treat the
Moroccan Jews cautiously was the belief that the latter, who controlled
much of the protectorate economy, could serve the Nationalists' war effort.
Hence, while trying to restrain the Falangists' and Carlists' excesses, the
military authorities, desperate to replenish their coffers but reluctant to
raise taxes, also extorted money from the Jews. In August 1936, the
Tetuán Jews had to pay 500,000 pesetas as "voluntary contributions" to
the rebels" treasury. In May 1937 they were again compelled to give
60,000 pesetas to the Nationalist cause.[128] The Jews were also forced to
hand over their merchandise, especially foodstuffs as well as jewelry and
gold. Those who refused to do so were subject to arbitrary arrest, forced to
drink castor oil or had their estates confiscated. Saguès asserted that the
Moroccan Jews were "forced to put their wealth and their activities to the
service of Franco".[129]

While most Jews of the zone were compelled to finance the war effort,
a small mercantile elite did back the Nationalists willingly. Such was the
case of the Banque Hassan. At the onset of the war the High Commissioner
Juan Beigbeder struck a deal with Jacob Benmaman, the agent in Tetuán
of the Banque Hassan of Tangier, who offered to finance the rebellion. A
new form of silver coinage known as the Hassani money was introduced in
the protectorate, soon to be replaced with paper notes. As a result of his

assistance Benmaman gained the favour of Beigbeder, which he used on his coreligionists' behalf. Ironically, the Nationalists' allies, the Italians, rewarded the owner of the Bank, Augustus Hassan, by throwing a reception in his honour and awarding him their highest decoration, the "Order of Christ".[130] Republican papers did not fail to note the hypocrisy of the insurgents who claimed that the rebellion was a crusade against the Jewish-Masonic conspiracy and yet were financed by a Jewish bank.[131]

The Balkans

The outbreak of the Civil War also affected the Spanish Jews who lived in the Balkans. Many of them rallied to the Republican cause. They felt sympathy for the Popular Front government, which had announced in March 1936 that it would revise article 23 of the Constitution to facilitate the naturalization of those Spanish Jews who had not benefited from the 1924 decree.[132] Maximo José Kahn, the Republic's representative in Greece, played an active role in promoting closer ties between the Barcelona government and the Sephardim of the Balkans. Born to a Jewish family of Frankfurt, Kahn immigrated to Spain in 1920. A strange twist of fate made him a collaborator of Giménez Caballero in the *Gaceta Literaria* from 1927 to 1929.[133] In September 1937, as the Republic's Consul in Salonica, he asked for permission to collect data on the Spanish Jews living in the Balkans and the Near East, on the grounds that they would play an important role in the reconstruction of Spain after the war.[134] Kahn recommended that the Republic designate two or three Sephardic intellectuals as its cultural delegates in every major centre of the region. Those delegates would then organize conferences and write articles on the Sephardic culture. They would administer Spanish libraries and create a monthly political review, which Kahn proposed to call "*Sefarad*". The delegates could serve the Republic's interests by gathering information on the "movement and possibilities of the capital invested by the Sephardim in banks, industries and commerce".[135] Although the Republican government found the plan interesting, it failed to materialize.

Kahn also encouraged the Republican authorities to send an envoy to the Second Sephardic Congress that was to take place in Amsterdam in May 1938. He viewed the gathering as an opportunity to distribute pro-Republican propaganda. He suggested that thirteen pamphlets be handed out, which would contrast the Republic's philosemitism with Franco's anti-semitism.[136] One of these leaflets was to discuss the economic situation of the Republic.[137]

The Republican authorities followed Khan's advice and sent two delegates to the Congress: Don Menahem Coriat, Professor of Talmudic Studies, and Edmundo Gruenebaum, President of the Jewish community of Barcelona. The Republicans felt the Congress was a success because the envoys from all over the world praised Coriat's speech, which stressed the full freedom enjoyed by the Jews in the Republican zone.[138] The Sephardim pledged an increase in the financial and material assistance to the Republic and promised that they would set up support committees. Two English delegates, Mr Beriro and Mr Da Costa, who worked for the Midland Bank and the Montagu Bank respectively, indicated that they were willing to arrange important financial transactions for the Republican government.[139]

The delegates of Nationalist Spain in the region noted with displeasure that the Sephardim had sided with the Republicans. In June 1938, the Francoist agent in Athens, Sebastiàn Romero de Radigales, declared that the Spanish Jews were "openly opposed" to the Nationalist cause. He noted that the most eminent person in the Sephardic community of Athens, Jacobo Saporta, had resigned as president of the Hispano-Hellenic League after that cultural association had sent a congratulatory message to Franco. The Jews of Salonica, Radigales asserted, "entertained royally the Red representative", Maximo José Kahn, himself "a Jew who had acquired Spanish citizenship".[140]

A number of Spanish Jews in Romania were equally hostile to the insurgents. In 1937, the Great Rabbi of Romania, Sabetay I. Djaen, sent a letter to the Republican Prime Minister, José Giral, expressing his unconditional support to the Republic. He revealed in his letter that he despised the Nationalists' representative in Bucharest, Pedro de Prat y Soutzo, who had been "blackmailing the Sephardic community to obtain money for the Francoist rogues".[141] The hostility was mutual. Referring to the Primo de Rivera's decree of 1924, Prat declared bitterly to the Nationalist authorities that the Sephardim were "unworthy of the honour" that the Spanish government had done them "by granting them the Spanish citizenship".[142]

At times the antisemitism of the Nationalist envoys fused with their francophobia. In August 1938, the envoy in Istanbul, Julio Palencia, wrote a letter which revealed this amalgamation. Palencia assessed that "without exception the Spanish Jews of the Balkans had supported the Reds" and had "expressed antipathy if not hatred" towards the Nationalist cause. The explanation to this hostility, Palencia believed, was that the Sephardim had "received a French education" and "shared the Gallic mentality".[143]

The Nationalist envoys were split on the attitude to adopt towards the Spanish Jews who had maintained political connections to the Republicans. Some delegates felt that they should be severely punished; others continued to believe that the Sephardim constituted a basis for the expansion of Spain in the Near East and that sanctions should be applied cautiously. Pedro de Prat y Soutzo clearly belonged to the first category. He held the view that the Spanish Jews of Romania who had used the services of the Republican delegates should be harshly sanctioned. He proposed "as maximal sanction the deprivation of nationality and, in other cases, fines correlated to both the seriousness of the action and to the person's means".[144] He implemented his own recommendations by withholding the passport of a Spanish Jew, who had had his documents renewed by the Republican legation. Other members of the Jewish community, who had had contacts with the Republicans, were forced to pay 50,000 Leu[145] as "voluntary contributions" to the Falange and the Nationalist Press and Proganda service.

Sebastiàn Romero de Radigales, the agent in Athens, asked the Foreign Ministry in Burgos whether he could issue certificates and passports to the Spanish Jews who had used the services of the Republican consulate in Salonica. He pointed out that the deprivation of documents would put those Sephardim in a difficult position given that they had to possess a passport in order to obtain a yearly resident permit in Greece. He asserted that it would be unfair to deprive of their documents the persons "whose only fault" had been to use the services of the Republican consulate at a time when the Nationalists did not have any representative in this city. On the other hand, he believed that those who have fought against the Nationalists deserved "a harsh punishment".[146]

The pragmatic envoy in Sofia, Carlos de Miranda, suggested that Nationalist authorities be merciful towards the Spanish Jews as they could "serve as a basis for any cultural or commercial venture" that the Nationalists might undertake in the Balkans in the future.[147] Carlos de Miranda contended that the Spanish Jews who had only used the services of the Republican legations to have their documents renewed should not be troubled. On the other hand, those who had been blatantly hostile to the Nationalists had to be punished either by having to pay a fine or by being deprived of their Spanish nationality. In fact they should be treated like any Spaniard who had supported the Republicans, regardless of the fact that they were Sephardic Jews.[148]

The Ministry of Foreign Affairs faced a dilemma. On one hand, it had to sanction "those compatriots, whatever their origin, who had fought against the [Nationalist] cause". On the other hand, the Foreign Minister, General Francisco Gómez Jordana, was anxious to maintain good relations with England and it was feared that "a punitive sanction might label the government as antisemitic".[149] Like Carlos de Miranda, he realized that Spanish Jews were likely to promote Spain's interests in the region in the aftermath of the war. The ministry resolved the matter by issuing a decree on 19 July 1938, which was "applicable to all Spaniards with no distinction of races".[150] The circular stated that the Spaniards who had supported the Republicans would not be assisted by the Nationalist representatives and that their documents would not be renewed.[151] They could obtain passports only to go to Spain where "the appropriate measures would be undertaken".[152] Another decree dating from 7 September 1938 proclaimed "that the Jews who had been openly opposed" to the Nationalist cause were "no longer considered Spaniards".[153]

Another question that the Foreign Ministry had to deal with was that of the military status of the Spanish Jews. In Sofia, Carlos de Miranda believed that they should be exempted from military service because the Spanish government would not be able to prevent the Jewish conscripts from settling in Spain after having fulfilled their military duties. He also noted that the conscription of Jews into the Spanish army stood in evident contradiction to the Nationalists' principles:

> *Would it be advisable to have these people fight on our side? Can the New Spain, which views itself as the heir of the Catholic Kings, admit in its ranks the sons of those she has expelled? It would seem illogical to ask them to return to Spain after four centuries to spill their blood for a cause that condemns them and for a religion that is not theirs.*[154]

Miranda suggested that the 1935 regulation, which exempted the Spanish nationals living in Latin America and the Philippines from military service, be applied to the Jews of the Balkans. The Foreign Ministry and the Ministry of Defense agreed to the proposal. But in exchange for the exemption the Spanish Jews had to pay a service tax of four thousand pesetas. The amount was lowered to 1,100 pesetas for those who were not in the position to pay.[155]

Nationalist Reactions to the Persecution of Jews Abroad

In an environment rife with antisemitism it was not surprising that the Nationalist press would approve the anti-Jewish legislations enacted in Germany and Italy. In an article entitled "Praise to Nazism", written on the fifth anniversary of Hitler's accession to power, *El ideal Gallego* declared that by getting rid of its enemy "Marxist Judaism", Germany had "reached the peak of greatness and nobility".[156] For the Francoists the Jews were to be

blamed for the degeneration of Europe and their expurgation was a prerequisite to the revival of the old continent. In the final pages of *Qué es "lo
nuevo"*, José Pemartín wrote that Hitler was "thoroughly right in his anti-
Jewish fight".[157]

In October 1938, after the Fascist Grand Council of Italy enacted a
number of racial laws, excluding Jews from the army and the civil service,
ABC wrote an article lauding the promulgation. According to the Sevillan
daily, the warmongering of the Jews and their "aid to Marxist Spain" had
elicited Mussolini's decision.[158] The Spanish press liked to remind its
readers that Spain had been at the vanguard in the fight against the Jews;
the Catholic monarchs, Isabella and Ferdinand, had initiated anti-Jewish
policies and the fascists and Nazi were only following suit. *El Pensamiento
Navarro* wrote about the "brillant foresight of the Catholic Kings, who were
centuries ahead of their time".[159] In the same vein, *ABC, Seville* noted that
"today Italy, like yesterday Germany [. . .] has adopted means similar to
those taken by our Catholic Kings four centuries ago."[160]

Francoist propagandists drew upon Spain's historical myths to interpret
the situation in Germany. They established a parallel between medieval
Spain and Hitler's Germany, labeling the Nazi antisemitic campaign a
"crusade against the enemies of Christianism", even though Nazi ideology
was based on paganism and was potentially anti-Christian.[161] In the
Nationalist reading, it was the Germans who were the victims of the Jews.
Pemartín, for instance, justified Hitler's racism as a defense against "the
satanical destructiveness of the Jewish people".[162] Similarly in the treatment of *Kristallnacht*, much was made of the murder of the third secretary
of the German embassy in Paris, Ernst von Rath, by a Jewish youth on 7
November 1938, but scant attention was paid to the anti-Jewish riots that
took place two days later. *Amanecer*, for instance, asserted that von Rath's
assassination was an "attack against the German nation" and that "nobody
should be outraged by the measures Germany had adopted to defend
itself".[163] *Amanecer* did not mention that 91 German Jews were killed, more
than 30,000 arrested and sent to concentration camps, and hundreds of
synagogues destroyed. Instead it insisted on the international reaction to
the pogrom, which provided evidence to the alleged power of the Jews. The
Jews, according to *Amanecer*, "could not resign themselves to accept their
well-deserved punishment" and "using their tentacles" they had launched
an "ignominious campaign against Germany".

Nationalist representatives stationed in Germany, Italy and Eastern
Europe echoed the view of the Nationalist press on the persecution of Jews.
Sentiment that Jews were responsible for the upsurge of antisemitism was
quite common and diplomatic dispatches made constant references to the

Jewish conspiracy. Hence, after the opening of a research centre on the Jewish Question in Munich in November 1936, Daniel Castel, the Spanish Consul, lauded Hitler's "rise against the reign of Israel". Castel was not alone in expressing understanding for the hatred felt towards the Jews. Writing about Italy's antisemitic campaign in the summer 1938, the Ambassador in Rome, Pedro García Conde, declared that "Jewish support for international communism" had ignited it.[164]

For these diplomats the problem was not that the Nazis and their allies were persecuting the Jews but that the expulsion of hundreds of thousands of people, some of whom held Spanish passports, might create some pressure for Spain. In September 1938, Mussolini issued a decree which revoked the citizenship of Jews naturalized after 1919 and ordered them, along with all foreign Jews, to leave Italy within the next six months. A number of Spanish Jews who had settled in Naples, Genoa and Rome had to depart Italy. They asked the Nationalist emissaries in those cities to issue them passports.

Fearing the "mass invasion of Nationalist Spain" by Jews, the Foreign Ministry in Burgos sent a circular to its envoys, which advised them to give out passports only to the Spanish Jews who had supported the Nationalist movement. As for the Jews who had been hostile to the insurgents, they would receive passports only to come to Spain. They would have to enter the country through predetermined border checkpoints and the Spanish police would have to be advised before their arrival so as "to take the necessary steps". The Foreign Ministry forewarned that future measures would have to be adopted either to compel those Spanish Jews to leave Spain or to control their activities in the Iberian Peninsula.[165]

The Spanish Ambassador in Berlin, Antonio Magaz, was also concerned about the immigration of Spanish Jews to Spain. In the aftermath of *Kristallnacht*, Jews in Germany felt growing pressure to emigrate as their chances of being deported increased.[166] On 23 November, Magaz wrote to the Spanish Foreign Ministry that it would be impossible to prevent the Jews who held Spanish passports from coming to Spain. He declared that the "infiltration" of Spain by "these people", who "because of their race, were undesirable", "could result in a number of unpleasant incidents".[167] José Rojas, an official in the Foreign Ministry, reminded Magaz that from a moral standpoint it was difficult to refuse entry into their fatherland to the Jews who possessed the Spanish nationality. He suggested that the Spanish Jews who had been naturalized after January 1924 be forced to demonstrate their loyalty to Nationalist Spain by fulfilling a number of obligations. They would have to register in the consulate and those of military age would have either to enlist in the Nationalist army or to pay a fine.

A fine would also be levied from those who had not supported the Nationalist movement. Spanish Jews who failed to fulfill those requirements would automatically lose their nationality.[168]

Magaz was not only concerned about the coming to Spain of the Spanish Jews but also about the possible immigration of German Jews. He wrote to the Foreign Ministry that since German Jews had a letter J stamped on their passports, a number of countries had began denying them visas. Magaz recommended that Nationalist Spain follow suit and adopt a new visa policy that would distinguish between German Aryans and German Jews.[169] In response to Magaz's report, the Nationalist authorities asked their representatives in Germany not to give visas to the holders of passports bearing a J without obtaining the prior authorization of the Foreign Ministry in Burgos.[170]

But the question of whether or not to grant Spanish visas to Jewish refugees from Germany did not end there. It resurfaced a few days later in a cable sent by the Ambassador of Nationalist Spain to Portugal, Nicolás Franco, brother of the *Caudillo*. Franco informed the Foreign Ministry that a number of German Jews had disembarked in Lisbon. Their Portuguese visas were only valid for a week and the German legation in Lisbon, in its eagerness to get rid of these Jews, asked that Spain grant them visas.[171] Nicolas Franco requested instructions from the Foreign Ministry. As revealed in his reply, Rojas, like Magaz, was concerned that "the mass emigration of Jews" to Spain would create a "Jewish problem" there. Rojas concluded the report by declaring that each visa demand would be considered individually.[172]

The Nationalist government was also unwilling to let Catholic non-Aryan refugees enter the country. This reluctance, coming from Catholic Spain, might be surprising. But as we have seen, during the 1930s a number of ultraconservative intellectuals, including Vallejo-Nágera and González Oliveros, had come to espouse eugenic theories and by the end of the Civil War the line separating Nationalist Spain's Catholic antisemitism from Germany's racism had become thinner. This was demonstrated by the Nationalists' reaction to the proposal, in January 1939, that 150,000 Romanian Jews, who had converted to Catholicism, be allowed to immigrate to Spain. The wholehearted support of the Vatican for the project and the fact that these well-to-do people planned to bring large sums of money to Spain did not mollify the position of Spain's Minister in Romania, Prat. In a report to the Foreign Ministry, he revealed that he opposed their coming to Spain on the grounds that "the baptismal waters" would not "greatly change the mentality and the race" of the Jews and that their entrance into Spain "would be similar to that of a plague of parasites".[173]

By denying the efficacy of baptism, Prat, like the Nazis, defined Judaism as a race rather than a religion. A converted Jew, he believed, would never cleanse himself of his Jewish taint. To the Nuncio in Bucharest, who told him that he favoured the immigration to Spain of these converts, Prat said that he was much more concerned about "Spain's own interests" and the "purity of the Spanish race" than about "the salvation of those Jews" who "like, the majority, if not the totality of their coreligionists must have been enemies of the Spanish cause".[174]

The rise of antisemitism during the Spanish Civil War reflected a deep-rooted prejudice against the Jews, which was bolstered by Nazi propaganda. Although all Nationalist factions embraced an antisemitic rhetoric, their attitude towards the Jews of Morocco and the Balkans varied significantly. While the pro-German Falange orchestrated arbitrary actions against the Jews in both the Peninsula and in Spanish Morocco some of the senior officers, like Orgaz or Jordana, tried to restrain these excesses as they were eager to maintain cordial reaction with Britain and realized that blatant anti-semitism could hurt the Nationalists' image there. They were also convinced that the Spanish Jews of Morocco and in the Balkans could give financial support to the Nationalist movement and maybe even serve Spain's expansion in the future. This opportunistic attitude would be exacerbated by the outbreak of World War II.

IV
A Policy of Contradictions
Germanophilia and the Revival of Philosephardism (1939–1942)

Spain's attitude towards the Jews during the first years of World War II was inconsistent. Although the Francoist propaganda continued to stir up anti-semitism at home, the regime also revived philosephardism by promoting ties with the Jewish communities of the Moroccan protectorate and Tangier, posing as defenders of the Spanish Jews living in French Morocco. While scores of books mention the antisemitic rhetoric of the Franco government, scholars have by and large underplayed the revivification of philosephardism or have failed to analyse this movement within the context of Spain's colonial ambitions.

The dictatorship's paradoxical attitude was partly due to the many faces that the "Jewish question" had in post-Civil War Spain. Not only did the new administration have to deal with the small Jewish community of Northern Morocco and with the few remaining Jews in mainland Spain, it was confronted, as a result of the outbreak of World War II, with a wave of refugees, desperate to go through Spain on their way out of Europe. Furthermore, the adoption of antisemitic measures throughout Europe made the issue of consular protection for Jewish Spanish nationals more pressing. Yet at the same time "the Jew" remained an abstract concept, the hereditary enemy, the "Other" who embodied the "Anti-patria" – the elements which had allegedly provoked the Civil War.

The regime's changing stance towards Jews was also related to the factional divisions between the pro-Axis Falangists on the one hand and the army officers, Catholic Church and monarchists on the other. The ministries and departments, which were controlled by the Falange, collaborated closely with the Germans and were particularly hostile to the Jews. Such was the case of the press and propaganda machinery and the secret police agency – the *Dirección General de Seguridad*. In contrast, military officers, who had built their careers in North Africa, were more favourably disposed towards the Jews, at least towards those of Morocco.

Matching these internal divisions were the regime's conflicting aims of institutionalizing repression and aligning itself with Germany while building a new empire in the Mediterranean basin. The ongoing anti-Jewish campaign was part of the regime's efforts to "purify" the country of the "Anti-Spain". The revival of philosephardism needs to be understood within the context of Spain's Mediterranean policy, more concretely within the ebb and flow of the Franco-Spanish relationship in Morocco. In an attempt to rationalize these contradictions the regime revived the distinction between the Ashkenazi and the Sephardic Jews, by pinning all ills on the former and arguing that the latter had been "cleansed" during their stay in Spain.

Pro-Axis Leanings and Imperial Ambitions

The Civil War left the Spanish Nationalists with a debt of gratitude towards Italy and Germany without whose aid their victory would have been impossible. The Franco regime's ideological affinity with the Axis powers was revealed in its adhesion to the anti-Comintern pact on 26 March 1939. Five days later and one day before the official end of the Civil War, on 31 March 1939, Franco signed a German–Spanish treaty of friendship with Hitler, providing for mutual consultation on all common interests and benevolent neutrality in the event of war.[1]

In the first months of peace interest shifted back to internal politics. How would General Franco succeed in keeping together the various factions, which had backed him during the conflict, but were likely to compete for predominance in a peacetime regime? The tensions between the Falangists, who were drawn from the middle and artisan classes and the military–monarchy group, which represented the governing classes of the old regime, soon became evident. The military–monarchist faction was resentful of the Germanophile spirit of the Falangist Party and its attempt to impose a National–syndicalist regime on Spain.[2] The pro-Axis Falange preached economic autarchy while the army group favoured opening up trade with Great Britain, France and the neutrals.

Army leaders and monarchists particularly resented Franco's brother-in-law, the pro-Axis Serrano Suñer, whose star was in the ascendant. He was at once Minister of the Interior, Vice President of the *Junta Politica* (practically head of the Falange) and in charge of the regime's propaganda. Tensions had run high between Serrano Suñer and the Anglophile monarchist General Francisco Gómez Jordana who was Foreign Minister from January 1938 to August 1939.[3] An equally bitter struggle went on with Jordana's successor, Juan Beigbeder, as the latter – though also a

Germanophile – tried to maintain a balancing act between Great Britain and Germany. In a report to the Foreign Office the British Ambassador in Spain, Samuel Hoare, noted that while Beigbeder wished to have good relations with Great Britain, the whole machine of the Ministry of Interior was mobilized against him.[4]

Official statements made by Serrano Suñer and Beigbeder about the Jews reflected their political sympathies. Whereas Serrano Suñer declared on 12 June 1939 that "Judaism was the enemy of the new Spain",[5] Beigbeder tried to dissipate Spain's image as an antisemitic country by flaunting its good relations with the Jewish community of Spanish Morocco. He told the President of the Export–Import Bank, Warren Lee Pierson on 29 August 1939 that there was "no Jewish problem in Spain" and that his own private secretary was "a Jew". Beigbeder also asserted that Spain's "ability to reconcile all creeds" was displayed in Spanish Morocco, where Catholic, Jew and Moslem lived "in entire harmony, none molesting the other".[6]

Like other Spanish officers who had built their careers in Morocco, Beigbeder regarded Moroccan questions as the most important in the world. "We are all Moors", he once said to Sir Samuel Hoare.[7] The need to further colonial expansion was also to the fore of the third point in the Falange's programme, which stated: "We have a will to empire. We affirm that the full history of Spain implies an empire".[8] Until 1940, the Falange's imperial ambitions had largely been metaphysical; the movement was more interested in the spiritual re-conquest of Latin America than in colonial expansion in Morocco. It was only after the end of the Civil War that the Falange proclaimed the mission of empire with vigour.[9] By then the aspiration to reconstruct Spain's empire in North Africa was a shared aim of the Spanish leadership, notwithstanding the rivalry between the Falange and the army.

The Francoists considered that Spain had received unjust treatment and that the treaties of 1904, 1912 and 1926 had diminished the zone of Spanish influence to advantage France. Drawing on the theories of 19th century *Africanistas* such as the Regenerationist social thinker Joaquín Costa, the Francoists argued in favour of a united Morocco closely associated to Spain on the ground that "strategically the establishment in Morocco of a people distinct from the Moors is contrary to the security of Spain".[10]

Setting their sights on Gilbraltar as well as Tangier, French Morocco and Northwestern Algeria, the Francoists did not attempt to conceal that imperial expansion in North Africa would come at the expense of France and Great Britain. Their latent hostility towards France was exacerbated by the perception that France had helped the Republicans during the Civil War and by the fact that France had given asylum to 450,000 Republican refugees. Franco–Spanish relations remained strained despite the appointment of Marshall Philippe Pétain as France's Ambassador in Spain in March 1939.[11]

The signature of the Non-Aggression Pact between Germany and the Soviet Union on 23 August gave Spaniards a rude shock and German prestige a serious blow. The fact that Spain's economy was in a shambles, the vast majority of Spaniards war-weary, and the army poorly equipped, prompted the Spanish government to give Marshall Pétain a verbal assurance of Spanish neutrality in the event of a European war on 30 August 1939. On 4 September, a decree was issued, which imposed on Spanish nationals the strictest neutrality in the conflict in accordance with the existing principles of international law.

Despite the announcement of neutrality, the pro-Axis orientation of the Spanish government was beyond doubt. The Germanophile atmosphere did not bode well for the 4,000 Jews who found themselves in Spain in the first days of World War II.[12] Most of them were stateless or of Polish nationality and lived in Barcelona where they numbered 500 in June 1940, against 5,000 on the eve of the Civil War. The synagogues and communal offices in Madrid and Barcelona were closed; Jewish marriages, burials and the rite of circumcision were prohibited. Religious activities were forced underground and the heads of the Jewish communities had to pledge not to continue their religious activities in the future. The situation prompted many Jews to convert.[13]

Under the guidance of the Germans, the press, which was controlled by the Falange, never missed an opportunity to launch an attack on the Jews. When the seventh edition of *The Protocols of the Elders of Zion* was printed in December 1939 the newspaper *ABC* reviewed it in glowing terms, declaring that the pamphlet constituted "a prophetic revelation of the evils that Spaniards have had to suffer".[14]

Among the many tracts inspired by the Protocols stood *¡Alerta! . . . Francmasonería y Judaísmo*. Its author, Juan Segura Nieto, pinned all of Spain's ills, from the loss of Cuba to the outbreak of the Civil War, on the Jews. "Jewish bankers from England and the United States", he wrote, "opened up their coffers" to finance the Cuban separatist movement.[15] While most of the Francoist anti-Jewish drive was directed against abstractions such as "International Jewry", and the "Judeo-Masonic conspiracy", Segura Nieto had the originality to target specifically the Sephardic Jews and to designate one man, the "Jew and Freemason" Pedro Moisés Sánchez Gali, as the leader of the conspiracy. According to Segura Nieto, Sánchez Gali had been an agent of the Republic's intelligence service, the *Servicio de Investigación Militar*. The Republican Defense Minister Indalecio Prieto had allegedly sent Sánchez Gali on a mission throughout Europe to convince fellow Freemasons to support the Republic. Viewing himself in the role of a fifteenth-century inquisitor general, Segura Nieto wrote:

> *I accuse: Indalecio Prieto of judaizing and of being a protector of the Freemasonry.*
>
> *I accuse: The Freemasons born in Spain and the Sephardic Jews { . . . } of being reprobate, spies, mercenaries and* condottieri *{ . . . }. I cry out for justice. Exemplary justice { . . . }. An eye for an eye! A tooth for a tooth!*[16]

In fact nostalgia for the Inquisition permeated the Francoist discourse. The new regime was bent on "purging" Spain of the "*Antipatria*", the "Anti-Spain", that is all things considered alien and foreign – specifically communism, liberalism and Freemasonry. In the cultural sphere, the dictatorship, which was convinced that the cure for Spain's "decline" was to shut out foreign ideas and to preserve national values, eulogized Catholicism, rural life and imperialism.[17]

Franco himself reiterated again and again his admiration for the Catholic Kings. He liked to remind Spaniards – and probably the Germans too – that Isabella and Ferdinand's policy towards the Jews had paved the way for the Nazi antisemitic legislation. In his End of Year radio broadcast of 31 December 1939 he declared:

> *We, who were freed of this heavy burden centuries ago by the grace of God and the clear vision of Ferdinand and Isabella, cannot remain indifferent before the modern rise of avaricious egoists who are so attached to their own earthly possessions that they sacrifice the lives of their sons more readily than their own base interests.*[18]

The Francoists continued to associate Jews with Communists and Freemasons. The Law for the Suppression of Freemasonry and Communism, which was promulgated on 1 March 1940, made it "a crime to belong to Freemasonry and to Communism" and stated that all the ills of Spain since 1800 could be traced back to "the joint action of Freemasonry and of the anarchising forces, served in their turn by hidden international forces",[19] a barely veiled reference to "International Jewry".

Foreign observers feared that the antisemitic propaganda might be accompanied by certain secret anti-Jewish measures. The Jewish rescue organization HICEM asked its representative in Portugal, Dr Augusto d'Esaguy, to investigate whether Spain was preparing legislation to expel the Jewish refugees who had settled there after 1931. D'Esaguy's report was far from being reassuring. "The situation of the Jews," he wrote in April 1940 "is getting worse every day." He held the pro-Axis Serrano Suñer responsible for their problems. While D'Esaguy did not think that the Minister of Interior was contemplating legislation against the Jews, he feared that "police measures" could be "carried out secretly" as to avoid alarming "universal public opinion".[20]

D'Esaguy witnessed the "enormous influence" that the Gestapo exerted over the Spanish security police, the *Dirección General de Seguridad*. The latter organization, which was in charge of issuing visas to Spain and residency permits, was particularly hostile to Austrian and German Jewish refugees.[21] The *Director General de Seguridad*, José Finat Conde y Escrivá de Romaní, Conde de Mayalde, was one of Serrano Suñer's henchmen. In the words of a foreign observer, he was a "blackguard of the worst type", who "did all Serrano's dirty work".[22] Mayalde had been awarded the Grand Cross of the Order of the German Eagle in May 1938. Spain returned the gesture in November 1939 by bestowing the Imperial Order of Yoke and Arrow upon Heinrich Himmler, in recognition for his contribution to the struggle against Spain's "enemies" during the Civil War.[23]

From the outset of the war, the national security office, the *Dirección General de Seguridad* (DGS), showed its determination to prevent the immigration of Jews to Spain. In May 1940 the members of the *Association Culturelle Sephardite* (Sephardic Cultural Association) appealed to Franco for Jews to be allowed to immigrate to Spain. Although it was addressed to Franco, the request was not given the *Caudillo*'s personal attention. Instead it was forwarded from the Foreign Minister to the *Dirección General de Seguridad*, who rejected it without giving any reason.[24] On 5 May 1941 the DGS ordered civil governors in all provinces to compile information on Spanish and foreign Jews living in the peninsula. The reports were to specify the economic activities of Jews, their political inclination and "the degrees of danger" they represented. The DGS urged governors to pay particular attention to the Sephardic Jews, who could easily pass for Spaniards.[25]

It was in Barcelona that the situation of the Jewish community was most precarious. Franco had appointed Wenceslao González Oliveros, as his first governor. Gonzalez Oliveros' program was to "purify" Barcelona of Marxism, separatism and French influences.[26] An ardent antisemite who had praised German racism in *Acción Española* in the early 1930s, he saw Jews as disseminators of foreign ideas. In December 1939, the civil government of Barcelona created a file on the Jews living in the city, a copy of which was given to the Gestapo.[27] A few incidents also took place in Mallorca. On 21 June 1940, the US consul in Barcelona reported that all German Jews had been given ten days to leave Majorca.[28] The Jews, who interpreted this campaign as a prelude to Spain's entrance in the war on the side of the Axis, tried to leave the peninsula. But like their co-religionists throughout Europe, they faced closed borders.[29]

The situation was different in the Spanish protectorate of Morocco where in 1940 there were 14,734 Jews, 8,058 of whom lived in Tetuán.[30] The Jewish communities of Northern Morocco and Tangier were eager to develop good relations with the Nationalist regime. When the Civil War ended *Spain*, the Franco government's propaganda magazine published in England, reported that the Jewish community in Tetuán had celebrated with "great solemnity" Franco's victory. It informed its readers that at the entrance of the Jewish quarter of the town shone an illuminated sign saying "Long live Franco, the Spanish victor" and that the celebration, at which two Moorish orchestras performed, went on until dawn.[31] On 18 December 1939, the Jewish community of Tetuán sent a delegation to Madrid. They met with Beigbeder and pledged their "unshakable loyalty" to Generalissimo Franco.[32] The outbreak of World War II did not alter the status of the Jews of the Spanish protectorate. No antisemitic legislation was enacted despite the repeated requests of the German consul in Tetuán.[33]

On the contrary, the spurt of Africanism was accompanied by a revival of philosephardism, as the Franco regime grew increasingly convinced that the Moroccan Jews, with their considerable economic power, could serve Spain's imperial ambitions. On that account the Spaniards went out of their way to persuade the affluent Jews of the protectorate that their interests and those of Spain coincided.[34] One gesture of friendship, albeit an incongruous one, was the awarding of the cross of Isabella the Catholic to the president of the rabbinic tribunal of Tetuán in January 1940.[35]

Colonel Tomás García Figueras, who was first the Secretary-General of General Carlos Asensio Cabanillas, the High Commissioner for the Spanish zone of Morocco and then the Delegate for Educational Culture, exemplified the regime's attempt to combine Germanophilia, Africanism and philosephardism. He had been the *Interventor* (the administrator) of the district of Larache during the Civil War and held considerable power in the zone. Although he was a friend of Serrano Suñer and was regarded by the British Consul General in Tangier as "thoroughly pro-German", García Figueras was also eager to promote Spain's ties to the Moroccan Jews. During the Civil War he objected to the antisemitic campaign in Larache, and after Franco's victory he deplored the fact that Spain had abandoned other Jews of the protectorate by failing to counteract French influence as promoted by the schools of the *Alliance Israélite Universelle*.[36] A Francophobe and staunch *Africanista* he drew a distinction between the Jews of Spanish Morocco and their co-religionists, against whom he made the standard anti-semitic statements. Thus, in 1939 he wrote that the Jewish population of the Spanish protectorate had been "purified by its contact with Spain" and that it was "unconnected to the methods and designs of universal Judaism", which was "the enemy of civilization".[37]

While they claimed to seek genuine entente with the Sephardim of Morocco, the Spanish authorities remained preoccupied with the continued sway that France held over the Jews of the zone. The Spaniards suspected the Jews of the protectorate of harbouring pro-Allied sentiments. On 1 May 1940, the Native Office in Tetuán reported that the town's most influential Jews were raising money to help fund the French war effort.[38] A few days later the Spanish authorities in Melilla accused the Jews of being hostile to the Franco regime and of manifesting pro-French and pro-British sympathies.[39]

The Spanish authorities also tried to minimize the role of the *Alliance Israélite Universelle*, which they regarded as the instrument of France's influence over the Jews of the protectorate.[40] In November 1939 the director of the school in El Ksar wrote to the director in Paris: "The Spanish authorities do not like us. They tolerate us. They are convinced that we are here in the service of France and that we disseminate French propaganda in our schools".[41]

Although they did not close the AIU schools, the Spaniards encouraged the Jewish children of the zone to attend the tuition-free *Hebreo–Español* (Jewish–Spanish) schools instead. But their efforts did not avail, the AIU school remained more popular with the Jews of Northern Morocco than the Spanish institutions.[42]

The Jewish population of the Spanish protectorate almost doubled after Spain seized Tangier in June 1940. Spanish military forces entered the international zone in the morning of 14 June 1940, when Italy had just joined in the war and France seemed defeated. That same day, the High Commissioner, General Asensio, informed British officials that the occupation of Tangier, which had been undertaken with the agreement of France, was of a provisional nature. The other chief guarantors of the international status of the zone – Great Britain, France and Italy – were belligerents; Tangier, the Spaniards alleged, had become the focus of conspiracy and unrest. They contended that the sole object of Spain's move was to ensure the strict neutrality of the zone and that there would be no interference with the existing international civil administration of the town and district.[43]

In Madrid, Beigbeder declared to the French Ambassador Comte Robert de la Baume that this arrangement, which was exceptional and temporary, would in no way be prejudicial to the permanence of the international regime. In stark contrast to Asensio and Beigbeder's soothing words, the Spanish press coverage of the news was imbued with a chauvinism that suggested the move was permanent.[44] The seizure of Tangier was only an initial step in the fulfillment of Spain's aspirations in Morocco. In the words of Samuel Hoare, "the Spanish troops", which had entered Tangier, "were made to appear as the advance guard of an army that was to conquer Morocco and recreate the African Empire of Charles V".[45] On the collapse of France, rumour was rife that Spanish troops had actually crossed the frontiers into French Morocco. Although this proved to be incorrect, it was believed that the Spaniards would soon act to recover that part of French Morocco up to the Sebou River, which they regarded as theirs by right.[46]

That the official explanation given at the time for the military occupation of the Tangier zone was inadequate was to become evident five months later, in November 1940, when the head of the Spanish occupation forces, Colonel Antonio Yuste, assumed the position of Governor General of Tangier. He abolished the Committee of Control and the Legislative Assembly. By the end of the year the international administration was dismantled.[47] Tangier was formally incorporated into the Spanish protectorate in Morocco on 15 March 1941 with the announcement through a *Dahir*, or native decree, that Tangier had become the sixth district of Spanish Morocco.[48]

When the Spaniards occupied Tangier, the Jewish community of Tangier had between 12,000 to 14,000 Jews. As the Franco regime consolidated its position in Tangier it abrogated the *Dahir* of February 1925 concerning the structural makeup of the Jewish council and institutions and all communal projects came under Spanish supervision. The communal leaders, who had previously been elected by the community, were now appointed by Spain and had to be either Spanish or Moroccan citizens.[49] Tangier's Jewish elite, which had developed some ties with the Francoists during the Civil War, continued to enjoy a privileged place. They maintained a large share of the import and export market for eggs, hides and manufactured goods and they still controlled the banking sector. The Spanish occupation, however, adversely affected the lower middle classes; the Spanish authorities imposed heavy taxes on their businesses and frequently refused them new licenses.[50]

The Jewish community of Tangier also included about two thousand refugees who had arrived in Tangier in the late 1930s.[51] Half were Sephardim, mostly from the Dodecanese Islands; the remainder had come from Poland, Italy, Germany and Austria.[52] The refugees from Central Europe did not integrate well within the Jewish community of Tangier. The affluent Sephardim feared that the refugees' political ideas and liberal customs would engender a wave of antisemitism and they called them disdainfully *los Polacos* (the Polaks).[53]

In May 1940, one month before the Spanish occupation, the Legislative

Assembly of the International Zone of Tangier had passed a law prohibiting the admission of more refugees.[54] According to a report sent by the Jewish community of Tangier to the War Refugee Board in 1944, the Franco regime was adamant in keeping Tangier's doors shut after its incorporation into the Spanish zone; with the exception of American citizens and British subjects, none could enter either Tangier or the Spanish Zone of Morocco unless they had been granted a special authorization from the Ministry of Foreign Affairs in Madrid.[55]

Among the few refugees whom the Spanish authorities exceptionally allowed to settle in Tangier after the outbreak of the war was the Reichmann family. The latter were ultra-Orthodox Hungarian Jews who would later found a great real estate empire, Olympia & York, which included such landmark skyscrapers as New York City's World Financial Center and Toronto's First Canadian Place. According to the family's biographer, Anthony Bianco, the Reichmanns probably obtained the Spanish Foreign Ministry's authorization to enter Tangier thanks to the intervention of Jacobo Salama, a wealthy Jewish merchant from Melilla, who had close ties to the Spanish administration.[56]

The First Wave of Refugees

In the meantime Germany's lightning victory over France and the subsequent occupation of Northern France by the German army in June 1940 brought a line of Jewish and non-Jewish refugees to the Pyrenean frontier. Refugees from Germany and Austria, who had already had a foretaste of French xenophobia, were particularly anxious to leave France. In fact 15,000 of them had been rounded up in the first days of the war on the ground that they were 'enemy aliens' and potential fifth columnists; they had been sent to join the Spanish republican refugees and members of the international brigades in the internment camps of Southern France.[57] The internees included luminaries such as the author Arthur Koestler, the novelist Lion Feuchtwanger, the philosopher and political scientist Hannah Arendt and the painter Max Ernst. In the words of Donna Ryan, the records of the internment centre of Les Milles in the Bouches du Rhône "read like a Who's Who in Weimar Germany and Interwar Vienna".[58]

After the fall of France, many of these refugees were released or escaped the camps. Their respite, however, was short-lived. According to Article 19 of the armistice, the French government agreed to surrender on demand any refugees from the Third Reich requested by the German government.[59] Their only chance was to leave France as quickly as possible. Following the closing of French seaports, refugees had to travel by train through Spain to Portugal. While the majority of refugees headed to Lisbon, from where they could arrange passage across the Atlantic, those with Cuban visas, planned to take Spanish boats from Vigo to Havana.[60]

Legal emigration from France was a Byzantine process: candidates needed entry visas from an overseas country, an exit visa from France, transit visas for crossing Spain and Portugal as well as paid ship passage. The Portuguese only granted visas to those who had an entry visa for some other country and emigrants could only apply for Spanish transit visas when they had the Portuguese document. Lisa Fittko, an anti-Nazi activist, remembers that "every country was afraid that the émigrés would settle in with them like bedbugs".[61]

In the summer of 1940 the majority of emigrants flocked to Marseilles, which held the main consulates of Vichy France. Some refugees had to stand in front of the Spanish consulate in Marseilles three nights in a row to get a transit visa.[62] Entry into Spain was regulated by two decrees. The first, promulgated on 11 May 1939, closed Spain's doors to foreign Jews, unless they had supported the Nationalists during the Spanish Civil War.[63] The second decree, issued on 1 May 1940, stated that Spanish consuls could no longer grant entry visas themselves; they had to telegraph visa applications to Spain and obtain permission from the DGS. However, Spanish consuls were still authorized to issue transit visas as long as the applicants possessed transit visas to Portugal.[64] This meant that the Spanish government only allowed Jewish refugees to transit through Spain on their way to Portugal.

Those who secured all required permits took the train from Marseille, spent the night in Narbonne and crossed the frontier in the border towns of Cerbère, on the French side, and Port Bou on the Spanish side. Once they had obtained the Spanish entry stamps, they traveled by train to Lisbon. The entire journey from Marseille to Lisbon took at least three days.[65]

Because of bureaucratic obstruction, French exit visas were difficult to obtain, especially for German and Austrian Jews who had been deprived of their nationality by the Third Reich and were now *apatrides* or stateless. While some *apatrides* managed to obtain false passports, many others had to leave France illegally by walking across the Pyrenees from Cerbère to Port-Bou. The long and arduous hike could take up to twelve hours.

Fortunately, in the first months after the armistice most refugees who entered Spain illegally had no difficulty with the Spanish border authorities. They just had to present themselves to the sentries in Port-Bou in order to obtain the Spanish entry stamp. Those who failed to do so, however, could be arrested for illegal entry and be interned.[66] The women were sent to regional jails while the men were confined to the Miranda de Ebro concentration camp close to the town of Burgos, which had originally been intended for the Republicans.[67]

Spanish border guards were easily bribed, with money as well as with tobacco, which was in shortage in post-Civil War Spain.[68] In his memoirs Varian Fry, the Marseille representative of the Emergency Rescue Committee, a US organization devoted to saving prominent refugees, recounted that he stuffed the bags of his *protégés* with packs of *Gauloises bleues* and *Gitanes* before they left for their journey across the Pyrenees. The trick seemed to work. After crossing the Pyrennes without a French exit permit, Lion Feuchtwanger's wife, Martha, tossed a pile of cigarette packs on the table of the Spanish customs house where she had stopped to obtain the entry stamp. As all Spanish officers lunged for them, one of the men stamped her paper without even looking at her.[69]

The attitude of the Spanish border guards towards the refugees tended to reflect their political sympathies. In her memoirs, Alma Mahler-Werfel, widow of Gustav Mahler and wife of the Austrian writer Franz Werfel, remembered her astonishment when upon her arrival in Port-Bou the customs house porters brought her wine, wished her good luck and cursed Franco and Mussolini. She wrote: "Catalonia was apparently still antifascist, and we took courage in spite of our great weariness."[70]

Not all refugees, however, experienced the same hospitality. The French composer Darius Milhaud, who crossed the French–Spanish frontier legally in the summer of 1940, was thoroughly searched by young Falangists "wearing scornful and triumphant expressions on their faces". Milhaud almost missed his train because they insisted on weighing every tube in his stock of homeopathic remedies and looked it up in the dictionary.[71]

A few refugees traveling on false passports had to pay large bribes to avoid arrest.[72] Others, who had booked trans-Atlantic passage on Spanish steamers, saw their visas to their final destinations expire as sailings were delayed. They were in a difficult situation since they had come to Spain for transit purposes only and were now compelled to remain for an indefinite period of time until these visas could be renewed. The cost of living in Spain being extremely high, most of these people exhausted their resources rapidly and came to depend on American welfare organizations. Although the Spanish government did not allow such organizations to operate in Spain, the Joint Distribution Committee managed to help Jewish refugees through the offices of Virginia Weddell, the wife of the US Ambassador.[73]

Despite those few incidents, Fry remained convinced that for most of the refugees the route through Spain was the best one.[74] All in all about 20,000 Jews passed through Spain and Portugal legally and illegally on the way to the Western Hemisphere between June and September 1940.[75] But that policy began to change in the late summer of 1940.

Throughout September Spain opened and closed its frontier several times. Sometimes the frontier was open for a few hours a day and sometimes it was open for a whole day. The refugees were trapped in France. Fry noted: "It would be hard to imagine a crueler way of torturing human being. Every opening meant hope renewed, every closing hope abandoned."[76] One victim of Spain's inconsistent policy was the German Jewish philosopher Walter Benjamin. Benjamin, who had a visa to the United States but had failed to secure a French exit visa, had decided to get into Spain illegally in late September with two other refugees. Since the route via Cerbère was now closely watched, they had to take a secret smuggler's path, known as *la route Lister*, because General Lister, of the Republican army, had used it for his troops during the Spanish Civil War.[77] Upon the group's arrival in Port Bou, after a ten-hour walk, the Spanish border authorities informed them that because they were stateless they would be taken back to France the next day.[78]

Walter Benjamin knew that his return to France would lead to his arrest and his dispatch to a French internment camp and then to a concentration camp in Germany. In despair, he took a large dose of morphine and died the following day. Spanish officials, who had found on Benjamin a letter of a recommendation from a prominent French clergyman, assumed that he was a Catholic and buried him in the Catholic cemetery of Port Bou. In a poignant epilogue the Spanish authorities allowed the rest of his group to pass through Spain immediately after his death.[79]

On 8 October 1940, Madrid issued a new decree, which ordained that Spanish Consuls could no longer grant any transit visas themselves but had to telegraph all visas applicants to Spain. Before doing that they had to verify that the applicant had a genuine overseas visa, a transit visa from Portugal and had paid a passage on a ship sailing from Lisbon on a fixed date.[80] Fry believed that "every name telegraphed to Madrid was submitted to a Gestapo agent, and no authorization for a visa would be granted until the Gestapo agent had given his consent".[81]

Given that the Portuguese consul had received similar instructions from Lisbon it became almost impossible to have all the visas valid at the same time. By the time the refugees had received the Spanish visa, their Portuguese visas or their visas to a final destination had generally expired.[82]

The Spaniards blamed Portugal for the change of border policy. The Conde de Mayalde told de la Baume that Spain had become reluctant to let

Jews travel through Spain because the Portuguese government was often turning them back at the Spanish–Portuguese frontier.[83] Fry, however, did not believe that the refugee bottleneck in Lisbon had motivated the Francoists. He was convinced that "the only adequate explanation of Spain's new regulations" was "a political one".[84]

Spain's new border policy must indeed be understood in the context of the Francoists' efforts to ingratiate themselves with the Germans. In the fall of 1940 Franco had become sure of Germany's ultimate success and he hoped to enter the war on the Axis side in return for the fulfillment of his colonial ambitions. Closing the borders to Jewish refugees was probably one way to establish Spain's credential as a worthy partner of Nazi Germany.

The increasingly pro-German leanings of the regime were reflected in the growing dominance of Serrano Suñer, who became Foreign Minister in October 1940, as well as in the exchange visits between Spanish and German leaders and in the closer collaboration between the Gestapo and the *Dirección General de Seguridad*. Hence, Mayalde came to Berlin in August 1940 to discuss the fate of the Republican refugees who had been captured by the Gestapo in occupied France. During their meeting Himmler proposed that Spain and Germany exchanged police liaison officers; his aim was to increase the Gestapo network in Spain to keep watch of the German refugees.[85]

In mid-September Franco sent Serrano Suñer on a mission to Berlin to negotiate the terms of Spain's entry in the war. In his discussions with the Nazi leadership, Serrano Suñer was forthright about Spanish aspirations in Northwest Africa, describing French Morocco as belonging "to Spain's *Lebensraum*". But Hitler and Ribbentrop, who had ambitions of their own in Morocco, informed him that a united Morocco under Spanish rule would come at the following price: the cession of one of the Canary Islands for a German base, and further bases in Mogador and in Agadir. The Germans also pressed for substantial economic concessions and participation in mining interests in Morocco.[86]

Despite his indignation at Germany's requests, Serrano Suñer invited Himmler to Madrid to give him advice on the liquidation of opponents and the capture of political refugees.[87] The *Reichsführer SS* arrived in Spain on 19 October and was greeted with much pomp and ceremony. During a dinner party held on 22 October, Mayalde expressed his desire for close cooperation between the Gestapo and the Spanish police against what he referred to as the "International Powers" – an allusion to the Judeo-Masonic-Bolshevik conspiracy.[88]

Consular Protection to the Spanish Jews

In the meantime the danger for Jews in France was becoming more pressing. On 27 September 1940, the Germans published a decree imposing on every Jew in occupied France the obligation to report to the police station where they would be entered in a special register. The decree defined a Jew as anyone who belonged to the Jewish religion as well as anyone who was the descendant of three grandparents of the "Jewish race".[89] A second order published on 18 October 1940 required that Jews registered their property at the French prefectures and established a system for nominating administrators of Jewish businesses.[90] The intention was clear: the confiscation of Jewish property in the occupied zone.

The decree also affected the 2,000 Spanish Jews who were registered at the Spanish consulate in Paris. Some of them approached the Spanish consulate shortly after the promulgation of the first German decrees. They wanted to know whether they had to be registered and to submit a list of their properties to the French police. The initial reaction of Bernardo Rolland, the Spanish Consul in Paris, was to object the imposing of antisemitic legislation on Spanish nationals on the grounds that no racial law existed in Spain. The Spanish Ambassador in Vichy, José Felix Lequerica, reported Rolland's attitude to Madrid on 8 November and asked the Foreign Ministry to formulate its position.[91]

The following day Serrano Suñer's reply, which was sent to Lequerica on the following day, clearly reflected the fact that the Foreign Ministry's position was very different from that of Rolland and was indifferent to the fate of Spain's Jewish nationals in France:

> You are requested to inform the Consul that his response to the German authorities is neither approved nor in an accordance with the viewpoint of this government. He must completely submit to these measures, he must not impede their enforcement, and he must keep a passive attitude. Although there are no racial laws in Spain, the Spanish government cannot prevent its Jewish subjects from being exposed to regulations of a general nature.[92]

Despite Madrid's dissuasive orders, the Spanish representatives in Paris were reluctant to give up the defence of the Spanish Jews' properties. The chargé d'affaires of the Spanish Embassy, Mario de Piniés, took advantage of Serrano Suñer's stopover in Paris on his way to Germany in December 1940 to point out the damage to Spanish interests bound to arise from the new antisemitic legislation. In a meeting with Barón de las Torres, Antonio Tovar and García Figueras, who were all accompanying Serrano, he explained that the aim of both the French and German authorities was to proceed to the confiscation of Jewish property. To allow this, he declared, would be the same as "to make a donation of no less than a few millions without receiving in exchange any compensation or any expression of gratitude for this generosity".[93] In order to prevent the exploitation of the situation by the French and German authorities, Piniés suggested that the Spanish consulate protect Jewish businesses. The Spanish Jews, in exchange, would make a donation to the Franco regime, which would contribute to Spain's "resurgence". The German authorities would be informed that Spain was willing to collaborate with their "*medidas de limpieza*" ("cleansing" measures) but could not give up its rights on its subjects.

On their way to Berlin, the Barón de las Torres, Antonio Tovar and García Figueras expounded Piniés' proposal to Serrano who approved it.[94] Did the philosephardic García Figueras play a particular role in convincing his friend Serrano to accept Piniés' suggestions? He might have thrown all his weight behind Piniés' argument as he must have realized that to give up the rights of the Spanish Jews in France would eventually force Spain to relinquish their rights in French Morocco, too, which could have far-reaching political and economic consequences.

But even without the backing of García Figueras, Piniés' proposal was likely to strike a chord with Serrano. Increasingly frustrated with Berlin and Vichy's refusal to indulge Spain's imperial ambitions, Serrano Suñer could only embrace a plan, whose tenet was to prevent the property of Spanish Jews from falling into French or German hands. On 26 December 1940, upon being informed that the German authorities had initiated the confiscation of the Spanish Jews' properties and were about to appoint commissioners to oversee them, Serrano Suñer instructed the Spanish Embassy in Paris to protect the interests of the Spanish Jews.[95] In accordance with these instructions, the staff of the consulate in Paris reached an agreement with the French and German authorities in the spring 1941 whereby Spanish commissioners, under the supervision of the Bank of Spain, would be appointed to oversee the businesses of Spanish Jews in both the occupied and unoccupied zones.[96]

There remained, however, some serious reservations regarding the defense of the Spanish Jews. A report drafted by the political department of the Foreign Ministry on 26 February 1941 emphasized the need to distinguish between three categories of Spanish Jews: those who had availed themselves of the 1924 decree and were unquestionably Spaniards those who had availed themselves of the decree but had failed to register in the population registry, as required by the citizenship law and finally those who had been Spanish citizens or *protégés* until 1924 but had missed the opportunity to avail themselves of the decree. The property of those in the first category had to be protected "because their defense was in the interest of Spain from an economic and political point of view". Each case in the second group would be considered individually. Finally, with regards to the third group, the Spanish authorities were to display "their willingness to collaborate" with the Germans "and to facilitate the implementation of the antisemitic measures" by "giving in completely". The message was clear: Spain would throw its protective mantle only over a few selected Spanish Jews.

By the summer of 1941 the situation of the Spanish Jews in France became hazardous. The opening of the Eastern Front on 22 June 1941 was accompanied by preparations towards the "Final Solution of the Jewish Problem" throughout Europe. In Paris, the French police, under German orders, conducted the first manhunts in August 1941. Among the 4,232 Jews arrested and transferred to the Camp of Drancy were fourteen Spanish nationals.[97] Rolland demanded that they be released at once but his repeated requests to the German officials and the French police were to no avail.

As the antisemitic campaign in occupied France intensified, Rolland began doubting whether the Spanish consulate would be able to protect its citizens there. He reported his doubts to the Ministry of Foreign Affairs on 10 September 1941, noting that soon the Spanish Jews would either be imprisoned in concentration camp or would be given a deadline to abandon the occupied zone. They would probably not be allowed to take their capital or large sums of money with them, which would "create another serious problem", a broad hint that the Spanish Jews, were they to be repatriated, could become a burden on Spanish coffers.[98]

While he was reluctant to repatriate the Spanish Jews to peninsular Spain, Rolland did not object to their repatriation to Spanish Morocco, possibly because there was already a well-established Jewish community there. In September 1941 he proposed to the Germans to send the 2,000 Spanish Jews living in France to Spanish Morocco provided that those detained in Drancy could come along. But the Spanish government and the German authorities failed to respond to Rolland's proposal and the fourteen Spanish citizens remained in Drancy.[99]

The Franco regime was equally reluctant to repatriate Spanish Jews from the Balkans. The DGS, in particular, remained virulently opposed to any Jewish immigration. The issue of Spain's consular protection in the Balkans was first raised in Romania. On 2 July 1940, the Spanish *chargé d'affaires* in Bucharest, Alfonso Merry del Val, reported that the upsurge of antisemitism in Romania would soon endanger the Spanish nationals there. Merry del Val reported that the pro-Franco sentiments of the one hundred Spanish Jews had earned them the hostility of their co-religionists and would justify their evacuation to Spain or to Spanish Morocco. He emphasized that they were affluent and therefore unlikely to become a burden on Spanish treasury.[100]

The Foreign Ministry's reply was sent on 2 August 1940. It had been drafted by Carlos de Miranda, the former Nationalist envoy in Bulgaria now working in the European department of the Foreign Ministry, who wrote that it was "neither desirable nor opportune to bring to Spain a large population, which even if it is Sephardic is, after all, Jewish". Yet he realized that Spain could "not ignore or completely abandon those of its citizens who, even if they were Jewish had efficiently contributed [. . .] to the victory of the Nationalist movement". Hence, Miranda declared, the evacuation of the Spanish Jews would be contingent on their attitude during the Civil War and that special permission would be needed in each case. Finally, Miranda expressed his reluctance to send the Spanish Jews to Morocco, where their presence could exacerbate the "traditional antipathy of the Moroccan people towards Jews". He would rather repatriate them to mainland Spain, where "it would be much easier to keep watch over them and to prevent their possible noxious activities".[101] Miranda's report was passed to the Interior Ministry and from there to the DGS. The reply, which was sent on 2 September 1940 to the Foreign Ministry, was adamant: the *Dirección General de Seguridad* considered that none of these requests for repatriation should be granted.[102]

Spanish intervention was also needed in Greece, in the sector of eastern Macedonia and parts of Thrace, which were placed under German control in April 1941. In Salonica, the centre of Sephardic culture in the Balkans, the 511 Spanish nationals were exempted from the antisemitic measures implemented by the Germans.[103] On 1 November 1941, Eduardo Gasset, the Spanish consul in Athens, informed the Foreign Ministry, through the intermediary of the Italian Embassy, that given the shortage of food supplies, some Spanish citizens wished to immigrate to Spain. Madrid gave the standard reply: a special permission would be needed in each case, contingent on the applicant's qualifications and on the place in Spain where he or she wanted to settle.[104] As the fate of the Jews of Greece continued to deteriorate, Eduardo Gasset informed the Foreign Ministry on 13 March 1942 that it would have to decide whether to continue protecting them or to abandon them. He suggested that if the Spanish government opted to defend them, it could in exchange ask them for some contributions to promote the cultural interests of Spain in Greece. Spain might thus be able to establish a centre for Spanish culture and archaeological research in Athens and compete with France, which had long had such a centre.[105] The answer of the Foreign Ministry is not known but Gasset's proposal is in itself noteworthy. It demonstrates again the opportunistic nature of the Franco regime's policy towards the Jews and its jealousy of France's ascendancy over the Sephardic Jews.

Spain's Colonial Ambitions and the Jews in French Morocco

In contrast to the situation in France and in the Balkans, the Spanish authorities adopted a pro-active approach in defending the rights of those of their nationals in the French Moroccan protectorate, who were affected by the antisemitic legislation of the Vichy regime. On 3 October 1940, the Vichy government published the first *Statut des Juifs* (Jewish Statute), which forbade Jews to hold any post in the public service, the officer corps of the armed forces, teaching, journalism, the theatre, radio and cinema.[106] The law, introduced in French Morocco through the *Dahir* of 31 October 1940, affected the 2,000 Spanish Jews living in the French protectorate.[107] The reaction of the Spanish diplomats to the *Dahir* must be understood within the context of Spain's efforts to squeeze out concessions from France in Morocco. In their campaign for imperial expansion, the Francoists used demographic arguments, pointing out that many Spaniards lived in French North Africa.[108]

On 31 July 1941, the Spanish Consul in Casablanca reported that the French authorities refused to recognize the naturalizations of the Spanish Jews on the grounds that they had not been obtained with the consent of the Sultan, as stipulated in the agreement signed at the Madrid conference of 1880. This meant, in practice, that the Spanish Jews living in French Morocco were set to lose their citizenship and be subjected to the antisemitic legislation. These Spanish Jews were persecuted, the Spanish consul in Casablanca, Jaime Jorro, believed, not because they were Jews but because they were Spaniards who, as such, constituted "a factor of economic penetration" in the French zone. Anticipating the impending enactment of further antisemitic decrees, Jorro asked the Foreign Ministry for instructions.[109]

Six days later, on 5 August 1941 another *Dahir* was issued to introduce Vichy's second *Statut des Juifs* of 2 June 1941. This decree enlarged the list of occupations prohibited to the Jews to include money lending and the real estate business. It also required that all Jews in the French protectorate register their persons, occupation and declare their property to the authorities.

On 22 September, Jorro sent a telegram to the Foreign Ministry asking whether the Spanish Jews could be exempted from the census. "I believe," he wrote "that from a Spanish point of view, it is not possible to accept France's policy and to abandon an important factor of political and economic penetration."[110] The same day, the French consul in Larache wrote a report, echoing some of Jorro's assertions: "The Sephardim are the most affluent elements in the Moroccan cities", he stated, "most of the important businessmen in Casablanca are either from Tangier or Tetuán".[111] On 29 September, Jorro visited his American colleague in Casablanca, H. Earle Russell, to sound out the attitude of the US government regarding the *Dahirs* affecting the Jews of Morocco. Russell informed him that in view of its constitutional traditions and ideas, it was unlikely that the American government would ever accept such legislation. Jorro, for his part, carefully refrained from giving any indication of what Spain's attitude might be.[112]

Jorro's dispatches indicated that the Spaniards' objection to the imposition of antisemitic legislation on their citizens arose from the need to protect their economic position and their prestige in the French zone rather than from ethical concern. In fact, explicit in all Spanish representatives' reports was both their belief in the enduring power of the Jews and their indifference to the fate of non-Spanish Jews. Thus, on 8 October 1941, the Spanish High Commissioner in Morocco, Luis Orgaz, wrote a report to the Foreign Ministry in which he contrasted the hostility of the French authorities towards the Spanish Jews originating from their zone to their "benevolent attitude" towards the French and Moroccan Jews.[113] On 30 October Orgaz sent another dispatch, asserting that the Resident General in French Morocco, General Charles Noguès, mindful of "the endless resources" of the Jews, had modified the Jewish statute in favour of the Moroccan Jews. The latter, in contrast to the Spanish Jews, no longer had to declare their property if its value did not exceed 50,000 francs.[114]

The opportunism of the Spanish representatives was not lost on the French. "Jorro is above all interested in protecting the properties of the Jews", wrote Noguès, in a report to the French Foreign Minister Admiral François Darlan, on 4 December 1941. The Spaniards' policy, Noguès added, had a double aim: one was to create a minority problem by increasing the number of Spanish nationals in French Morocco, the other was to enhance Spain's economic position there; Spain's overall aspiration being to substantiate its claims in Morocco. To that end, Jorro was trying to convince the well-to-do Jews of French Morocco to go to Tangier or the Spanish protectorate, where they could obtain Spanish nationality. He promised them that in return the Jewish statutes promulgated by the Vichy regime would not affect them.[115]

The defense of the Spanish Jews of French Morocco was accompanied by a philosephardic campaign in Spain. In 1941, the Ministry of Education in Madrid opened the *Escuela de Estudios Hebraicos* (School for Hebrew Studies), which began publishing the journal *Sefarad*. In the fall of 1941 Garcia Figueras conducted a vast campaign among the Jews of the Spanish protectorate for the subscription to *Sefarad*.[116] His activities came to the notice of the French representatives in the zone and to the Ambassador in Madrid, Francois Pietri, who wrote to Vichy a report about the aim of *Sefarad*, noting that Spain was "trying to flaunt its knowledge of the Semitic civilizations in Africa so as to appear as the protector of the Jewish communities of Morocco".[117]

The first issue of *Sefarad* made clear that the rekindling of philosephardism did not imply the outright rejection of Nazi antisemitism:

> *It was not in Spain that Judaism acquired the materialistic character that some of its segments evince; it was in Provence, in the Pagan Italy of the Renaissance and finally in the frozen valleys of the Batavian coast, under the rationalistic north wind, that this havoc began.*[118]

Hence, as they trod carefully between their friendship with Nazi Germany and their renewed interest in the Moroccan Jews, the Francoists revived the distinction between Sephardic and Ashkenazi Jews, praising the former and pinning negative stereotypes on the latter. The Sephardic Jews, they asserted, had been "purified" by their stay in Spain. This notion was expressed in the autobiographical film-script *Raza*, which Franco wrote between the end of 1940 and the beginning of 1941. In the following passage, the hero José Churruca, his mother and his sister, Isabel, walk by the synagogue of Santa María la Blanca in Toledo. A dialogue ensues:

> THE MOTHER –*This is the famous synagogue, isn't it José?*
>
> JOSÉ – *Yes, another place full of evocations.*
>
> ISABEL – *What can the Church of the Jews evoke?*
>
> JOSÉ – *Of the Jews? { . . . }. Who knows! The synagogues, the mosques and the Churches were passed around. The Jews, the Moors, the Christians lived here and in contact with Spain they were purified.*
>
> THE MOTHER – *The Moors and the Jews, my son?*
>
> JOSÉ – *It is true. I have told you, not long ago, the chivalrous gesture of the Moors in front of Doña Berenguela. Instead of one of these temples, a synagogue, which had housed Saint James, had been built. The Church fathers say that when the Pharisees decided that Jesus had to die they wrote to the most important syna-*

gogues to get their approval. Not only did the Spanish Jews refuse to do so, they protested and after Jesus' death they sent ambassadors who asked that St James come to Spain to preach the Gospels.[119]

The passage shows that although Franco did not adopt Nazi racism, he did not deviate from traditional Christian anti-Judaism and still accused the Jews of being guilty of deicide. To accept the Spanish Jews as Spaniards he had to declare that they had not taken part in the crucifixion. He argued that the Spanish Jews had asked St James to come to Spain to evangelize them, a hint that they felt no loyalty towards their brethren and that they were willing to convert. Thus it seems that Franco was willing to claim as Spaniards the Spanish Jews only by denying their identity as Jews.

That attitude reverberated in the Spanish press. In June 1941 *El Mundo* justified Spain's treatment of the Moroccan Jews by arguing that the latter did "not serve the aims of international Judaism" and that they had neither "infiltrated the state's administrative apparatus, nor invaded the liberal professions".[120]

In fact, the Franco regime oscillated almost schizophrenically between the philosephardic campaign and the crusade against the "Judeo-Masonic-Bolshevik" conspiracy. The Nazi invasion of the Soviet Union in June 1941, and the ensuing decision of Franco to send the Blue Division of Falangist volunteers to fight the Russians, further reinforced the atmosphere of anti-communism in Spain. On 24 June, *Amanecer* published an editorial welcoming the dispatch of the Blue Division to the Eastern front. Identifying the Jews, Freemasons and Bolsheviks with diseases, the Falangist daily asserted that both Spain and Germany had been "vaccinated against the same Judeo-Masonic virus: Communism".[121]

In *España y el mar* (Spain and the sea) Franco's *éminence grise*, Carrero Blanco, asserted that the war against the Soviet Union was part of the age-old "struggle of Christianity against Judaism".[122] Carrero Blanco used antisemitism as a canopy to express his hostility not only to the Soviet Union but also to the Western Allies. In a report he wrote to Franco in 1941, he asserted that the "Anglo-Saxon-Soviet front" was "really the front of Jewish power" and that the aim of Judaism was "to provoke a dis-astrous situation which would result in the collapse of the Christian civilization".[123] Carrero Blanco reiterated the accusation that the Jews were both Bolsheviks and unscrupulous capitalists who disregarded national borders, "brandishing simultaneously the weapons of separatism and internationalism".[124]

The spectre of another expulsion of the Jews from Spain continued to loom large in the first years of the war. In February 1941, the wife of the

American Ambassador, Virginia Chase Weddell, reported to the American Jewish Joint Distribution Committee in New York that several German Jews who had been living in Majorca for fifteen years had been arrested and ordered to depart. They were released after her intervention on the condition that they would leave Spain. Those who could not depart were subsequently imprisoned in the concentration camp of Miranda de Ebro.[125] That same month the US Consul in Barcelona, AC Frost, reported the uneasiness of the Jewish community as rumours abounded that the Spanish authorities planned, under the instigation of the Gestapo, to expel all Jews living in Spain. The Jews were attempting frantically to obtain visas for countries on the American continent.[126] In January 1942, the vice-secretary of the Falange and close follower of Serrano Suñer, José Luna, declared at a public meeting: "We shall proceed to the expulsion of the Jews with the firmness that may be necessary, consistent with the doctrine of unity."[127] In April 1942, the police of Barcelona arrested several Jews whom the Falangists had denounced as having fought for the Republicans and who were suspected of being fifth columnists for the Allies.[128]

As the tide of war turned in favor of the Allies, the suspicion increased that the Jews of Spanish Morocco were harbouring pro-Allied sentiments and the Spaniards put many of them under surveillance.[129] In May 1942, the DGS charged that the Jews of Tangier were volunteering to fight with the Allied forces and were working for the British intelligence service.[130] Oddly enough, even the Jews who had supported the Nationalists during the Civil War were now believed to be at the service of the Allies. The Hassan family, for instance, whose bank had funded the Francoist uprising, was suspected of financing the French war effort, disseminating pro-Allied propaganda among the Muslims and plotting with the English and American diplomatic representatives to re-establish the international status of Tangier. In June 1942, the Spanish police in Tetuán considered expelling Augusto and Joe Hassan but realized that it was impossible because the former was the Portuguese Consul in Tangier and the latter the Portuguese vice-consul in Larache.[131]

Jewish refugees in Tangier were in a particularly precarious situation. Most of them were Ashkenazi Jews and since they could not serve Spain's imperial ambitions, they were merely tolerated by the Spanish authorities. They had to face the ever-increasing influence of the Germans in Tangier. In March 1941, the Spaniards had permitted Germany to establish a consul general in the Mendoub's palace; the main function of this official was to spy upon the activities of the Allies in North Africa.[132] In August 1942, several Jewish refugees from Central and Eastern Europe sent a letter to the American Joint Jewish Distribution Committee in New York to complain about the increasing influence of the Germans over Spaniards. They reported being harassed by the Spanish police, which asked them when they intended to leave Tangier. As the majority of refugees did not have visas to another destination, they said that they would depart Tangier at the end of the war. They were then informed that if they did not leave Tangier within three or four months they would be given "board and lodging free of charge in some brand new concentration camp".[133] All in all the Spanish authorities did not carry out their threats but a number of stateless refugees, among them former Hungarian nationals, were expelled without being given any reason. The American *chargé d'affaires* in Tangier, Charles Burke Elbrick, believed that some of these persons were expelled out of suspicion of being Allied agents.[134]

Some members of the diplomatic corps were also hostile to the Jews, even to those who were Spanish nationals. Lequerica, for instance, was reluctant to defend Spanish Jews in Vichy France on the grounds that they were Spain's eternal enemies, allied to both the Soviet Union and the democracies. In March 1942 he shrugged off a request from the Foreign Ministry that he insist on Spain's right to appoint Spanish commissioners to oversee the businesses of Spanish Jews in Vichy France. In his response to the Foreign Ministry, Lequerica commended Vichy's antisemitic legislation. "This delegation," he wrote, "has never pretended to object to France controlling the lot of French Jews and to it defending itself against the Jews of other countries who have established themselves on its territory." In his view, it was not appropriate for Spain, which was "at war against one of the principal forces of international Judaism: Russian Bolshevism", to join the United States and Great Britain in the defense of the Jews.[135]

Although he agreed to defend the economic interests of the Spanish Jews Lequerica did not believe, in contrast to *Africanistas* such as García Figueras, that they could contribute to Spain's regeneration let alone promote its colonial expansion.

As the French administration in Morocco continued to refuse acknowledging Spanish naturalizations, Lequerica brought the issue to the attention of Vichy in February 1942, to no avail. The Spaniards' stratagems in French Morocco continued to worry the French authorities. On 4 February, Noguès dispatched an intelligence report to Darlan, entitled "Spanish action on Jewish elements", which originated from Casablanca. The report stated that the Falange backed Jorro. Thus, during a visit to Casablanca, the chief of the Falange exterior, Aragón, had met up with the notables of the Jewish community. "The Falange," he had reportedly declared, "has now forgiven the Jews for the support they have given the Republicans." Aragón had pledged that Spain "would not abandon the Jews of its zone (Tangier included) even if they found themselves in the French zone" and that "it will grant them its protection".[136] This rhetoric could only irritate the French authorities. "The presence of a foreign (racial) minority in this country," Noguès wrote to Darlan on 11 February 1942, "could cause us a serious problem, by threatening our authority in the zone."[137]

Faced with the resoluteness of the French government, Lequerica came up with an original idea: Spain could retaliate by adopting hostile measures against the French Jews living in Tangier and the Spanish protectorate.[138] Lequerica's malicious proposal, again reflecting the Francoist hostility to non-Spanish Jews, was not implemented and the issue of Spanish naturalizations remained a thorn in Franco–Spanish relations in Morocco until the Allied landing of November 1942.

The deterioration of the situation of the Jews of France during the second half of 1942, with the massive manhunts in both zones and the deportation that ensued, failed to move Lequerica. On the contrary, he vilified prominent clerics, such as Cardinal Pierre Gerlier in Lyon and Monsignor Jules – Gérard Saliège, the archbishop of Toulouse, who openly expressed their opposition to the arrests of thousands of Jews.[139] The prelates' protests resounded through the country and abroad, prompting Lequerica to devote several detailed memoranda on what he called "the philo-israelite" ardour of the French clergy. The Spanish Ambassador denounced Saliège and Gerlier as Spain's "old enemies" who had protected "red murderers" during the Civil War.[140] He sneered at their protests, which, he believed, were motivated by their Germanophobia, their desire for revenge, and their willingness "to support with all possible means the anti-German coalition backed up by the Jews' financial power". Their criticisms, Lequerica asserted, were ill-founded, as "only eleven thousand Jews" had been arrested, who were foreign citizens whom "the French government had the right to send back to their countries of origin". The all-powerful Jews, Lequerica concluded, had orchestrated the campaign of the French clerics. "It is," he wrote "always the privilege of the Jew to arouse this excessive compassion, to organize it and to exploit it."[141]

Spain's attitude towards the Jews in the first half of the war was linked to the political factors that directed its policy during those days. The climate of repression, the regime's identification with the fifteenth-century Catholic Kings and the influence of Nazi Germany called for a continuation of the antisemitic rhetoric of the Civil War. Not only public discourse but also diplomatic dispatches were replete with references to the machinations of "International Jewry", which demonstrate the wide acceptance of antisemitic stereotypes among Francoist officials. Yet, the Franco regime's dreams of restoring the grandeur of imperial Spain prompted it to promote a rapprochement with the Spanish Jews of Morocco, by rekindling philosephardism.

Despite their claims that the Sephardim had no part in the "Jewish conspiracy", the Francoists suspected the Spanish Jews in Northern Morocco of being fifth columnists at the service of the Allies and put a number of them under surveillance. The opportunistic nature of Spain's philosephardic policy was demonstrated in its attitude towards its Jewish citizens living in France and the Balkans, who found themselves the victims of antisemitic persecution. While the Franco regime agreed to handle the confiscation of their businesses, it did not ask that they be exempted from other antisemitic measures. Proposals from Spanish diplomats serving in France, Greece and Romania to transfer to Spain the Spanish Jews whose lives were in danger, were opposed by the Foreign Ministry and the *Dirección General de Seguridad*, which feared the entry into Spain of refugees, who, even though there were Sephardic, were after all Jewish.

V
Welcoming the "Conspirators"
1943–1945

In the second half of the war, antisemitism remained an integral part of the Franco regime's rhetoric. In the aftermath of Operation Torch in November 1942, the Jews became specifically identified with the United States and Great Britain, whose military had crushed Madrid's imperial dreams.

While antisemitism influenced the way the Spaniards viewed the war, it was not used to persecute the Jewish refugees who flocked to Spain in the winter of 1942–1943. Even as the Franco regime insinuated the danger of allowing such a large number of "conspirators" into Spain, local Spanish officials treated them humanely, an impression borne out by the testimony of Jewish refugees themselves. The regime's basic policy towards Jewish refugees did not change during the war: Jewish refugees would be allowed to transit through Spain but would not be allowed to settle there. So reluctant was Madrid to have a Jewish community establish itself in Spain that it refused to provide haven to its own Jewish citizens from the areas of occupation. Like the other refugees they were allowed only to go through Spain "like light goes through glass" and the Franco regime exerted much pressure on the rescue organizations to expedite their departure from the country.[1]

After the fall of Mussolini in the summer of 1943, Madrid became increasingly concerned about its image in the foreign press, which it believed was controlled by the Jews. Interest in improved public relations prompted Spanish officials to seek to develop a relationship with representatives of the World Jewish Congress and to have them publicize the myth of Spain's extensive activities to rescue Jews.

Operation Torch and the "Anglo-American–Jewish Conspiracy"

The landings of Anglo-American forces on the shores of Morocco and Algiers, and in the vicinity of Dakar, on 8 November 1942, known as

Operation Torch, marked a turning point for Spain. The fact that Allied forces had landed precisely on the territories in French Morocco and Algeria that Spain coveted, put an end to the dictatorship's imperial ambitions there. Franco had lost his chance. Some extremists in the government such as the Director-General of foreign policy, José María Doussinague, suggested that Spain should seize upon the opportunity presented by Torch to enter the war on the Axis side.[2] In the same vein the Secretary General of the Falange, José Luis de Arrese, insisted that the Franco regime collaborate with Germany and Italy to guarantee Spain's colonial ambitions.[3]

While the Falangists might have initially considered occupying the portions of French Morocco on which Spain laid claims, the celerity with which the American troops spread themselves over the French territory and the opposition of the monarchist officers put an end to these schemes.[4] By shifting the strategic balance in the Mediterranean, Operation Torch demonstrated the mounting strength of the Allies to the Franco regime. While many Spanish officials, including Franco, remained convinced of the ultimate victory of the Axis, the Allied landings forced them to realize the necessity for the regime to observe the greatest prudence to avoid provoking allied military action against Spain. The dictatorship's aim was now to safeguard Spain's territorial integrity by maintaining the good will of the Germans and avoiding clashes with the Allies. To that end, Spain conducted a dual policy, ingratiating itself with both parties.[5] Its attitude towards the Jews reflected this Janus-faced foreign policy.

The regime's greater caution, however, was not synonymous with neutrality. The Spanish press continued to be dominated by German propaganda and accused the Allies of having provoked the World War II.[6] Hostility towards the United States and Great Britain was conflated with antisemitism. The newspaper *Pueblo*, for instance, wrote about the influence of the "circumcised flock" on US politics.[7]

An anonymous pamphlet, *La garra del capitalismo judío* (The grip of Jewish capitalism), published in 1943, denounced the warmongering manoeuvers of the Jewish plutocracy, which allegedly controlled the media, politics and economics of the United States and Great Britain. It charged that there had been an alliance between the British government and the Jews since Cromwell's rule and decried the fact that the British Empire was in the hands of "Jews" and "Judaizing aristocrats".[8]

The pro-Axis bias of the dictatorship was particularly evident in Spanish Morocco and Tangier, where the aftermath of Torch was characterized by a tightening of Hispano–German relations. The appointment of the Germanophile General Juan Yagüe as commander of the Spanish forces in

Melilla facilitated the rapprochement.[9] According to the British Consul General in Melilla, Gore Edwards, the hostility of Spanish officials was such that Melilla had to be considered "enemy territory".[10] The situation was no better in Tangier. There too the Spanish authorities were upset that Spain's chance of taking over French Morocco had vanished. They were also concerned about possible Anglo-American incursions into Spanish Morocco – despite specific reassurances from the US and British Ambassadors, Carlton Hayes and Samuel Hoare, to the Spanish authorities. Spanish officials in Tangier mounted an anti-British campaign, interfering with the circulation of the English language newspaper, *The Tangier Gazette*, and the private affairs of British citizens.[11]

In Tangier and Spanish Morocco, Allied sympathizers, among whom were a number of Jews, were under constant surveillance and could be arrested at any time. In a memorandum on Allied activities in Tangier, written in July 1942, the *Dirección General de Seguridad* in Madrid had charged that a large number of foreign Jews in Tangier worked for the British Intelligence Service. The memo also charged that the Jewish community of Tangier was distributing English propaganda and that a certain number of Jews were volunteering with the Allied forces.[12] In a note written in December 1942 the headquarters of the Tangier police asserted that the Jews of Tangier had played an important role in the preparation of the operation and that five of them had been "awarded military by the Yankee authorities" for the role they had played in the preparation of the landings.[13]

Among the named suspects was once again Joe Hassan whose bank had financed the Nationalist uprising. It was clear that the Nazis had a hand in creating an atmosphere of suspicion. In mid-December 1942 the head of German intelligence in Spanish Morocco, Recke, asked the local head of counterespionage to arrest all suspected American and British agents.[14] Suspicion that the Jews of Tangier sympathized with the Allies prompted the Spanish authorities to raid a synagogue during services, as well as several Jewish homes. Fifty-five Jews were apprehended and incarcerated without evidence for trial, on charges of "communist" activities. Five Hungarian refugees were ordered expelled.[15]

The British Consul General in Tangier, Alvary Gascoigne, to whom Jews appealed for help, wrote that a "reign of terror among the Jews, alleged republicans and suspected Red sympathizers of Spanish nationality" had started again. Gascoigne believed that the cracking down was due to the fear, sparked by British landing in Tripoli, that the Allies were about to make a landing in Spanish North Africa and that a Republican rising might take place in Spain or in Spanish Morocco. Hence additional Spanish troops were brought to Tangier and machine-guns and anti-aircraft guns were placed at key points in the city.[16]

The atmosphere of repression continued throughout the winter and spring of 1942–1943. The Spaniards ordered all stateless Jews and all Jews who had arrived in Tangier during the past five years to register themselves with the Spanish authorities. The injunction caused panic among the Jewish refugees as rumours abounded that registration would be followed by deportation.[17] Spain continued to suspect the Jews of conducting pro-Allied activities. One allegation was that the Jewish community of Tangier had collected 25,000 francs for the British Red Cross.[18]

The situation of the Jewish community continued to deteriorate after the Axis forces surrendered in Tunisia in May 1943. The Spanish authorities reported that the Jews of Tangier had organized a party to celebrate the arrival of the Allies in Tunis and that they were now speaking only English.[19] In Tetuán, the rabbi of the main synagogue was suspended for three months for offering a thanksgiving prayer on the occasion of the Allied victory.[20]

The level of suspicion reached its height at the end of May when the Spanish authorities arrested hundreds of young Jews and Muslims for having allegedly enlisted at the French consulate general of Tangier for military service in the Free French forces. In reality, the Spanish police summoned anyone who was associated with the Allies, most notably Jewish employees of British institutions such as the *Tangier Gazette*. Gascoigne believed that the Spaniards' objectives in making the arrests were not only to put a stop to recruiting for the Free French forces but also to destroy an imaginary fifth column, which could assist an Anglo-American disembarkation in Tangier.[21] As living embodiment of the Jewish-Communist-Anglo-American conspiracy, the arrested youth were sent to the concentration camp of Khemis el Anjera where they received the same kind of "purifying" treatment as political prisoners: they were shaved and subjected to forced labour.[22] However, they were quickly released after the head of the US legation in Tangier, James Rives Childs, and the Permanent Under-Secretary of the Foreign Office in London, Sir Alexander Cadogan, expressed their indignation to the Spanish authorities.[23] On June 3, the military governor General Uriarte informed representatives of the Jewish community that the boys would be "pardoned".[24]

Yet the Jews remained under close surveillance. In September 1943, the Spanish authorities reported that the Jews of Tangier were celebrating the Italian armistice so euphorically that they had turned the Jewish-owned "Hollywood" cabaret into "a bacchanal".[25] In October a number of incidents of vandalism against Jews in Tangier led the Board of Deputies of

The only one that is missing.
– Is it possible?

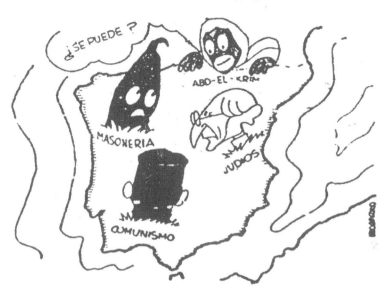

Los Hijos del Pueblo, 26 January 1933.

Page of a passport with stamped French, Portuguese and Spanish visas issued to Raya Markon, a Jewish emigré from Vilna, and her son, Alain.

Reichsführer SS Heinrich Himmler meets with the Minister of Foreign Affairs, Ramon Serrano Suñer during his visit to Madrid (20 October 1940). Suñer invited Himmler to Madrid to give him advice on the liquidation of opponents and the capture of political refugees.

Investiture of José Felix de Lequerica as Foreign Minister (12 August 1944). In his previous position as Spanish Ambassador in Vichy, Lequerica had been unwilling to defend Spanish Jews in Vichy France on the grounds that they were Spain's eternal enemies.

The Oskenhandler family, Jewish refugees from Poland, receiving clothing from the Joint Distribution Committee distribution centre in Tangier (1944).

British Jews to protest to the Spanish Ambassador in London, the Duque of Alba.[26]

The Spaniards also kept an eye on the situation in French Morocco. Spanish newspapers, which in the first years of the war had denounced the anti-Jewish legislation enacted in the French protectorate on the grounds that the Moroccan Jews had no part in the "Jewish conspiracy", now decried the fact that along with the Freemasons, the Jews of Morocco and Algeria were recovering their rights. In January 1943, *El Español* charged that there were 170,000 more Jews in Algeria than in 1940 "swarming in big businesses", and that 45 per cent of the leather industry was in the hands of the "undesirable race", even though in reality the situation of the Jews in Algiers remained precarious.[27] According to *El Español*, the culprit behind the "Jewish invasion" was the recently arrived US army, which counted among its ranks more Freemasons than any other army in the world.[28]

Wary of the Committee of National Liberation, formed by General Charles De Gaulle and General Henri Giraud in the spring of 1943 in Algiers, Francoists claimed that it was in the hands of a Jewish-Bolshevik conspiracy whose ultimate aim was to transform French North Africa into a Soviet Republic.[29] The Spanish press saw evidence of Jewish influence on the Gaullist administration in the reintroduction of the Crémieux Decree, which gave rights of citizenship to Algerian Jews and had been suspended by the Vichy regime. *El Mundo*, for instance, wrote in December 1943 that "the reestablishment of the decree was logical in view of the political significance of the groups which most actively support General De Gaulle".[30] Clearly, the myth of the Judeo-Masonic conspiracy was still alive and was now used to delegitimize the Free French. To it were tied also the US, whose landings in North Africa had thwarted Spain's colonial ambitions.

Dealing with the Refugees

While the Spanish authorities in Morocco were concerned with the pro-Allied activities of the Jewish community in Tangier and Spanish Morocco, Madrid was warily watching the developments on the Pyrenean frontier. In response to Torch, the Germans invaded Vichy France on 11 November 1942. Hitler declared that the armistice was still in effect and that Vichy remained sovereign. However, the situation of the Jews in the formerly unoccupied zone changed radically, as the enhanced powers of the German police meant that the danger of arrest now spread into most of France.[31] At the same time, exit visas were no longer issued and both the American refugee organizations and the US consulates had to close down.[32]

As their prospects for emigration disappeared a number of Jewish refugees fled into Spain. Also fleeing Vichy France were escaped prisoners of war, Frenchmen of military age trying to get to North Africa to join Henri Giraud or Charles de Gaulle as well as forced-landed and shipwrecked Allied military personnel.[33] The two groups overlapped significantly as a number of Jewish refugees hoped to join the Allied forces. Hence the question of refugees became closely connected to the question of prisoners of war.[34]

The flight from France involved a long and difficult trek, which lasted about three days. Usually refugees traveled in small groups. They hired smugglers on the French side and were passed from farmhouse to farmhouse, traveling at night and sleeping during the day. The Germans caught only a small percentage of the refugees. The greatest danger for them lay on the Spanish side where Civil Guards and custom officers were waiting at every border. Even those who slipped by were picked up by the Spanish police when trying to buy foodstuffs or obtain lodgings in the nearest village. A few refugees who feared imminent arrest voluntarily presented themselves to the Spanish police.[35]

In the first days of the exodus from Vichy the Spanish authorities deported some of these refugees back to France.[36] The Director of the Intergovernmental committee on refugees, Sir Herbert Emerson, urged the Spanish Ambassador to Great Britain to persuade his government to refrain from sending refugees back to France. On 17 November, the Spanish Ministry of Foreign Affairs informed the British Embassy that orders had been sent to the Spanish border authorities not to turn the refugees back to French territory. These reassurances resulted in an increased flow of refugees: by the end of November, fifty of them were arriving in Spain each day. In late December 1942, the European director of the Joint Distribution Committee, Joseph Schwarz, estimated that there were 10,000 refugees in Spain, half of whom were Jewish; the large majority came from Austria, Germany and Poland.[37]

Early in 1943, the American Friends Service Committee, the Joint Distribution Committee and the Unitarian Service Committee agreed to cooperate in caring for stateless and other unprotected refugees in Spain. They established the "representation in Spain of American relief organizations" under the direction of David Blickenstaff. The organization was recognized by the Spanish Government as the agency principally concerned with the welfare of stateless and unprotected refugees.[38]

In January 1943 the Spanish government also began to pay attention to the representations made by the World Jewish Congress (WJC). The Congress's claim to represent "the permanent address of the Jewish people", albeit contested by other Jewish organizations, was taken seriously by the Spaniards. Soon Madrid came to treat the WJC as the recognized body of world Jewry and as their favoured interlocutor on the matters regarding Jewish refugees. In January the Duque of Alba met with a representative of the WJC in London, Ben Rubenstein, whom he already knew. Alba expressed the sympathy of the Spanish government with the plight of the Jews, qualifying the Nazi policy as "lunatic" and gave the WJC the solemn assurance that no Jew finding refuge in Spain would be repatriated to any German occupied territory. He also promised that the Spanish government would resist any pressure on the part of the Germans to introduce anti-Jewish legislation in Spain. Alba also pledged that Jews finding refuge in Spain would not be molested in any way.[39]

While they were no longer threatened with forcible return to France, Jewish refugees were thrown into local prisons on the ground that they had crossed the frontier without papers. Notorious for their harsh conditions, Spanish prisons were at the time less suited than ever for the reception of foreign refugees, as they were still overcrowded with political prisoners.[40] After a few weeks in prison, Jewish men were sent to the concentration camp at Miranda while Jewish women remained in prison for an indefinite length of time.[41]

The story of the Theodore family illustrates this pattern. Henry Theodore crossed the French border with his wife and two children on 28 November 1942. After walking for three nights and hiding out during the daytime they gave themselves up to the Spanish authorities. Theodore and his elder son were promptly sent to prison in Lerida where they remained one week after which they were transferred to Miranda. His wife and younger son were sent to prison in Madrid.[42]

The camp of Miranda de Ebro, near the town of Burgos, was under the control of Spanish military authorities. In his memoirs, Samuel Hoare described Miranda as a "veritable Noah Ark" of every type of refugee.[43] To it were sent any foreigners who entered Spain illegally. Members of the International Brigades had been interned there since the end of the Civil War in April 1939 – some from as far back as 1937. They were mostly Poles, Yugoslavs and Balts, who had been deprived of their citizenship by their respective governments and left to languish in Miranda. Kept in separate barracks, the International Brigadiers were forced to do all the demeaning work in the camp.[44]

When Theodore arrived at Miranda in early December 1942, there were about 3,500 men interned there. By the end of the month the number had swollen to around 4,300. The camp had been constructed to hold 1,500 people and according to a relief worker the conditions "were beyond description".[45] Inmates were crowded in barracks according to their nationality. Men were sleeping in dis-used latrines because of the lack of space. In his report on Miranda, however, Theodore wrote that while the sanitary arrangements left much to be desired, the food and treatment in Miranda were much better than in the French concentration camps.[46] The difference was probably due to the fact that the Allied representatives were particularly interested in their nationals interned in Miranda. They sent them large amount of supplies and money and exerted pressure on the Spanish government to treat them well. Hence upon learning that a Dutch prisoner, suffering from tuberculosis, was compelled to sleep with the other internees, Hoare warned Jordana that an exposure of the conditions in Miranda in the press would cause a public scandal in Great Britain and the United States.[47]

Local Spanish officials, policemen and camp guards did not discriminate against the Jews. While the Spanish authorities asked each prisoner his religion, they did not treat the Jews differently from the other detainees. Eli Rubin who was interned for two years in Miranda noted the contrast between the official antisemitic rhetoric and the relative tolerance of the camp's authorities:

> As to the treatment of the Jews, never during all these years there has been any discrimination between the Jewish and the other internees. This is for the European continent, indeed an outstanding fact, considering the sympathies of the Spanish authorities for the Axis doctrines and considering, moreover, the ceaseless German antisemitic propaganda work in Spain.[48]

In Miranda the manifestations of antisemitism experienced by the Jewish refugees came from their fellow prisoners rather than the Spanish guards. The Poles, who had the largest group in the camp, were particularly hostile to the Jewish inmates. In November 1942, they received the wave of Jewish refugees, many of whom originated from Poland, with a hail of rotten onions, tomatoes and stones. They bawled out: "What are you doing here? Go to Palestine! Jews go to Palestine". A Polish delegation proposed that a special camp should be set up for the Jews inside Miranda, on the grounds that it was impossible for a Polish Catholic to live together with so many Jews. The commandant of the Spanish camp told the delegation that to him all prisoners were equal, Catholics or not Catholics.[49] The fact that an orthodox rabbi from Poland was allowed to lead daily services and was the sole internee not obliged to attend the roll-calls is yet another indication that the attitude of Miranda's commandant towards the Jews was relatively tolerant.[50] When rumors of an impending German attack swept the camp, causing alarm among the Jewish refugees, the commandant promised that if it happened he would throw open the gates of the camp straightaway.[51]

Although they were not mistreated, the refugees in Miranda were prone to boredom and frustration. One refugee wrote: "Every morning when one gets up one puts oneself the same eternal question: Shall we never leave from here?"[52] Another detainee remembers: "I had felt that risking life and limb on the Pyrenees would spell freedom. There was supposed to be a joyful ending now, not the drab disappointment of this dumb internment."[53] For months – and in some cases years – the inmates followed the same routine. At seven sharp every morning they had to attend the *bandera*, the ceremonial hoisting of the flag. With their arm raised in the fascist salute the prisoners were obliged to sing the three anthems of Franco's Spain: the monarchist, the Carlist and the Falangist to the accompaniment of a band, composed of prisoners and led by a German Jew. The counting of prisoners would then begin. The task often took hours because the semi-literate Spanish soldiers never came up with the same numbers. The rest of the day was punctuated by breakfast, lunch and dinner as the prisoners formed queues to receive either a loaf of bread or a metallic-tasting soup with tiny morsels of meat or potato floating about.[54]

Allied nationals received food packages as well as a weekly allowance of about 35 pesetas from their diplomatic representatives.[55] Many stateless Jews, of German, Austrian, Polish, Czech and other origins, who like all other refugees had had their money confiscated by the Spanish police, declared themselves to be nationals of Allied countries in order to receive assistance.[56] In the early days of immigration from France, the Allied embassies and legations were not strict in the distribution of food and financial help to nationals other than their own. But gradually, as true nationalities were determined, they weeded out non-nationals from their relief rolls.[57] Despite the occasional packages they received from the American Jewish organization, the Joint Distribution Committee, the stateless Jews were worse off than the other refugees. They took to trading: buying cigarettes and food from other prisoners and reselling them later when the prisoners had run out of supplies.[58]

The sole purpose for which prisoners were released from Miranda, however, was to leave Spain. The Spanish authorities wanted the refugees to be removed from Spanish soil as soon as possible. Prisoners were released only after all the arrangements had been completed for their evacuation; they were expected to go directly from the camp to the frontier. While Allied governments could make the necessary arrangements for exit, transit, transportation and destination visa of their nationals, the stateless Jews found themselves in a catch-22 situation. They had to obtain their individual visas yet it was impossible for them to do that before leaving the camp, because visas had to be applied for in person.[59]

Another problem for the stateless refugees was to find a destination. Immigration into the United Kingdom and the United States was on the basis of individual selection and could take considerable time to arrange. The process of obtaining visas for Latin America was also long and while Palestine could accept approximately six hundred refugees there was no transportation to get them there. Sir Herbert Emerson suggested that the Allies open a clearance camp in North Africa, near Casablanca, but the US military authorities opposed the proposal.

Despite the apparent goodwill of Jordana and of his staff, the refugee situation reached an impasse in the months of February and March 1943. Allied representatives became increasingly frustrated by the slowness with which prisoners were released from Miranda. While the civil authorities in the province of Navarre displayed a friendly attitude to the newly-arrived refugees by accommodating them into hotels, the pro-German Ministries of War and Interior were obstructive and held up releases from Miranda. The War Ministry resented Allied interest in what it regarded as the exclusively military administration of the camp. For its part, the Ministry of Interior pointed out that the detainees had broken Spanish law in entering prohibited areas, in having no papers and in possessing foreign currencies. It also claimed that there was no evidence that the men were escaped prisoners of war and refugees, and that they could be Red agents who were entering Spain to stir up a revolution. Hoare believed that behind the War and Interior Ministries stood the Falange, which insisted that the released prisoners might in the future be fighting against the Spanish Blue Division in the Russian front.[60] The question of the prisoners in Miranda added to tensions within the regime. Exasperated with the obstructiveness of the Minister of Interior Blas Pérez, Jordana asked him to shorten the detention time of the foreign detainees in Miranda, as the situation was causing an international outcry.[61]

Meanwhile, the Spaniards were secretly discussing with the Germans the steps to be taken for closing the Spanish frontier. In February, the Germans asked the Spaniards to reinforce frontier control in the Pyrenees and offered a bounty of 200 pesetas for every escapee that would be sent back to France.[62] In March, the Nazis decided to set up a zone of thirty kilometres on their side of the frontier in which all suspects would be arrested and they asked the Spaniards to create a similar zone.[63] The recent signature of an agreement between Spain and Germany, whereby the Reich promised military aid to Spain,[64] made the Spanish government amenable to German pressures. Furthermore, the pro-Axis Ministry of

War and Ministry of Interior supported the closing of the frontier.[65] On 25 March, the Spanish government ordered the complete closure of the Pyrenees frontier to any person not in possession of legal documentation. At the same time, the *Dirección General de la Seguridad* instructed the Civil Governor at Gerona and the Military Governor of Irun that all foreigners entering Spain clandestinely had to be sent back to France where they would be handed over to the Germans.[66] The explanation provided was that the constant clandestine crossing of the Pyrenees was causing much disturbance and that the refugees were mounting anti-Spanish campaigns upon leaving Spain.[67]

The Allies were infuriated. Both the British and American Ambassadors in Madrid made representations to Jordana. Hoare was quick to remind the Spaniards that during the Civil War, the French government had allowed Spanish military personnel who had escaped from the Republican zone to return to the Nationalist zone. He told Jordana that he could not believe that the Spanish Government would make a complete reversal of a policy that had been so beneficial to it during the Civil War. Meanwhile in Great Britain, Prime Minister Winston Churchill informed the Duque of Alba that the handing back of refugees would destroy good relations between Great Britain and Spain.[68]

Throughout the spring of 1943, there were indications that the regime's enthusiasm for the Axis was still alight. The pro-German propaganda of the Falange hindered Jordana's efforts to follow a policy of neutrality.[69] In April, the Falange drafted a statement that was published throughout the Spanish press and drew a parallel between the Spanish Civil War and World War II:

> The war that took place in Spain, like the current conflict, was a civil war in both the European and universal sense, it was a conflict between fascism and antifascism. On one side the Jews, the Freemasons, the democrats, the liberals, the communists, and the anarchists; on the other side Spain, Italy and Germany. On a much larger scale the situation is repeated today.[70]

On a few occasions Franco himself delivered antisemitic diatribes, conflating Judaism with US capitalism and Russian Bolshevism. Hence, in April 1943, he transmitted a letter to Pope Pius XII, which Roosevelt had purportedly written to Stalin, claiming the document provided evidence that "International Freemasonry and Judaism require that their members carry out a programme of hatred against Christian civilization".[71] A few weeks later, on 4 May at Huelva, the *Caudillo* denounced the "propaganda machines promoting the interests of capitalism, Judaism and Marxism".[72]

"Like Light Through Glass"

In addition to making frequent references to the Jewish conspiracy, the Spanish press continued to draw a distinction between the Sephardic and the Ashkenazi Jews. *El Mundo*, for instance, wrote in September 1943 that "because of their customs and their mentality" the Sephardic Jews were "superior" to their Ashkenazi brethren and that they did not participate "in the political movements of the Jews".[73]

The regime's philosephardic rhetoric faced a test in the spring of 1943, as it was confronted with the question of the repatriation of the Jews who held Spanish citizenship and lived in German occupied countries. The latter had until then enjoyed preferential treatment and been protected from harassment, but the plan for the systematic extermination of Jews in occupied Europe had put their fate on the agenda of the German authorities. Their future was the subject of much debate between the German Foreign Ministry, which was determined to maintain cordial relations with the neutrals, and the Reich Main Security Office (RHSA), which was eager to promote the process of extermination of the Jews.[74] On 26 January, the German Embassy in Madrid had informed the Spanish Ministry of Foreign Affairs that, after 31 March, Spanish Jews living in France, Belgium and the Low Countries would no longer be exempted from the anti-Jewish measures: they would be interned and deported along with their co-religionists. The Spanish government was thus urged to carry out the repatriation of its Jewish nationals by that date.[75] A similar announcement was conveyed to the Swiss, Portuguese, Swedish and Turkish governments.[76]

The German Embassy's note was sent to the Director-General of Foreign Policy, José Maria Doussinague. Doussinague, it must be remembered, was no stranger to the subject: in 1930 he had written a report entitled "economic Sepharadism". Loaded with antisemitic references, his study had stressed the need to use the Sephardic Jews as agents of Spain's commercial penetration in the Balkans.[77] Doussinague's reaction to the German proposals of repatriating the Spanish Jews was consistent with his opportunism. On 28 January, he wrote to Jordana that by abandoning its Jewish nationals in German occupied territories, the Franco regime would aggravate the hostility of the Allies towards them, particularly that of the United States. Doussinague's other utmost concern was that the Spanish Jews' property, which he considered "part of Spain's national heritage", would not be delivered into the hands of the Germans.

Doussinague's response to the German proposal also revealed that he had not shed any of his prejudices against the Jews. Hence, he wrote to Jordana, that because of their "race, money, Anglophilia and Freemasonry" the Jewish nationals would "plot all kinds of intrigues". Therefore, while he objected to letting the Spanish Jews be included in deportation, he recommended that they should not be allowed the right to return to Spain. He proposed two alternative solutions: either they should be repatriated to their country of birth in the Balkans, or they should be given a visa to a destination other than Spain.[78] Doussinague's recommendations were to provide the framework for Spain's policy towards its Jewish nationals. In early February, Doussinague instructed the new Spanish Ambassador to Germany, Ginés Vidal, to obtain for the Spanish Jews entry visas to Greece, Turkey or any other country.[79] The Spanish position was much less generous than that of other countries. Faced with the same German proposal, the Swiss had begun evacuating their nationals and the Italians had announced their decision to repatriate all their Jewish citizens from France, Belgium and Holland by the end of March.[80]

In any event, Doussinague's plan to have the Spanish Jews either evacuated to their country of origin in the Balkans or immigrate to another destination was wholly unrealistic. As both Vidal and the Spanish Consul in Paris, Bernardo Rolland, pointed out, there was a law in Turkey prohibiting Jewish immigration and the other Balkan countries had also promulgated antisemitic laws.[81] No alternative destination could be found: Switzerland and Argentina had slammed the door on Jewish immigration, while Portugal refused to let the Spanish Jews in on the grounds that Spain itself did not want to accommodate them. Rolland suggested that Spain explored the opportunities for immigration in other Latin American countries and asked Germany to postpone the final date for repatriation.[82]

Throughout February, the Spanish Foreign Ministry came under increasing pressure to evacuate its Jewish nationals. On 27 February, a group of Spanish Jews living in Paris wrote an emotional letter to Bernardo Rolland in which they expressed their dismay at Spain's decision to deny them refuge. "If Spain refuses asylum to its own nationals", they asked, "how will another country grant it to them?" The letter indicated that the number of Spanish Jews in Paris was relatively small: about 250 people, all of whom had sufficient means, and hence would not become a burden on the Spanish economy. The Spanish Jews also pointed out that they requested asylum to Spain only on a temporary basis. They would seek to immigrate to Latin America, where many of them had relatives.[83] Echoing the letter of the Spanish Jews was a letter from Ambassador Vidal suggesting that the government grant them transit visas, which would allow them to wait in Spain until they receive a visa that would enable them to travel to another country. On 6 March, the German Embassy in Madrid announced that Berlin would not authorize the Spanish Jews to travel to their country of birth or to any country other than Spain.[84]

This last argument must have struck a chord with Doussinague. On 9 March 1943, he recommended to Jordana that the dictatorship grant its Jewish nationals the right to come to Spain. Repatriation, however, remained out of question: the Jewish nationals would be allowed no more than to transit through Spain like all other refugees. They would be separated from each other and confined to assigned residences. In addition, Doussinague asserted that the number of Spanish Jews allowed in Spain should not exceed 250 persons. Doussinague's decision was once again motivated by political opportunism: he wrote to Jordana that the regime's refusal to grant the Spanish Jews protection "could have a negative impact on Spain's image abroad".[85]

Jordana's attitude was no more generous. He adopted Doussinague's recommendations but imposed further conditions on the entry of Spanish Jews to Spain. In a cable to Vidal, he announced that the Spanish Jews would have to produce the documentation to prove their full Spanish citizenship. In practice this meant that they would have to be listed in the citizens' register of the consulates, which had been established under the Primo de Rivera decree of December 1924. This condition severely limited the number of potential repatriates: in France, for instance, fewer than a third of the 3,000 Jews registered at the Spanish consulates had the full documentation to prove their Spanish citizenship.[86] Jordana's second condition was that the Spanish authorities would select their places of residence in Spain and they would be under police supervision throughout their period of stay there.[87]

Not content with limiting the number of those entitled to repatriation, Madrid wanted to receive the firm assurance that the Spanish Jewish nationals would not linger in Spain. On 18 March 1943, Germán Baráibar, chief of the European section of the Ministry of Foreign Affairs, informed Hayes that the Spanish government would grant transit visas and necessary identity papers to the Spanish Jews if the Joint Distribution Committee guaranteed that they would leave Spain within four to six weeks after their arrival. Hayes replied that the JDC had no power to grant visas and that the organization could attempt to obtain visas only for countries that might be willing to accept immigrants. The impression Hayes received from the conversation was that Spain was interested in its Spanish nationals "for reasons of propaganda value".[88] Finally, Jordana asked the representative of the JDC in Spain, David Blickenstaff, to guarantee that his organization would do everything possible to obtain immigration visas for the Spanish

Jews.[89] However, the conditions established by Jordana to limit those entitled to repatriation were not deemed sufficient by José Felix de Lequerica,
the Spanish Ambassador in Vichy. In early April, Lequerica tried to undermine the rescue of Spanish Jews further by suggesting that the evacuees be
selected on the basis of their income, social status, contacts with communists and Freemasons, as well as their attitude towards the Nationalists.[90]

Although the Spanish Ministry of Foreign Affairs ignored Lequerica's
suggestions, it continued to drag its feet on evacuating and repatriating its
nationals. In July 1943, Alfonso Fiscowisch, Spain's new Consul in Paris,
announced that 79 Jewish nationals fulfilled the requirements of the
Ministry of Foreign Affairs.[91] The group finally arrived in Spain on August
11. The refugees were assigned to residence in the main provincial capitals:
Zaragoza, Burgos, Avila, Valladolid, Granada and Logroño. They were
under close police surveillance and were not allowed to travel without
permission. Neither were they authorized to work as they were regarded as
privileged aliens sojourning in the country in transit before their emigration.[92] The Spanish government considered that it was the responsibility
of the Joint Distribution Committee not only to secure visas for the group
of refugees but also to pay for all their living expenses while they were in
Spain.[93]

The reports that the police in Zaragoza sent to the *Dirección General de la
Seguridad* demonstrate that the Spanish Jews from Paris were considered
subversive elements. Thus a police memorandum dated from 9 September
1943 noted:

> *The staff of this brigade confirms that the Sephardic Jews have a lot of contact
> with the local workers and soldiers, to whom they constantly speak. In view of
> their {the Jews'} extremist ideas, they are considered dangerous. They openly
> admit that they are communist and they spread propaganda against the totali-
> tarian states. It would be advisable to take some steps to prevent this type of
> behaviour.[94]*

The solution advocated by the Spanish government was to remove the
Spanish Jews from Spain without delay. In fact, the Ministry of Foreign
Affairs ordained that its Jewish nationals living in German-occupied countries would not be able to come to Spain until David Blickenstaff had taken
the necessary steps to evacuate the group that had arrived from France.[95]
Blickenstaff, however, was meeting a number of difficulties in trying to
assist the Spanish Jews in their emigration from Spain. For one thing, the
Ministry of War had extracted five or six members of the party who were of
military age, compelling them to do military service in Spain. The families
of these men were naturally reluctant to leave Spain. In addition, a number

of Spanish Jewish nationals insisted on remaining in Spain until the end of
the war. Among their objections to leaving the peninsula were the claims
that they were Spanish citizens with the right to enjoy the privileges of
Spaniards on Spanish territory, that they lacked the economic means to re-
establish themselves in a new country as immigrants, and that they had left
in France fortunes and businesses to which they intended to return at the
end of the war.[96] The insistence of the Franco regime to evacuate the Spanish
Jews infuriated both Blickenstaff and Hoare, who considered that since
those Jews were acknowledged to be Spanish nationals, the Spanish authorities had no right to refuse them admittance and residence in the country.

The Spanish government's refusal to admit other groups of Spanish Jews
in the peninsula had particular repercussions for the Spanish Jewish
community of Salonica. The Nazi deportation of the Greek Jews of Salonica
had begun in March 1943. By May more than 48,000 Jews had been sent
to Poland.[97] Jewish nationals of neutral countries, including 511 Spanish
nationals, had been left unharmed. However, on 30 April the German
Embassy in Madrid warned that the Spanish Jews would be deported unless
Spain evacuated them by 15 June 1943. The German authorities in Greece
expressed their willingness to facilitate the immigration of the Spanish Jews
to the Peninsula even though they were ultimately convinced that Spain
took no interest in the fate of its Jewish citizens residing in Greece.[98]

In early May, the Spanish Consul General in Athens, Sebastiàn Romero
Radigales, asked Madrid for instructions. Romero Radigales put forward a
number of arguments to justify Spain's intervention on behalf of its Jewish
nationals. He suggested, for instance, that if the immigration of the Spanish
Jews to Spain was considered unsuitable, they could settle in Spanish
Morocco where there already existed a Jewish community. He also noted
that the Italians were protecting their own Jewish nationals and were planning to evacuate them to Italy. Finally, he warned the Foreign Ministry that
a refusal to allow the Jews in Spain would lead to "a violent campaign
against Spain in many countries, given the enormous influence" that Jews
held "throughout the world". He feared that the campaign in turn "could
be exploited" by the exiled Republicans.[99]

The Spanish government's initial response to the question of the repa-
triation of the Spanish Jews of Salonica was positive. On 20 May, the
Ministry of Foreign Affairs informed Romero Radigales that the Spanish
Embassy in Berlin would grant entry visas to Spain to the Jews who had
fully documented Spanish citizenship. For the next weeks, the Spanish
Sephardim prepared their departure, liquidating their businesses and
entrusting their properties to close associates. At the same time, Romero
Radigales tried to find a means of transporting the Spanish Jews from

Salonica to Spain. He negotiated with the Swedish *chargé d'affaires* the transportation of the Spanish Jews to Spain on Swedish boats, which were run by the International Red Cross and brought food to Greece.[100]

In mid-July, the Spanish government abruptly shifted its position. On 17 July, Vidal informed Romero Radigales that the Franco regime could not accept the repatriation of its Jewish nationals and that visas would only be granted in exceptional cases. A few days later, the German authorities, exasperated with the Spaniards' delays in evacuating their nationals, informed Vidal that the Spanish Jews would be deported to Germany on grounds of military security. Distressed by the news, Romero Radigales tried to do everything that he could to assuage the lot of his *protégés* by asking the Germans to spare the children and the elderly from deportation. At the same time, he negotiated with the Italian consulate the possible evacuation of the Spanish Jews to Athens, which was in the Italian zone of occupation. The German authorities rejected both suggestions.[101] They considered that the Jews had to be either repatriated to Spain or transferred to a camp in the Reich.[102] On 20 July a Spanish diplomat in Berlin, who was clearly distraught by his government's refusal to evacuate the group, forewarned Doussinague of the consequences of Spain's policy of abandonment. He wrote:

> If Spain { . . . } refuses to welcome these members of the Spanish colony abroad, even though they possess Spanish nationality and have settled all formalities imposed by our legislation, we condemn them automatically to death. This is the sad reality and we cannot conceal it to ourselves { . . . }.
>
> I understand perfectly well that we do not want to see such a large number of Jews entrench themselves in Spain, even though they are in theory and practice Spanish.
>
> I cannot give up the belief that we can save them from the horrible death that awaits them. We could welcome them in our country and place them in a concentration camp, which in the given circumstances will seem to them like heaven.[103]

The pleas fell on deaf ears as Jordana insisted that the Spanish Jews be allowed only to transit through Spain on their way to Portugal or the United States.[104] Once again the position of the Spanish government stood in contrast to that of other countries: Switzerland, Turkey, Argentina and even Germany's ally, Italy, had evacuated their Jewish nationals from Salonica.

On 29 July, in the face of Spain's refusal to repatriate its Jewish nationals, the Germans assembled 366 Spanish Jews in the detention camp of Baron Hirsch suburb.[105] They were deported to Bergen-Belsen on 2 August. Fortunately for them, the Nazis decided that they would not be treated like the other Jews there. In fact the Germans viewed the internment of the

Spanish Jews in Bergen-Belsen as an interim solution as they reckoned, that under Allied pressure, the Spaniards would repatriate their Jewish nationals within the next three months. Hence the *Einsatz Kommando* at Salonica and the camp *Kommando* in Bergen-Belsen were instructed to treat the Spanish Jews in a way that could not give any cause for serious complaints and "undesired propaganda" in case they were later granted an exit permit to Spain.[106]

Shortly after the deportation of the Spanish Jews of Salonica, another volte-face by the Franco regime seemed to prove the Germans right and presage that the Jews would be repatriated to Spain in the near future. On 5 August, the Spanish Ministry of Foreign Affairs suggested that the Spanish Jews of Salonica be evacuated in groups of 25. The Germans rejected the proposal, insisting that they be repatriated in one group.[107] In September, Spain and Germany reached an agreement whereby the Spanish Jews would be repatriated in two groups of roughly 180 people.

By then, the Spaniards had probably realized that the evacuation of their Jewish nationals was in the interest of Spain's public relations. The fall of Mussolini in late July pointed to a victory of the Allies and to difficulties for Franco. Accordingly, the regime was trying to dissociate itself from the Axis. The Spanish press was placed on a neutral basis and Jordana informed Hayes that Spain would withdraw the Blue Division.[108] To improve their image abroad, the Spaniards began promoting the myths of the non-anti-semitism of the regime and its extensive activities to rescue the Jews. On 4 August, Alba told the representatives of the World Jewish Congress in London, Ben Rubenstein and AL Easterman, that the time was now appropriate to inform the public "of the part that Spain had played in giving asylum to Jewish refugees".[109]

In October 1943, the Laurel incident, occasioned by a telegram of congratulations that Jordana sent to José Laurel, Japan's new puppet governor in the Philippines, led the US media, including the *New York Times*, to press for a tougher line with Madrid.[110] Convinced that the American press was in the hands of the Jews, Jordana commissioned the Falangist leader and close associate of the late Onésimo Redondo, Javier Martínez de Bedoya, to write a piece on the "militant anti-racism" inherent in the Falange's program.

In early November, Jordana dispatched Bedoya as press attaché to the Spanish Embassy in Lisbon. His assignment was to establish contacts with the Jewish organizations, particularly with the World Jewish Congress and to reach a "gentlemen's agreement with them", whereby Spain would provide help to the Jewish refugees and the WJC would campaign to improve Spain's image abroad. One of the reasons Jordana was eager to strike an accord with the WJC was his frustration in dealing with the Joint Distribution Committee, which he considered to be too closely connected to the US State Department. Jordana hoped to reach a universal agreement with the Jews and the WJC, which presented itself as the recognized body of world Jewry and seemed to be the right partner.[111] In addition, both the Spanish Ambassador in Washington, Juan Cárdenas, and the Duque of Alba in London, enjoyed warm relationships with WJC officials, who tended to overstate Spain's assistance to Jewish refugees. Hence, in June 1943, one of the WJC representatives in the US, Rabbi Maurice Perlzweig, declared in a coast-to-coast radio broadcast that in proportion to its resources and population, Spain had done "a great deal" more for Jewish refugees than the United States and Great Britain. Perlzweig, who was disappointed at the attitude of the Western allies towards the Jews, seemed to believe genuinely that the Franco regime was doing everything it could to help endangered Jews; he also wanted the Spaniards to be committed publicly to the rescue of Jews.[112]

Bedoya's mission in Lisbon was surrounded with secrecy: neither the brother of the *Caudillo*, Nicolás Franco, who was then Ambassador in Lisbon, nor the pro-German Arrese, who, as Secretary General of the Falange, was responsible for the Spanish press, were informed of it. Besides Jordana, the only person who knew the real purpose of Bedoya's assignment was the chief of the European section of the Ministry of Foreign Affairs, Baráibar, who had been dealing with the question of the repatriation of the Spanish Jews.[113]

In the meantime, negotiations over the Jews of Salonica were protracted throughout the autumn of 1943 as the Franco regime continued to refuse to evacuate the Spanish nationals from Bergen-Belsen as long as the group, which had come from France in August, remained in Spain. The principal aim of the Spaniards was to avoid the concentration of Spanish Jews in the peninsula.[114]

The opportunism of the Spanish authorities did not escape the notice of EA Walker of the Foreign Office Refugee Department. On 20 September he commented:

> *The attitude of the Spanish government seems to be ambivalent. We know that for the past year at least the Spaniards have been giving somewhat perfunctory protection to Sephardic Jews in the Balkans on the grounds that it would seem, of their being Spanish speaking, and that they are therefore touched with the sacrosanct "Hispanidad". On the other hand, the Falange, not to mention the traditional antisemitic bias of the Spaniards, is probably in favour of the Nazi methods where Jews are concerned.*

We are thus faced with an attempt to gain credit by rescuing Jews and to save expense by getting rid of them after having done so.[115]

In addition to refusing to assume responsibilities for its Jewish nationals, the Spanish government also added to the refugee problem by serving expulsion orders to the Jews who had entered the country in 1933 or even earlier. The latter were told that they had to leave Spain immediately or risk imprisonment in concentration camps even though some of them had married into Spanish families or had sons serving in the Spanish army.[116] The British Embassy in Madrid considered that through this "retrograde policy" the Spanish government itself was creating a refugee problem in the same way as the Vichy government had done in the days prior to the occupation of the Vichy zone.[117]

By the end of 1943, the Spanish Jews from Salonica had still not been repatriated to Spain. In early November, the German authorities warned that if they were not evacuated to Spain they would be deported to Poland.[118] The pro-German Doussinague in the Ministry of Foreign Affairs blamed the situation on Blickenstaff for having failed to provide destinations for the Spanish Jews who had come from France. He threatened that if arrangements were not made soon, not only would those who had arrived be thrown into prison but also, others would not be allowed into Spain. E. A. Walker was scandalized. He minuted:

The action of the Spaniards in expelling their own nationals is comparable in quality, though not in scale, with that of the Germans who have pushed out their nationals in great numbers. No reasonable motive can be imputed to this action.[119]

The situation was finally resolved in early December 1943 as Monsignor Boyer-Mas, who dealt with the evacuation of French refugees in Spain, accepted the inclusion of the group of Spanish Jews for evacuation to North Africa into the next French convoy. The group assembled in Malaga. They were given a final warning on their departure: following the instructions of Doussinague, the *Dirección General de la Seguridad* notified them that their behaviour after leaving Spain would affect the regime's repatriation policy towards the other Spanish Jews. They were told that any criticism of the Spanish government would lead Spain to give up the pending negotiations with the German government for the arrival of other Spanish Jews to the Peninsula.[120]

Meanwhile a number of Spanish Jewish refugees from France were forced to stay in Spain as the pro-German Minister of War, General Carlos Asensio, compelled them to do military service in the peninsula. At the same time, their families were threatened with being thrown into prison if they did not leave Spain. The incongruousness of the situation prompted Hayes to ask Jordana to release the Jewish refugees from their military obligations.[121]

A few days later, Jordana wrote to Asensio to suggest that the Spanish Jews be exempted from military duty. In his letter, he explained Spain's policy towards its Jewish nationals, stressing Franco's personal reluctance to see the Spanish Jews settle in Spain:

> *The problem is that the several hundreds of Jews with Spanish nationality who are in Europe right now are either in concentration camps or bound for them. We cannot let them settle in Spain because it does not suit us and the Caudillo does not authorize it. Yet at the same time we cannot abandon them in their current situation and ignore the fact that they are Spanish citizens as this could bring about a press campaign against us overseas, particularly in the United States and result in serious international difficulties. In light of this situation, we have considered bringing them in groups of one hundred. Only after one group leaves Spain – going through the country like light goes through glass, without a trace – do we allow a second group, which in turn would be evacuated to let others come. With this system it is clear that in no case will we allow the Jews to remain in Spain.*[122]

Now that the group from France had been evacuated from Spain, the Franco regime was making arrangements for the repatriation of the Spanish Jews from Salonica who were stranded in Bergen-Belsen. Spanish officials were eager to find further destinations for the group even before it had arrived in Spain. Doussinague informed Blickenstaff that the arrival of Jewish nationals from Salonica would be contingent upon the confirmation by the JDC of their departure date; in effect the Spanish Jews would not be allowed to stay in Spain and would have to go directly to the port of embarkation.[123]

At the same time, Spanish officials had grown so convinced that Blickenstaff was incapable of handling the emigration of the Jewish Spanish nationals on his own that they tried to find alternative emigration destinations. Hence, on 30 December, Jordana wrote to the High Commissioner General Orgaz, to ask him if the Spanish Jews from the Balkans could settle in Spanish Morocco. In his letter, Jordana explained the dilemma in which Spain was caught and expressed again his fear of a campaign against the regime: "On the one hand," he wrote "Spain cannot get filled with Jews, on the other we cannot refuse them the protection to which they are endowed as Spanish citizens even if we wish to do so because it would spark an anti-Spanish campaign overseas and Spain would be accused of copying German antisemitic policy."[124]

In his response, Orgaz expressed scepticism about the "Spanishness" of the Jewish nationals, noting that "the Spanish nationality had been granted without rhyme or reason". He discouraged the regime from evacuating the Spanish Jews to Morocco on the grounds that the Spanish authorities could face the opposition of the Muslim population and that the Jews of the zone had not identified with the Nationalist Movement. He recommended that Spain negotiate with Great Britain their immigration to Palestine.[125] What Orgaz did not realize was that the British government was equally worried about the effects of a mass movement of Jews to Palestine. Hence, while Hoare encouraged Jordana to evacuate the Salonica Jews, he informed him that the British government would not be able to permit the emigration of the entire group to Palestine but would have to admit them on a case-by-case basis.[126]

Even though they had not found a final destination for them, the Spaniards carried out the repatriation of the Spanish Jews from Salonica in February 1944. The first group arrived at the French border town of Port-Bou on 7 February. After a delay of 36 hours – during which the German authorities threatened to re-embark them – they finally entered Spain. The second group followed a few days later. By then the 365 Jews of Salonica had spent six months in Bergen-Belsen.[127] Jordana hoped that Spain would immediately capitalize on the repatriation of its Jewish nationals. On 19 February, he asked the Spanish Ambassador in Washington, Juan Francisco de Cárdenas, to publicize their arrival in the United States in order "to counteract the anti-Spanish campaign, which attributed a racist policy to the regime".[128]

In the meantime, after Italy's capitulation in September 1943 Germany took over the areas in Southern Greece, which the Italians had formerly occupied. The Jews had been safe while Italy occupied the zone as the Italians were completely opposed to the German policy of deporting the Jews. In October, the Germans issued a decree ordering all Jews to register and began to make plans to deport them. On 23 March 1944, the Germans rounded up the Jews of Athens for deportation to Auschwitz.[129] That night, 155 Spanish Jews of Athens were arrested by the German police and driven to the Haidari camp on the outskirts of Athens. They were herded on to a train to Bergen-Belsen in the first week of April. Despite the protests of Romero Radigales, the elderly, the children and the sick were included in the deportation.[130]

The fate of the Spanish Jews of Athens raised considerable concern among the representatives of the World Jewish Congress. On 6 April the WJC delegate in Lisbon, Isaac Weissman, wrote to the Spanish Ambassador in Ankara that the Spanish Jews of Athens were guaranteed immigration visas to Palestine if they could reach Istanbul. Weissman asked that the

Spanish authorities open negotiations with the German authorities, with the object of obtaining permission for these persons to come to Turkey.[131] Similar pleas were made to the Duque de Alba in London and to Cárdenas in Washington. The WJC strove to appeal to the highest echelons of the Spanish government. On 8 April, through the intermediary of Bedoya, Weissman met with Nicolás Franco and asked him to intervene in favour of the Jews of Athens. During the meeting, Nicolás Franco provided some important clues about the calculating attitude of his brother toward the "Jewish question". He explained to Weissman that Spain was not antisemitic and that the *Caudillo* was very interested in the Jewish question, particularly in the Sephardic Jews. He also claimed that despite German endeavours, Spain had not introduced antisemitic laws because his brother wanted to avoid introducing measures which might involve difficulties for the Jews in Tangiers, where banking and commerce were in their hands.[132]

To convince Spain to intervene on behalf of the Spanish Jews of Athens, Weissman played on the traditional stereotype about the Jews by overstating their leverage on the Anglo-American journalistic sphere. Hence, he promised that in return for Spain's intervention, all the major British and American newspapers would publicize the regime's actions and praise "Spain's humanitarian generosity".[133] On 11 April, Bedoya wrote to Jordana about the potential public relations coup:

> My dear General, I believe that we have in our hands an important card to play, which could completely disconcert our enemies. While we will win sympathies abroad we will not compromise ourselves in any way since the actions we have been asked to undertake on behalf of the Jews correspond to the moral obligations of a neutral power and are inspired by Catholic thought.[134]

That same day Jordana asked Vidal to demand the German authorities to allow the Jews of Athens to proceed to Palestine via Istanbul.[135] However, by the time Vidal received Jordana's instructions, the Spanish Jews had left the Haidari camp near Athens; they had been deported to Bergen-Belsen. Hence, Vidal informed Jordana that in terms of logistics it would be easier to evacuate the group to Spain than to Turkey.[136] In accordance with the policy it had formulated, Madrid chose to wait until the refugees from Salonica were removed before repatriating the group of Athens. In June, after the Jews of Salonica had been transported to the Fedala refugee camp near the city of Casablanca, the Franco regime agreed to evacuate the Spanish nationals detained in Bergen-Belsen.[137] Madrid made arrangements for their passage through Vichy France but the situation in France after the Allied troops' disembarkation rendered it impossible.

Jordana died on 3 August 1944. In September, Hayes wrote to the freshly appointed Foreign Minister, Lequerica, urging him to make use of all possible means to evacuate the Jews of Athens. Hayes suggested that if the repatriation of the Jews of Athens to Spain turned out to be infeasible the Spaniards should request that Switzerland temporarily admit them. In November 1944, the Swiss Embassy in Berlin informed the Germans that it would accept the passage of the Athens Jews through its territory. However, the plan failed due to German obstruction and the Jews of Athens remained in Bergen-Belsen until the arrival of the Allied forces on 13 April 1945.[138]

In the meantime, the ever-energetic Weissman had decided to organize the rescue work of Jewish children living in hiding in France. On his intervention, the State Department authorized its consular officers in Spain and Portugal to issue one thousand immigration visas to refugee children from France.[139] In Toulouse the chiefs of the French-Jewish partisan group, *Armée Juive* (Jewish Army) established the *Service d'évacuation et de regroupement des enfants* (SERE, Evacuation and Relocation Service for Children) whose objective was to evacuate the children across the Pyrenees to Spain and Portugal.[140] Weissman obtained Portugal's permission to house them temporarily. In May 1944, thanks to the mediation of Monsignor Boyer-Mas and Jean Chatain, a former French consular officer, Jordana had agreed to allow the evacuation of 500 children through Spain. He had also given permission for the creation of reception centres in Barcelona and Madrid for these children.[141] The operation came to an end after the Allied liberation of Southern France in the summer of 1944: by that time about 100 children had transited through Spain.[142]

The next rescue operation took place in Hungary. Until spring 1944, the 762,000 Jews living in Hungary had been relatively safe for, in spite of being a member of the Axis, the Hungarian government had rejected German demands to introduce the wearing of the yellow badges for the Jews and to deport them to Poland. The situation changed dramatically in March 1944 after German troops invaded Hungary and the pro-German Sztojay government was installed. The process of ghettoization began almost immediately. By July about 445,000 Jews had been deported to Auschwitz. These Jews came mostly from the provinces as the Germans opted not to deport the Jews of Budapest for the time being out of concern that the presence of foreign diplomats there would make it impossible to conceal the annihilation of Hungarian Jewry.[143] Aware that the lives of the Hungarian Jews depended on the presence of the greatest number of foreign observers, the War Refugee Board instructed Hayes to urge Madrid to increase its Spanish diplomatic and consular personnel in Hungary.[144]

Like other neutral countries, Sweden and Switzerland, Spain became involved in rescue activities only after the deportations from the provinces were completed.[145] The Franco regime entered the picture on the initiative of Renée Reichmann, a wealthy Hungarian Jewish refugee, who had been sending food parcels, under the aegis of the Spanish Red Cross, to the inmates of concentration camps in German-occupied territories. Aware that about four hundred refugees in Tangier were on the waiting list for the next boat to Palestine and that the JDC was planning the emigration of two hundred Jews to Canada, Mrs Reichmann hoped that the Spanish government would allow into the city an equal number of Hungarian Jewish children. On 22 May, at her initiative, a number of Jewish dignitaries asked Orgaz to authorize the emigration of five hundred Hungarian children ranging in age from two to fifteen. Orgaz responded a day later. He agreed to forward the request to the Ministry of Foreign Affairs but sticking to the regime's policy he insisted that the departure of the five hundred refugees would have to precede the arrival of the Hungarian children.[146] Mrs Reichmann also called on the US *chargé d'affaires*, Rives Childs, to support her plan. In the ensuing meeting, Orgaz informed Childs that he had forwarded the request to the Spanish Foreign Ministry with a favourable recommendation.[147] Finally, on 20 July, Jordana instructed the Spanish legation in Budapest to issue visas for five hundred children and seventy adults to care for them, but he insisted that the departure of the refugees had to precede the arrival of the children.[148] The Joint Distribution Committee agreed to assume the expenses of the rescue plan and the International Red Cross (IRC) undertook to help arrange the refugees' transportation to Tangier. As the German authorities refused to grant them transit visas, the Jewish children were assembled and transferred into houses under the joint custody of the IRC and the Spanish legation.

Throughout the summer of 1944, the Franco regime was responsive to the various demands that they act to save the Jews. In July, Madrid accepted the American and British request to allow 1,500 Jews of Budapest to enter the peninsula on their way to Palestine and promptly instructed its new *chargé d'affaires* in Budapest, Ángel Sanz Briz, to issue the visas.[149] In August, the Vatican representative, Angelo Rotta, had prompted the representatives of the neutral countries including Spanish *chargé d'affaires* in Budapest, Ángel Sanz Briz, to formulate a common declaration urging the Hungarian authorities to cease all deportations.[150] In September, emboldened by her earlier success, Mrs Reichmann requested another 700 visas from the Spanish authorities but this time for Jewish adults in Budapest. She again appealed to Childs, who obtained Orgaz's agreement. Orgaz forwarded the demand to Madrid indicating that, given the circumstances of the war, the visas were merely intended to protect the Jews of Budapest as they probably would not be able to come to Tangier.[151] That argument probably struck a chord with the Ministry of Foreign Affairs, which instructed Sanz Briz to issue the visas.

Meanwhile, the situation in Budapest was deteriorating dramatically. On October 15, after Horthy announced Hungary's withdrawal from the war, the Hungarian fascist organization, the Arrow Cross, staged a coup with the support of the Germans. A spree of violence directed against the Jews of Budapest took place in the aftermath of the coup. As the Soviet troops were advancing inexorably westwards, thirty-five thousand Jews were mobilized to dig trenches and construct defense fortifications.[152] Following the coup of the Arrow Cross, the threat of deportation inspired the neutral countries to actively help rescue a considerable portion of the Jews of Budapest. Hence Raoul Wallenberg, the third secretary of the Swedish legation, issued about 17,000 protective passes to Hungarian Jews, many of whom were housed in the buildings protected by the Swedes.[153]

In Washington the WJC representatives petitioned Cárdenas to ask the regime to extend its protection over the persecuted Jews. In Lisbon, Weissman appealed to Nicolás Franco, who urged Madrid to provide assistance to the Jews of Hungary on the grounds that it would provide Spain with good publicity.[154] The request prompted Lequerica to instruct Sanz Briz to extend Spain's protection over the Jews of Budapest.[155] As a result, Sanz Briz safeguarded the lives of about 2,300 Jews by providing them with protective documents such as ordinary Spanish passports, limited validity passports or with letters of patronage and by sheltering them in safe houses.[156] Sanz Briz established that letters of protection would be issued to all persons requesting them, without regard to social status and connections. In order to be protected it was sufficient to claim "Sephardic origin", or any degree of family relationship or commercial interests in Spain.[157] In November 1944, Sanz Briz saved thirty of his *protégés* whom the Germans had dragged into a death march with thousands of other Jews.[158]

In December 1944, as Soviet troops approached Budapest, Sanz Briz, who feared for his safety, left Hungary for Switzerland. His protégés, however, were not left unprotected: Giorgio Perlasca, a volunteer in the Nationalist forces during the Spanish Civil War who had used his connections to the regime to secure a job with Sanz Briz, appointed himself Spanish *chargé d'affaires*. From 1 December 1944 to 16 January 1945, the day the Red Army occupied Budapest, he directed the Spanish legation and continued to safeguard the Spanish *protégés*. Because communication between Spain and Hungary had become impossible, Madrid did not know anything about the activities of the "bogus consul".[159]

While the Spanish legation in Budapest was active in safeguarding the lives of the Budapest Jews, minor collaboration with Nazi Germany continued in Spain throughout 1944. Hence in early June 1944, in the Province of Huesca, a number of refugees were refused entry into Spain and were handed over by Spanish frontier officials to German border patrols. In one incident, on 11 June in Bielsa, the border authorities were forced to rescind the expulsion orders after one of the refugees' attempt to commit suicide caused the public indignation of the villagers.[160] On 18 July 1944, the eighth anniversary of the military rising, a group of fifteen Falangists, including some former members of the Blue Division, forcing their entry at pistol-point-burst into the offices of the Jewish Joint Distribution Committee in Barcelona and vandalized the premises.[161] Until the end of the war there continued to be diatribes against the Jews in the Spanish press. Hence in late 1944, *Haz*, the journal of the Falangist student organization the *Sindicato Universitario Español*, denounced the Jews as the main beneficiaries of the war.[162]

Meanwhile the Franco regime remained determined to prevent the Sephardic Jews from settling in Spain after the end of World War II. Madrid published two decrees on 24 July and on 10 October 1945, which confirmed that anyone who did not receive citizenship by means of the Primo de Rivera decree of December 1924 or who was not listed in the citizens' register could not be considered a citizen of Spain. Madrid also pledged to facilitate the repatriation of those who held genuine Spanish citizenship to their country of origin. The avowed aim of the decrees was to "avoid the entrance and settlement in Spain of those Sephardic Jews who previously lived abroad".[163]

After the Allied landings in November 1942 and more particularly after the fall of Mussolini in the summer 1943 Spanish officials had to reconcile their antisemitic beliefs with a more pragmatic foreign policy. Using the Jews to improve Spain's image abroad had a compelling attraction. The idea of reaching a "Gentleman's agreement" with the worldwide Jews to present a positive image of Spain abroad, particularly in the United States, was a logical consequence of the overestimation of Jewish power in Francoist thought that derived from the *Protocols of the Elders of Zion*. For a short while, the strategy seemed to be a good one. Spain saw its greatest propaganda victory at the World Jewish Congress conference, in Atlantic City in November 1944, where a resolution was passed acknowledging Spain's assistance to Jewish refugees.[164]

In the long term, however, using the Jews was not as easy as it might have seemed. In October 1945, Franco Salgado called Martinez de Bedoya and told him that the government was outraged by the anti-Franco press

campaign that had been launched throughout the world and that seemed
to indicate that Martinez de Bedoya had not demanded anything in return
for Spain's assistance to the Jews.[165] Bedoya grew convinced that the failure of the World Jewish Congress to fulfill its part of the "Gentleman's
agreement" was due to the combined scheming of the Republican government in exile and the Soviet government, which could not tolerate a
rapprochement between Franco's Spain and the "worldwide Jewry".
According to Bedoya, the WJC was receptive to the pressure emanating
from Moscow because it hoped to obtain Soviet support for the establishment of a Jewish state in Palestine.[166] Despite this setback Bedoya did not
give up hope of building good will with the Jewish community. His rea-
soning remained the same: diplomatically isolated Spain had to avoid
antagonizing the Jews given the fact "that the principal means of propaganda were in Semitic hands".[167]

Madrid's decision to grant Spanish nationality to the Sephardic Jews
living in Egypt and Greece who were under Spanish protection, must be
read within this context. Under the treaties that the Second Republic had
reached with Greece and Egypt in the 1930s these protected Jews were set
to lose the Spanish consular protection in 1949. In December 1948, Franco
published a decree permitting those affected to apply to Spanish embassies
to request the status of "Spanish citizens abroad". The decree affected about
seven hundred people but many of those on the list in Greece had died in
the Holocaust.[168]

The timing of the measure was chosen carefully. Israel had obtained
international recognition from a large number of governments. Madrid
interpreted the development as additional proof of the power of the Jews.
Hence no time was lost in using the decree to promote Spain's image abroad.
An article published in the state-sponsored *Sefarad* review announced: "This
decree proves once more Spain's elevated international conduct, to which
racism is unknown."[169]

At the time Franco coveted admission to the United Nations. The veto
pronounced against the dictatorship by the UN resolution of 1946 was an
obstacle to obtaining aid from the Marshall Plan, which the regime desper-
ately needed to weather the economic crisis.[170] By granting Spanish
nationality to the Sephardic Jews, the regime hoped to enlist the assistance
of "International Judaism" in opening the doors of the United Nations to
Spain.

Other gestures of goodwill towards the Jews included granting authorization to open a synagogue in Madrid in January 1949. The synagogue,
however, was quartered in a private house with no sign to indicate that it
was a place of Jewish worship, as the public celebration of non-Catholic

ceremonies was prohibited by the *Fuero de los Españoles* (Spanish Bill of Rights) of July 1945.[171]

These efforts were to no avail as Abba Eban, Israel's newly appointed representative to the UN, opposed the cancellation of the diplomatic ban of Francoist Spain, which was discussed in the General Assembly in May 1949. The vote caused much anger in Spain: *Arriba* accused Israel of having "knifed [Spain] in the back with unprecedented rancor and ingratitude unknown in history" and Franco felt personally wounded by the vote.[172]

Ambivalence continued to characterize the Franco regime's attitude towards the Jews after the war. While trying to rebuild its image by courting "International Jewry", Spain served as a refuge for a number of Nazi war criminals and their collaborators. Among the most prominent were Louis Darquier de Pellepoix, Commissioner General for Jewish Problems in Vichy France between May 1942 and February 1944, and Léon Degrelle, founder of Christus Rex, a Belgian fascist organization, and leader of the Belgian section of the *Waffen-SS*.[173] Sentenced to death in 1944, he managed to escape to Spain in May 1945. Always opportunistic, the Franco regime hoped to capitalize on the extradition of Nazi war criminals to put an end to its diplomatic isolation. Hence, in exchange for the hand-over of Degrelle, it demanded the restoration of full diplomatic relations between Spain and Belgium, a condition that was deemed unacceptable by the Belgian Foreign Minister, Paul-Henri Spaak.[174] As a result, Madrid refused to extradite Degrelle, who spent the rest of his life in Spain where he was naturalized in 1954, taking the name León José de Ramírez Reina.

Other key Nazi refugees included Reinhard Spitzy, a former SS agent and aide to Foreign Minister Joachim von Ribbentrop, Hans Lazar, chief of Nazi propaganda in Spain and Otto Skorzeny, the Nazi colonel who had rescued Mussolini from his imprisonment after his overthrow. The Spanish Church helped the war criminals, some of whom had important business interests in Spain, and knew key figures in the regime. Darquier was protected by General Antonio Barroso y Sánchez Guerra, and Spitzy hid for three years in the monastery of San Pedro de Cardeña in Burgos. Through the intermediary of General Yagüe, Spitzy traded the designs of Germany's anti-aerial rocket program to the Spanish army in exchange for money and false papers, which enabled him to go to Argentina.[175]

In fact many Nazi criminals and collaborators used Spain as an escape route to Latin America, particularly to Argentina. In March 1945, Carlos Fuldner, a German-Argentine, former SS intelligence officer, who had served as lieutenant and German-Spanish interpreter in the Blue Division, fled to Madrid to set up a network aimed at bringing Nazi war criminals to Argentina.[176] Fuldner enjoyed the protection of the Spanish elite, particularly of Blue Division veterans, such as the journalist Víctor de la Serna, whose namesake father, a pro-Nazi journalist, had denounced the Basque separatists as "Jews" after the bombing of the Basque market town of Guernica by the German Condor Legion in April 1937.[177] Both Charles Lesca, the editor of the notoriously French antisemitic weekly *Je suis partout* and Pierre Daye, a leader of the Belgian Rexist party and close associate of Degrelle, who had fled to Madrid in the last days of the war, were instrumental in setting up a Nazi escape route from Spain to Argentina.

The group often gathered at the German-owned Horcher restaurant in Madrid, where there were joined by Francoist intellectuals such as Manuel Aznar and Eugenio d'Ors, who both stood as character witnesses for Daye's Spanish residency application. The fugitives were so closely tied up with the Spanish political and intellectual elite that asking for their arrest seemed pointless. In fact when Lesca prepared his departure to Argentina in August 1946, he was invited to the Bilbao home of the former Foreign Minister José Felix de Lequerica, who feasted him with a delicious lunch and expensive wine.[178] After his escape to Argentina in 1947, Daye maintained a close friendship with Franco's ambassador to Buenos Aires, José María de Areilza, who even allowed him to use the Embassy's diplomatic pouch for communicating with fellow Nazi collaborators in Madrid. "The beautiful Spanish Embassy has replaced the Belgian Legation which disowns me", Daye wrote in his memoirs.[179]

The war criminals that remained in Spain lived there openly; their presence was conspicuous. In fact far from trying to conceal their presence in Francoist Spain, some Nazi fugitives actively encouraged Spanish extreme right agitation and promoted revisionist views. In an interview with *L'Express* in 1978, Darquier claimed that the only creatures that were gassed in Auschwitz had been lice; he called the Holocaust a "Jewish invention".[180] Similarly, Degrelle became the spiritual mentor of the neo-Nazi organization *Círculo Español de Amigos de Europa* (Spanish Circle of Friends of Europe), known as CEDADE, which published a number of his books, including "Memoirs of a Fascist", which denounced "the myth of the six million Jews" as a "propagandist stunt designed to extort gold from the Germans".[181] In 1985, Violetta Friedman, a survivor of Auschwitz who had later immigrated to Spain, filed a law suit against Degrelle who had declared on Spanish television: "if there are so many Jews at present, it is difficult to believe they are alive and kicking after the gas chambers". The court ruled against Friedman in the first trial and in a subsequent appeal. After a long legal battle during which CEDADE provided support to Degrelle the Constitutional Court finally convicted Degrelle of libel in 1991.[182]

Epilogue

The Contradictions and Hypocrisy of Francoist Policy

Between 1898 and 1945, Spanish antisemitism was based on two powerful myths: the myth of the *Reconquista*, which was deeply rooted in Spanish culture, and the myth of the Judeo-Masonic-Bolshevik conspiracy, which was largely imported from France. Constant references to the machinations of the Jews and lauding of the Edict of Expulsion not only in public statements but also in diplomatic dispatches suggest that far from being just a mere rhetorical device, antisemitism was pervasive among Francoist officials. The Franco regime's adherence to the myth of the *Reconquista* largely explains its reluctance to allow Jews, including Spanish nationals, to settle in Spain during World War II. It simply did not want to undo one of the achievements of the Catholic Kings – the expulsion of the Jews from Spain.

The myth of the *Reconquista* and the myth of the Judeo-Masonic-Bolshevik conspiracy were constantly evolving with Spain's domestic issues and geopolitical interests as Jews were identified with the enemy *du jour*. Thus, during the Second Republic and the Civil War, left-wing leaders, as well as Catalan and Basque nationalists were denounced as the descendants of the *conversos*. It was alleged that in order to enact revenge on Spain for the forced conversion of their forefathers, they were co-conspiring with the Freemasons and the Jews to bring about the country's downfall. Conversely, the radical right portrayed itself as the spiritual heir of the Catholic Kings who would revive the Inquisition "to purge" Spain of the Judeo-Masonic-Bolshevik conspiracy.

The persecution of Jews from the 1930s was also reinterpreted through the lens of the twin myths of the *Reconquista* and the myth of the Judeo-Masonic-Bolshevik conspiracy. Ultraconservative intellectuals drew a parallel between Weimar Germany and medieval Spain, claiming that both were in the hands of Jews. According to this analysis, Hitler had had no choice but to emulate the Catholic Kings, Isabella and Ferdinand, and to expel the Jews.

Throughout the period, myths about Jews were frequently modified to adapt to Spain's policy in Morocco. The colonial discourse of the Spanish radical right between 1898 and 1936 often associated Jews and Muslims, describing them as the archetypal "Others" of the Catholic Spaniards. Jews were portrayed as natural allies of the Moors. It was alleged that they had given a helping hand to the Moors during the *Reconquista* and had assisted Abd-el Krim, the rebel leader of the Rif tribes of Morocco. Yet, the opportunism of the Spanish radical right led it to emphasize the shared past of Spaniards with either Jews or Muslims when convenient. Hence, to recruit Moroccan troops during the Civil War, the Spanish Nationalists stressed Spain's Islamic past, while trying to channel Moroccan nationalism against the Jews. Later on, during World War II, Spain's colonial drive in North Africa prompted the Francoists to promote a rapprochement with the Spanish Jews of Morocco by rekindling philosephardism. The opportunistic nature of the regime's philosephardism was revealed during World War II as the dictatorship opposed proposals from Spanish diplomats serving in France and the Balkans to transfer to Spain the Spanish Jews whose lives were in danger.

Spain's international relations were critical in affecting the image of the Jews. Thus, from the turn of the century to World War II the Spaniards associated the Jews with France, which was at once the initiator of the process of Jewish emancipation and Spain's archrival in Morocco. Antisemitism and anti-Gallicism often proceeded hand in hand and the liberal ideas that abounded in Spain in the early twentieth century were blamed on the Judeo-Masonic-Bolshevik-French conspiracy. During World War II, the display of US military and economic strength prompted the Franco regime increasingly to identify the Jews with the new superpower rather than with France. Despite the frequent invectives against the Anglo-American-Bolshevik-Jewish foe, this association was to be beneficial to Jewish refugees as the Franco regime believed that aid to the Jews, even if limited, was in the interest of Spain's public relations.

The cynical position of the Spanish radical right towards the Jews was not unique. Brazil's policy towards the Jews during the 1930s, as demonstrated by Jeffrey Lesser, was equally opportunistic.[1] In the early 1930s, officials in the populist government of Getúlio Vargas were adamantly opposed to the notion of admitting members of the "Jewish race" into Brazil, on the grounds that they were closely linked to the Communists. In addition it was considered that as "non-Europeans" they could not contribute to the "whitening" of the Brazilian people, which the government desired. Between 1935 and 1938, the authorities did everything to keep the numbers of Jewish refugees low. This policy culminated in the enactment in 1937 of a secret circular banning the issuance of visas to all persons of "Semitic origin".[2]

However, despite the ban over four thousand Jews legally entered Brazil in 1939. By then a number of policymakers, including Brazil's Foreign Minister, Oswaldo Aranha, who had been among the officials supporting the secret circular, had become eager to build goodwill with the US government in order to obtain trade and loan agreements. The stereotypical images of Jews as financially astute and internationally potent, which had been previously used to justify their exclusion, were increasingly viewed as indicators of Jewish usefulness for Brazil's economic development and to polish the country's image abroad. Aranha's public relations stunt was more successful than that of Javier Martinez de Bedoya: in the aftermath of World War II, while Israel opposed the cancellation of the diplomatic ban on Francoist Spain, Brazil was considered a friend of the Jews and in Tel Aviv a street was named after Aranha.[3]

Also similar to Spain's wartime policy towards the Jews was that of Japan. In Japan, too, images of the Jews did not derive from experience but from translated antisemitc literature such as *The Protocols of the Elders of Zion*, mixed with strains of indigenous xenophobia.[4] Yet Japan did not carry out German antisemitic policies during World War II. Its policies towards the Jews were characterized by "self-interested neutrality", combining overt antisemitism with pragmatic measures. While antisemitism was an integral part of Japanese ultranationalist rhetoric and all of Japan's major papers carried antisemitic articles, which denounced the "Anglo-American-Jewish enemy", Japanese officials did not persecute Jews. In fact, Japan provided asylum for 18,000 Jewish refugees in Shanghai. Such a policy was judged to best serve Japan's war aims. A number of Japanese officials believed that they could enlist Jewish power to build the Japanese empire and to cooperate in the creation of the New Order in Asia.[5]

Closer to Spain, the same contradictions could be found in fascist Italy's policy towards the Jews. Obsessed with the immense power and influence of "International Judaism", Mussolini asked Italian diplomatic legations to send him extensive reports on all activities of Jewish communities in Europe and America, including rabbinical councils. In October 1938, the *Duce* enacted racial laws and introduced a policy of social discrimination against the Jews. Yet by the middle of 1942, Italian diplomats and military began to protect the interests of Italian Jews in areas of Southern France, Greece, Croatia and Tunisia, which Italy had conquested.[6]

This policy was motivated by political, economic and colonial considerations. As Daniel Carpi has demonstrated, Mussolini tried to make use of the Jews to promote his country's interests in the Mediterranean region. In

Tunisia, for instance, Italian consular representatives insisted that the Vichy laws were not be applied to the 5,000 Italian Jews. The existence of this community was one of the main arguments the Italians used to substantiate their claim over Tunisia. Hence the Italian authorities tried to preserve the social position of their Jewish citizens and to prevent their property from falling into French hands. At the same time, however, fundamentally Mussolini's regime remained as antisemitic as that of Franco.

In the aftermath of World War II, the Franco regime insisted on the non-existence of racism in Spain and argued that the country's Holocaust record was one of the features that distinguished it from the fascist and Nazi regimes. Yet a comparative perspective shows that the attitude of Franco's regime towards the Jews during the war closely resembled that of other authoritarian repressive regimes like Mussolini's Italy, Imperial Japan and Vargas's Brazil. In fact, the cynicism and hypocrisy of Francoist policy towards the Jews barely masked the dictatorship's underlying antisemitism, which was one of the many fascistic features that linked it to the Axis.

Notes

Introduction   The Interplay of Political Myths, Foreign Policy and Colonial Ambitions

1   Francisco Franco, *Textos de doctrina política: palabras y escritos de 1945 a 1950* (Madrid, 1951), p. 35.
2   Paul Preston, *Franco: A Biography* (London, 1995), p. 562.
3   Quoted in Haim Avni, *Spain, the Jews and Franco* (Philadelphia, 1982), p. 1.
4   Diplomatic Information Office of the Spanish Ministry of Foreign Affairs, *Spain and the Jews* (Madrid, 1949), p. 5.
5   Ibid., p. 9.
6   Anthony D.Smith, *Myths and Memories of the Nation* (Oxford, 1999), p. 58.
7   Georges Sorel, *Reflections on Violence* (New York, 1961) as quoted in Henry Tudor, *Political Myths* (London, 1972), p. 14.
8   Raoul Girardet, *Mythes et mythologies politiques* (Paris, 1986).
9   On the elaboration of these myths see José Àlvarez Junco, "The nation-building process in nineteenth century Spain", in Clare Mar-Molinero and Angel Smith (eds), *Nationalism and the Nation in the Iberian Peninsula: Competing and Conflicting Identities* (Oxford, 1996), pp. 100–1.
10 See Marie-Aline Barrachina, *Propagande et culture dans l'Espagne Franquiste: 1936–1945* (Grenoble, 1998), pp. 29–31. Bernd Rother also writes about the regime's anti-Judaic feelings, Bernd Rother, *Franco y el Holocausto* (Madrid, 2005), pp. 405 and 407.
11 Gavin I. Langmuir, *History, Religion and Antisemitism* (Berkeley, 1990), p. 297. See also Gavin I. Langmuir, *Towards a Definition of Antisemitism* (Berkeley, 1996), Chapter 14.
12 See for instance Sebastian Balfour, *Deadly Embrace: Morocco and the Road to the Spanish Civil War* (Oxford, 2002).
13 Ivan Davidson Kalmar and Derek J. Penslar, "Orientalism and the Jews: an introduction" in Kalmar and Penslar (eds), *Orientalism and the Jews* (Lebanon, NH, 2005) pp. xiii–xl.
14 Balfour, *Deadly Embrace*, p. 10.
15 See Ignacio Tofiño Quesada, "Spanish Orientalism: uses of the past in Spain's colonization in Africa", *Comparative Studies of South Asia Africa and the Middle East*, 23: Nos. 1–2 (2003), pp. 141–8 and Balfour, *Deadly Embrace*, pp. 161–3.
16 On the dictatorship's utilization of the past, see Tofiño Quesada, "Spanish orientalism", and Carmen Ortiz, "The uses of folklore by the Franco regime", *Journal of American Folklore*, 1999, 112 (446), pp. 479–96.

17 See chapter 3.

I   Degeneration, Regeneration and the Jews (1898–1931)

1   See Henry Kamen, *The Spanish Inquisition: A Historical Revision* (London, 1997). While Kamen estimates that no more than forty thousand Jews left Spain, J. H. Elliot, *Imperial Spain: 1469–1716* (London, 1990) believes that between 120,000 and 150,000 Jews fled the country.

2   See Joseph Kaplan "Jews and Judaism in the social and political thought of Spain in the sixteenth and seventeenth Century", in Shmuel Almog (ed.) *Antisemitism Through the Ages* (Oxford, 1988), pp. 153–61.

3   Kamen, *The Spanish Inquisition*, pp. 290–1.

4   Avni, *Spain, the Jews and Franco*, p. 7.

5   Caesar Aronsfeld, *The Ghosts of 1492: Jewish Aspects of the Struggle for Religious Freedom in Spain, 1848–1976* (New York, 1976) p. 18 quoting the *Jewish Chronicle* (27 November 1868). According to Aronsfeld, the sum corresponds to about 1,600 million pesetas.

6   Javier Vidal Olivares and Pedro Pablo Ortuñez, "The internationalisation of ownership of the Spanish railways companies, 1858–1936", *Business History*, Vol. 44, No. 44 (October 2002), p. 29.

7   C. R. Pennell, *Morocco Since 1830: A History* (London, 2000), pp. 64–5.

8   *Jewish Chronicle* (24 February 1860) quoted in Joseph Jacob Lichtenstein, *The Reaction of West European Jewry to the Reestablishment of a Jewish Community in Spain in the 19th Century*, Ph.D. dissertation, Yeshiva University (New York, 1962), p. 35.

9   Juan Bautista Vilar, "L'ouverture à l'Occident de la communauté juive de Tétouan 1860–1865", in Sarah Leibovici (ed.), *Mosaiques de notre mémoire: Les Judéo Espagnols du Maroc* (Paris, 1982), pp. 99–100.

10 Lichtenstein, *The Reaction of West European Jewry*, Chapter III.

11 *Jewish Chronicle* (8 January 1864).

12 See Lichtenstein, *The Reaction of West European Jewry*.

13 *Jewish Chronicle* (28 April 1876).

14 *Jewish Chronicle* (23 April 1869).

15 *Jewish Chronicle* (28 April 1876).

16 Avni, *Spain, the Jews and Franco*, p. 14.

17 The two projects are discussed by Isidro Gonzalez, *El retorno de los judíos* (Madrid, 1991).

18 H. Ramsden, *The 1898 Movement in Spain: Towards a Reinterpretation with Special Reference to En torno al Casticismo and Idearium Español* (Manchester, 1974), pp. 30–7.

19 Ibid., p. 67, p. 138, pp. 207–208 and Sebastian Balfour, *The End of the Spanish Empire 1898–1923* (Oxford, 1997), pp. 66–7.

20 Mary Nash, "Social eugenics and nationalist race hygiene in early twentieth century Spain", *History of European Ideas*, Vol. 15, No. 4–6 (1992), p. 743.

21 Pulido's racial ideas are analysed by Joshua Seth Goode, *The Racial Alloy: the*

Science, Politics and Culture of Race in Spain, 1875–1923, Ph.D. dissertation, University of California (Los Angeles, 1999).

22 Ángel Pulido Fernández, *Españoles sin patria y la raza sefardí*, 4th edn (Granada, 1993), p. 34 and p. 530.

23 Ibid., p. 50.

24 Ibid., pp. 26–30.

25 Ibid., p. 30 and p. 225 translated by Goode, *The Racial Alloy*, p. 320.

26 See John M. Efron, "Scientific racism and the mystique of Sephardic racial superiority", *Leo Baeck Institute Yearbook*, Vol. 38 (1993), pp. 75–96.

27 Pulido, *Españoles sin patria*, p. 18 translated by Goode, *The Racial Alloy*, p. 318.

28 Pulido, *Españoles sin patria*, p. 60.

29 Ibid., pp. 538–9.

30 Ibid., pp. 42–3.

31 Ibid., p. 21 and p. 550.

32 Benjamin Braude, "The myth of the Sefardi economic superman", in Jeremy Adlman and Stephen Aron (eds), *Trading Cultures: The Worlds of Western Merchants, Essays on Authority, Objectivity and Evidence* (Turnhout, 2001).

33 Esther Benbassa and Aron Rodrigue, *The Jews of the Balkans: The Judeo-Spanish Community, 15th to 20th Centuries* (Oxford, 1995), p. 85.

34 André Chouraqui, *L'Alliance Israélite Universelle et la renaissance juive contemporaine* (Paris, 1965), p. 161.

35 Benbassa and Rodrigue, *The Jews of the Balkans*, p. 4.

36 Pulido, *Españoles sin patria*, p. 608.

37 *Diario de Sesiones de las Cortes* (3 December 1904) (Senate), No. 51. Vol. II.

38 Jacques Bigart, "Choses d'Espagne" in *L'Univers Israélite* (11 November 1904), pp. 270–5.

39 Ibid., p. 218.

40 *Jewish Chronicle* (24 April 1931).

41 Aronsfeld, *The Ghosts of 1492*, p. 26. and Ranaan Rein, *In the Shadow of the Holocaust and the Inquisition: Israel's Relations with Francoist Spain* (London, 1997), p. 50.

42 See Matilde Morcillo-Rosillo. "España y los sefarditas de Salónica durante el incendio de 1917", *Sefarad* Vol. 59, No. 2 (1999), pp. 353–69.

43 Pulido, *Españoles sin Patria*, p. 480.

44 Translation of Maura Gamazo, *La cuestión de Marruecos desde el punta de vista Español* (Madrid, 1905), pp. 33–4 in James A. Chandler, "Spain and her Moroccan protectorate", *Journal of Contemporary History*, Vol. 10 (1975), p 302.

45 Sebastian Balfour, "Spain and the Great Powers in the aftermath of the disaster of 1898", in Sebastian Balfour and Paul Preston (eds), *Spain and the Great Powers in the Twentieth Century* (London, 1999), p. 17; Norman Goda, "Franco's bid for empire: Spain, Germany, and the Western Mediterranean in World War II", in Raanan Rein (ed.), *Spain and the Mediterranean since 1898* (London, 1999), p. 170.

46   On Spain's policy in Morocco see Balfour, *Deadly Embrace.*

47   Carolyn Halstead and Charles Halstead, "Aborted imperialism: Spain's occu-
      pation of Tangier 1940–1945", *Iberian Studies*, Vol. 7, No. 2 (Autumn 1978),
      pp. 53–71.

48   Balfour, "Spain and the Great Powers after 1898", pp. 21–2.

49   José Antonio de Sangróniz, *Marruecos, sus condiciones físicas, sus habitantes y las
      instituciones indígenas* (Madrid, 1921), p. 162.

50   Henk Driessen, *On the Spanish Moroccan Frontier: A Study in Ritual Power and
      Ethnicity* (Oxford, 1992), pp. 93–4.

51   Michael M. Laskier, *The Alliance Israélite Universelle and the Jewish communities
      of Morocco 1862–1962* (Albany, New York 1983), p. 45 and p. 80 and Leland
      Bowie, "An aspect of Muslim–Jewish relations in late nineteenth-century
      Morocco: a European diplomatic view", *International Journal of Middle East
      Studies* 7 (1976), pp. 3–19.

52   Ernesto Giménez Caballero, *Notas marruecas de un soldado* (Madrid, 1923), pp.
      176–179.

53   Ortega, *Los hebreos en Marruecos* (Madrid, 1919), p. 326.

54   Ibid.

55   Ibid., pp. 338–9.

56   Ibid., pp. 343–5.

57   Sebastian Balfour and Pablo La Porte. "Spanish military cultures and the
      Moroccan wars 1909–1936", *European History Quarterly*, Vol. 30, No. 3 (July
      2000), pp. 307–33.

58   Balfour, *Deadly Embrace*, p. 14.

59   Ortega, *Los hebreos*, p. 3.

60   Public Record Office, Kew London (hereafter PRO) FO 371/1694 W50674,
      letter from General Marina to A. Pimienta and Pinhas Asayag, Acting
      President and Secretary of the Israelite community in Tangier (26 September
      1913).

61   PRO FO 371/1694 W50674, letter from H. White, Tangier (28 October
      1913).

62   On Berenguer see Preston, *Franco*, p. 25.

63   Spain's imperial project also included the founding of primary schools for
      Muslim children. See Geoffrey Jensen, "Toward the 'moral conquest' of
      Morocco: Hispano-Arabic education in early twentieth-century North
      Africa", *European History Quarterly*, Vol. 31 No. 2, pp. 205–29.

64   MAEF Série Maroc-Tunisie (1917–1940) Sous-série Maroc, Vol. 826,
      communiqué from the vice-consul in Larache and El Ksar (15 November
      1919).

65   Laskier, *The Alliance Israélite Universelle* , p. 164.

66   Archives of the Alliance Israélite Universelle, Paris (thereafter AAIU)
      Microfilm Bobine MA 40, Maroc XIE 177–92, letter from Albert Benaroya,
      to AIU Paris (24 May 1912).

67   AAIU Bobine MA 40, Maroc XIE 177–92, letter Benaroya to AIU (5 October
      1913).

68 AAIU Bobine MA 40, Maroc XIE 177–92, letter from Benaroya (16 February 1912).

69 AAIU Bobine 18, Maroc III C 10, letter from Benaroya (12 June 1912).

70 AAIU Bobine MA 40, Maroc XIE 177–92, letter Benaroya (27 October 1913).

71 AAIU Bobine MA 40, Maroc XIE 177–92, letter from Benaroya (15 February 1912).

72 AAIU Bobine 18, Maroc III C 10, letter from the Jewish community (11 June 1912).

73 AAIU Maroc MA 40, XIE 177–192, letter from YD Semach to AIU (18 May 1916).

74 AAIU Maroc MA 40, XIE 177–192, letter from Sémach (18 May 1916).

75 MAEF Série Maroc-Tunisie (1917–1940) Sous-série Maroc, Vol. 826, yearly report from M. Levy, director of the AIU school in Tetuán (2 August 1920).

76 Laskier, *The Alliance Israélite Universelle*, pp. 11–12.

77 MAEF Correspondence Politique et commerciale, Série Maroc-Tunisie, Sous série Maroc, Vol. 217, letter from Victor Monge to Mr Fornes chargé d'Affaires of the French consulate in Tangier (28 August 1918).

78 Halstead and Halstead, "Aborted imperialism", p. 54

79 Serels, *A History of the Jews of Tangier*, p. 108.

80 Ibid., p. 114.

81 MAEF Correspondence Politique et commerciale, Série Maroc-Tunisie, Sous série Maroc, Vol. 381, Protection Indigène, letter from the plenipotentiary minister delegate to the General Residency in Rabat to the Minister of Foreign Affairs in Paris (2 June 1924).

82 *ABC* (28 April 1924).

83 Manuel Ortega, *El Doctor Pulido* (Madrid, 1922), p. 332.

84 Avni, *Spain, the Jews and Franco*, p. 27.

85 Isaac Guershon, "La Revista de la Raza: organo del filosefardismo Español", *Raices*, No. 8 (1994), pp. 58–61.

86 Lorenzo Delgado Gómez-Escalonilla, *Imperio de papel: acción cultural y politica exterior durante el primer Franquismo* (Madrid, 1992), pp. 1–19.

87 Archives of the Ministerio de Asuntos Exteriores Español Madrid, Spain (hereafter MAEE), R725/ 80.

88 MAEE R725/ 80, letter from the Duque of Amalfi (20 March 1922).

89 MAEE R725/ 80, letter from the Duque of Amalfi (28 February 1922).

90 José Antonio Lisbona, *Retorno a Sefarad. La política de España hacia sus judíos en el siglo XX* (Barcelona, 1993), p. 36.

91 See copy of *La Gaceta de Madrid* (21 December 1924) in MAEE R7330/122.

92 Ibid.

93 Aronsfeld, *The Ghosts of 1492*, p. 34.

94 MAEE R728/1, Memorias del Señor Caballero sobre los Sefardies (July 1931).

95 José Antonio de Sangróniz, *La expansión cultural de España en el extranjero y principalemente en Hispano-América* (Madrid, 1925), pp. 65–6.

96 Ibid., p. 67.
97 Ibid., p. 69.
98 Ibid., p. 71.
99 Douglas W. Foard, *The Revolt of the Aesthetes: Ernesto Giménez Caballero and the Origins of Spanish Fascism* (New York, 1989), p. 37.
100 Giménez Caballero, *Notas marruecas*, pp. 176–9.
101 Foard, *The Revolt of the Aesthetes*, pp. 65–8.
102 Ibid., p. 98.
103 *La Gaceta Literaria* (1 October 1929).
104 *La Gaceta Literaria* (15 February 1931).
105 *La Gaceta Literaria* (1 September 1929).
106 MAEE R728/1 Memorias del Sr Giménez Caballero sobre los sefardies.
107 Herbert Rutledge Southworth, *Antifalange: estudio crítico de "Falange en la guerra de España: la unificación y Hedilla" de Maximiano García Venero* (Paris, 1967), p. 33.
108 Ibid., p. 34.
109 *La Gaceta Literaria* (15 July 1931), as quoted in Foard, *The Revolt of the Aesthetes*, p. 99.
110 MAEE R515/7, El Sefardismo Economico (22 March 1930).
111 Ibid.
112 Ibid.
113 Ibid.
114 Marcelino Menéndez Pelayo, *Historia de los heterodoxos españoles* 2nd ed (Madrid, 1963), p. 471.
115 Ibid., p. 475.
116 Ibid., p. 16.
117 César Peiró Menéndez, *Arte de concocer a nuestros judíos* (Barcelona, 1916), p. 9, p. 14 and p. 51.
118 Ibid., pp. 20–45. On antisemitic rhetoric about the Jewish body see Sander Gilman, *The Jew's body* (New York, 1991).
119 Peiró Menéndez, *Arte de concocer*, p. 133 and p. 148.
120 Isidro González, "L'antisemitisme en l'Espanya contemporània", *L'Avenç* 18 (1995), No. 198, p. 59.
121 *El Siglo Futuro* (12 September 1899).
122 Peregín Casabó y Pagés, *La España judía* (Barcelona 1891), pp. 100–7.
123 Juan Vázquez de Mella y Fanjul, *Obras completas, Vol. 7: discursos parlamentarios* (Barcelona, 1932), p. 314.
124 Manfred Böcker, *Antisemitismus ohne Juden: die Zweite Republik, die antirepublikanische Rechte und die Juden. Spanien 1931 bis 1936* (Frankfurt, 2000), p. 64.
125 Joaqin Girón y Arcas, *La cuestión judáica en la España actual y en la Universidad de Salamanca* (Salamanca, 1906), p. 84, p. 86 and pp. 137–8.
126 Ibid., pp. 111–15.
127 Ibid., p. 117.
128 Ibid., pp. 135–6.

129 *El Pensamiento Español* (28 February 1920) reprinted in Juan Vázquez de Mella y Fanjul, *Obras completas, Vol. 3: odeario* (Barcelona, 1931), p. 221.

130 Ibid.

131 Africano Fernández, *España en África y el peligro judío: apuntes de un testigo* (Santiago, 1918), p. 244.

132 Ibid., pp. 221–40.

133 Ibid., p. 195 and p. 258.

134 Ibid., p. 189.

135 Ibid., p. 190.

136 Ibid., p. 195.

137 Ibid., pp. 248–9.

138 Avni, *Spain, the Jews and Franco*, p. 28.

139 José Luis Martínez Sanz, "Reflejo en España del antijudaismo Aleman prehitleriano", in M. Espadas Burgos and F. Ruiz Gomez M (eds), *Encuentros en Sefarad: actas del congreso internacional "los judíos en la historia de España"* (Ciudad Real, 1987), p. 359, quoting *ABC* (30 January 1919).

140 On the rise of European antisemitism in the wake of the Bolshevik revolution see Almog, *Nationalism and Antisemitism*, pp. 79–99.

141 *El Pensamiento Español* (28 February 1920).

142 José L. Rodríguez Jiménez, "Los Protocolos de los Sabios de Sión en España", *Raices*, No. 38, p. 28.

143 For the genesis of the *Protocols* see Norman Cohn, *Warrant for Genocide: the Myth of the Jewish World Conspiracy and the Protocols of the Elders of Zion* (London, 1967) and Stephen Eric Bronner, *A Rumor about the Jews: Reflections and Antisemitism and the Protocols of the Elders of Zion* (New York, 2000).

144 David L. Kertzer, *The Popes Against the Jews: the Vatican's Role in the Rise of Modern Antisemitism* (New York, 2001), pp. 267–8.

2   Anti-republican Antisemitism (1931–1936)

1   Michael Seidman, *Republic of Egos: A Social History of the Spanish Civil War* (Madison, 2002), pp. 17–18.

2   On the prevalence of conspiracy theories in the Third Republic see D.L.L Parry, "Articulating the Third Republic by Conspiracy Theory", *European History Quarterly*, Vol. 28, No. 2 (1998,), pp. 163–88.

3   Regarding the social psychological functions of conspiracy theories see Carl F. Graumann and Serge Moscovici, *Changing Conceptions of Conspiracy* (New York, 1987).

4   On that subject see Isidro González Garcia, *Los judíos y la Segunda República 1931–1939* (Madrid, 2004).

5   Quoted in Shlomo Ben-Ami, *The Origins of the Second Republic in Spain* (Oxford, 1978), p. 224.

6   Stanley Payne, *Spain's First Democracy: the Second Republic, 1931–1936* (Madison, Wisconsin, 1993), p. 31.

7　*L'Univers Israélite* (1 May 1931).
8　Quoted in *L'Univers Israélite* (1 May 1931).
9　Decree reproduced in Iacob M. Hassán (ed.), *Actas del primer simposio de estudios sefardíes* (Madrid, 1976), Appendix 4, p. 590.
10　*Jewish Guardian* (15 May 1931).
11　*L'Univers Israélite* (15 May 1931).
12　*Jewish Guardian* (29 May 1931).
13　*Jewish Guardian* (3 July 1931).
14　*American Hebrew* (19 June 1931) and *Jewish Chronicle* (26 June 1931).
15　*Jewish Guardian* (26 June 1931), *Jewish Chronicle* (1 May 193) and (9 October 1931).
16　MAEE R516/4, letter of Rabbi Djaen to Alejandro Lerroux (14 August 1931).
17　MAEE R516/4, letter from the Spanish representative in Cairo (10 June 1931).
18　*American Hebrew* (1 July 1931).
19　*Jewish Guardian* (12 June 1931).
20　*El Siglo Futuro* (8 June 1931).
21　*El Siglo Futuro* (30 December 1931).
22　MAEE R516/4, letter of Gabaldón to the Minister of State (18 May 1931).
23　MAEE R516/4, entrada y estancia de judíos en España de 1929 a 1935.
24　*Jewish Chronicle* (29 July 1932).
25　Joseph Harrison, *The Spanish Economy in the Twentieth Century* (London, 1985), pp. 79–85.
26　*American Hebrew* (1 July 1932).
27　*L'Univers Israélite* (15 May 1931).
28　On Yahuda see Chapter 1.
29　MAEE R516/4, translation of an article published in the Judeo-Spanish paper of Salonica, *La Acción* (31 January 1934).
30　*American Hebrew* (1 July 1932).
31　Ibid.
32　*The Reform Advocate* (12 December 1931).
33　Quoted by Avni, *Spain, the Jews and Franco*, p. 34.
34　Ibid., p. 35.
35　*El Debate* (29 December 1931).
36　Ibid.
37　*Jewish Chronicle* (22 January 1932).
38　*El Siglo Futuro* (8 June 1931) and (10 June 1931).
39　*Acción Española* (15 January 1932).
40　*El Debate* (2 December 1932).
41　*Jewish Chronicle* (6 January 1933).
42　See Giménez Caballero's report in Chapter 1.
43　MAEE R698/1, Report of Agustin de Foxá (18 October 1932).
44　Theodor Herzl himself believed that the existence of the *Alliance Israélite Universelle* perpetrated the antisemitic myth that there was an international

Jewish conspiracy to dominate the world. See Laskier, *The Alliance Israélite Universelle*, p. 195.

45 On the rise of Zionism in the Balkans and the struggle between Zionists and Alliancists see Esther Benbassa and Aron Rodrigue, *Sephardi Jewry: A History of the Judeo-Spanish Community, 14th–20th centuries* (Berkeley, 1999) Chapter 4.

46 MAEE R698/1, report of Agustin de Foxá (18 October 1932).

47 Ibid.

48 *L'Univers Israélite* (15 May 1931) and *Jewish Chronicle* (21 October 1932).

49 Laskier, *The Alliance Israélite Universelle*, p. 209.

50 *B'nai B'rith magazine* (April 1933), p. 223.

51 MAEF Correspondence Politique et commerciale, Série Maroc-Tunisie, Sous série Maroc (Vol. 381), letter from Urbain Blanc plenipotentiary minister to the General Residency in Morocco to the French Prime Minister (2 June 1924).

52 *El Debate* (22 December 1932).

53 AAIU, Fonds Moscou, E07.4, annual Report Moise Levy to the President (25 July 1932).

54 AAIU, Bobine MA 172, Maroc LXXVII-e, letter from Moise Levy (7 November 1933).

55 Ibid.

56 On Germany's boycott and anti-Jewish legislation, see Lucy Dawidowicz, *The War Against the Jews, 1933–1945* (New York, 1976), pp. 63–90 and Leni Yahil, *The Holocaust: The Fate of European Jewry* (New York, 1990), pp. 53–67.

57 MAEE R516/4, letter from Ginés Vidal to the State Minister (8 April 1933).

58 MAEE R516/4, note from the State Ministry (3 May 1933).

59 MAEE R516/4, letter from Gómez Ocerín (4 May 1938).

60 Ignacio Bauer, "Les Juifs en Espagne", *Revue Juive de Genève* (June 1936).

61 MAEE R516/4, letter from Salvador de Madariaga (26 April 1933).

62 Avni, *Spain, the Jews and Franco*, p. 37.

63 Preston, *Comrades* (London, 1999), p. 148.

64 Aronsfeld, *The Ghosts of 1492*, p. 42, quoting the *American Jewish Year Book*, 36 (1934–1935), p. 97.

65 Thomas F. Glick and José M. Sánchez Ron, *La España posible de la Segunda República: la oferta a Einstein de una cátedra extraordinaria en la Universidad Central* (Madrid, 1983), p. 18.

66 *El Debate* (12 April 1933).

67 *El Debate* (11 April 1933) and Jacobo Israel Garzón, "Judíos en España en los años treinta: Segunda República y Guerra Civil", *Raíces*, No. 26 (1996), p. 67.

68 Paul Preston, *The Coming of the Spanish Civil War: Reform, Reaction and Revolution in the Second Republic 1931–1936*, 2nd edn (London, 1994), pp. 93–4.

69 Paul Preston, *Doves of War: Four Women of Spain* (London, 2003), pp.323–4.

70 Paul Preston, "Alfonsist monarchism and the coming of the Spanish civil war", in Martin Blinkhorn (ed.), *Spain in Conflict: Democracy and its Enemies*, p. 179.

71   Raúl Morodo, *Acción Española. Origenes ideológicos del franquismo* (Madrid, 1980), p. 63.
72   Ibid., gives an inventory of the backers, pp. 65–73.
73   Lisbona, *Retorno a Sefarad*, p. 92.
74   Preston, *Franco*, p. 90.
75   Preston, "Alfonsist monarchism", p. 164.
76   Rodríguez Jiménez, "Los Protocolos", p. 31.
77   José Rodríguez Jiménez, *Historia de la Falange Española de la JONS* (Madrid, 2000), p. 98. On Redondo see Preston, *Doves of War*, pp. 209–32.
78   *Libertad* (14 March 1932)
79   In 1882, the French Abbé Chabauty published a book, which included two letters that were allegedly written in 1489 by the Rabbi of the Jews of Arles and the Prince of the Jews of Constantinople, who spoke of the Jews rising up to "dominate the world". These letters have come to be known as the letter of the Jews of Arles and the letter of the Jews of Constantinople. It is believed that these letters were probably written in Spain as a satirical comment on the *Marranos*. See Norman Cohn, *Warrant for Genocide*, p. 51.
80   *Acción Española*, Vol. II, No. 10 (May 1932).
81   Álvarez Chillida, *El antisemitismo en España*, p. 316.
82   On Jouin see Norman Cohn, *Warrant for Genocide*, p. 183 and David Kertzer, *The Popes Against the Jews*, p. 268.
83   Rodriguez Jimenez, "Los Protocolos".
84   Ibid., p. 131.
85   Ibid., p. 132.
86   Ibid., p. 133.
87   Balfour, *Deadly Embrace*, pp. 197–202.
88   *La Legión* (1 January 1931) quoted in Julio Gil Pecharroman, *Conservadores subversivos: la derecha autoritaria Alfonsina 1913–1936* (Madrid, 1991), p. 82.
89   *El Siglo Futuro* (3 June 1935) quoted in Álvarez Chillida, *El antisemitismo en España*, p. 323.
90   Tusquets, *Orígenes*, pp. 41–2.
91   Javier Tusell, *Historia de la democracia cristiana en España, Tomo I: antecedentes y C.E.D.A* (Madrid, 1974), p. 227.
92   José Antonio Primo de Rivera, *Escritos y discursos, obras completas* (Madrid, 1976), pp. 329–30.
93   José Maria Albiñana, *España bajo la dictadura republicana: crónica de un período putrefacto* (Madrid, 1933), pp. 179–81 and pp. 221–3.
94   *El Siglo Futuro* (26 February 1935).
95   Payne, *Spain's First Democracy*, p. 41.
96   Albiñana, *España bajo la dictadura republicana*, p. 221.
97   Mary Vincent, *Catholicism in the Second Spanish Republic: Religion and Politics in Salamanca 1930–1936* (Oxford, 1996), p. 219 quoting *Estrella del mar* (1932), p. 370.
98   Ramiro de Maeztu, *Defensa de la Hispanidad* (Madrid, 1934), pp. 206–7.

99 Ibid., p. 211.

100 Raúl Morodo, *Acción Española*, pp. 152–9.

101 Ernesto Giménez Caballero, *Genio de España: exaltaciones a una resurreción nacional y del mundo*, 8th ed (Barcelona, 1983), p. 104.

102 Ramiro de Maeztu, *Frente a la República*, 8th ed (Madrid, 1956), p. 219.

103 On French antisemitism and its labeling of the Jew as "oriental" see Pierre Birnbaum, *Antisemitism in France: A Political History from Léon Blum to the Present* (Oxford, 1992), pp. 99–105.

104 *Informaciones* (24 March 1933) as quoted in Mercedes Semolinos, *Hitler y la prensa de la II Republica* (Madrid, 1985), p. 222.

105 *JONS* (1 May 1933) quoted in Marie-Aline Barrachina, *Propagande et culture*, p. 32.

106 *Jewish Chronicle* (23 March 1934).

107 *El Debate* (17 October 1933) quoted in Paul Preston, *The Coming of the Spanish Civil War: Reform, Reaction and Revolution in the Second Spanish Republic 1931–1936* (London, 1994), p. 71.

108 *Jewish Chronicle* (23 March 1934).

109 Ibid.

110 Payne, *Spain's First Democracy*, p. 193. On the uprising see also Adrian Shubert, "The epic failure: The Asturian revolution of October 1934", in Paul Preston (ed.), *Revolution and War in Spain: 1931–1939* (London, 1985), pp. 113–37.

111 Quoted in Julio Rodríguez-Puértolas, *Literatura fascista española: volumen I historia* (Madrid, 1987), p. 70.

112 See Sebastian Balfour, *Deadly Embrace*, pp. 251–4.

113 *Informaciones* (28 October 1934) quoted in Manfred Böcker, *Antisemitismus ohne Juden: die Zweite Republik, die antirepublikanische Rechte und die Jude; Spanien 1931 bis 1936* (Frankfurt, 2000).

114 César González Ruano, *Seis meses con los Nazis* (Madrid, 1933), p. 14.

115 *ABC* (20 April 1932).

116 *ABC* (20 May 1933).

117 *El Debate* (10 March 1933) quoted in Mercedes Semolinos, *Hitler y la prensa*, p. 223.

118 *Acción Española*, Vol. V, No. 25 (March 1933).

119 *Acción Español*, Vol. V, No. 26 (May 1933).

120 Raúl Morodo, *Acción Española*, p. 73.

121 *Acción Española*, Vol. VIII, No. 44 (1 January 1934), p. 781.

122 Ibid., p. 789

123 René Llanas de Niubó, *El Judaísmo* (Madrid, 1935), p. 123.

124 Álvarez Chillida, *El antisemitismo en España*, p. 314.

125 Wiener Library, Document Series 684: Antisemitism in Spain –Reports and Correspondence 1936–1938. Excerpts of the letters from Juan Perez Martín to the Deutschlandsender Reichsender (4 June 1935) and to the Reichs-Rundfunk-Gesellschaft (27 November 1935).

126 *Archives Israélites* (10 May 1934).

127 *Jewish Chronicle* (4 January 1935).

128 *El Sol* (20 April 1935).

129 Virgilio Sevillano Carbajal, *La España { . . . } de quién? Ingleses, franceses y alemanes en este pais* (Madrid, 1936), pp. 210–11.

130 *El Sol* (20 April 1935).

131 HICEM was a Jewish emigration organization based in Paris. It was formed in 1927 with the merger of three organizations: the New-York based HIAS (Hebrew Immigrant Aid Society), the ICA (Jewish Colonization Association), which was established in Great Britain to assist East European Jewish emigrants, and the Berlin-based Emigdirect (United Committee for Jewish Emigration). HICEM is an anacronym for HIAS, ICA and Emigdirect.

132 Isaac Guershon, "La Revista de la Raza: Organo del Filosefardismo Español", *Raices*, No. 8 (1994), pp. 8–61. On CIAP and *La Gaceta Literaria* see chapter 1.

133 *El Siglo Futuro* (4 April 1934) quoted in Martin Blinkhorn, *Carlism and Crisis in Spain 1931–1939* (London, 1975), p. 179.

134 *Informaciones* (30 April 1936) quoted in Lisbona, *Retorno a Sefarad*, p. 98.

135 *El Siglo Futuro* (9 February 1933) quoted in Blinkhorn, *Carlism and Crisis*, p. 179.

136 *Jewish Chronicle* (4 January 1935).

137 Payne, *Spain's First Democracy*, pp. 234–5.

138 *American Hebrew* (22 March 1935).

139 Ibid.

140 *El Debate* (26 October 1935).

141 Llanas de Niubó, *El judaismo*, p. 112.

142 *Jewish Chronicle* (7 December 1934).

143 *ABC* (16 March 1935).

144 *El Debate* (26 October 1935) and (31 January 1936).

145 *El Debate* (31 August 1935).

146 Henry Buckley, *Life and Death of the Spanish Republic* (London, 1940), p. 180.

147 Payne, *Spain's First Democracy*, p. 247.

148 On the Stavisky Affair see Serge Bernstein, *Le 6 Fevrier 1934* (Paris, 1975).

149 *Heraldo de Madrid* (5 December 1935).

150 *El Debate* (25 October 1935).

151 *La Nacion* (30 October 1935).

152 Quoted in Jesús Pabón, *Cambó: parte primera 1918–1930* (Barcelona, 1969), p. 532. On Macià see Alfons Maseras, *La nostra gent Francesc Macià* (Barcelona, 1946).

153 *La Nacion* (30 October 1935).

154 Payne, *Spain's First Democracy*, p. 210.

155 Wiener Library, Document Series 684: Antisemitism in Spain, letter from Ignacio Bauer to the Centraal Joodschinformatebureau (9 December 1935).

156 Mary Vincent, "The Spanish Church and the Popular Front: the experience of Salamanca province", in Martin S. Alexander and Helen Graham, *The*

173

French and Spanish Popular Fronts: Comparative Perspectives (Cambridge, 1989), p. 84.

157 *El Siglo Futuro* (10 January 1936) quoted in Manfred Böcker, *Antisemitismus ohne Juden*, p. 303.

158 *ABC* (11 February 1936).

159 *Gracia y Justicia* (4 January 1935) quoted in José A. Ferrer Benimeli, "La Prensa fascista y el contubernio Judeo-Masónico-Comunista" in José Antonio Ferrer Benimeli (ed.) *Masonería y periodismo en la España conemporáneo* (Zaragoza, 1993), p. 215.

160 *The American Hebrew* (20 April 1936).

161 *The American Hebrew* (3 April 1936).

162 *La Vanguardia* (30 March 1936).

163 *El Siglo Futuro* (24 April 1936).

164 See Girardet, *Mythes et mythologies politiques*, p. 61.

165 Paul Preston, "Alfonsist monarchism", p. 163.

3 Antisemitism as a Weapon of War (1936–1939)

1 See Álvarez Chillida, *El antisemitismo en España*, Chapter 12.

2 Balfour and La Porte, "Spanish Military Cultures", p. 314.

3 See Chapter II.

4 Preston, *Franco*, p. 123.

5 Ibid., p. 78.

6 Ibid., pp. 122–3.

7 Emilio Mola, *Tempestad, calma, intriga y crisis*, 2nd edn (Madrid, 1932), p. 159.

8 Francisco Franco, "Xauen la triste", *Revista de Tropas Coloniales*, No. 19 (July 1926), p. 146.

9 *Palabras del Caudillo, 19 Abril 1937–7 Diciembre 1942*, 3rd edn (Madrid, 1943), p. 102.

10 On the antisemitism of *Acción Española* see Chapter II.

11 *Domingo* (11 December 1938).

12 *Domingo* (22 May 1938).

13 David Diamant, *Combattants juifs dans l'armée républicaine espagnole, 1936–1939* (Paris, 1979), pp. 43–51.

14 Albert Prago estimates the number of Jewish Brigadiers between 7,000 and 10,000 in "Jews in the International Brigades", in Alvah Bessie and Albert Prago (eds), *Our Fight: Writings by Veterans of the Abraham Lincoln Brigade, Spain 1936–1939* (New York, 1987) while Arno Lustiger regards 6,000 as a more likely figure in "The Jews and the Spanish war", in Ricardo Izquierdo Benito, Uriel Macías Kapón and Yolanda Moreno Koch (eds), *Los judíos en la España contemporánea: historia y visiones 1898–1998, VIII curso de cultura Hispanojudía y Sefardí de la Universidad de Castilla-La Mancha* (Castilla la Mancha, 2000), p. 179.

15 Josef Toch, "Juden im Spanischen Krieg 1936–1939", Zeitgeschichte, April 1974, quoted by Lisbona, *Retorno a Sefarad*, p. 80.

16   Prago, "Jews in the International Brigades", p. 97.

17   Zvi Loker, "Balkan Jewish volunteers in the Spanish civil war", *Soviet Jewish Affairs*, Vol. 6, No. 2 (1976), p. 74.

18   Lustiger, "The Jews and the Spanish war", pp. 179–80 and Colin Schindler, "No pasaran: the Jews who fought in Spain", *Jewish Quarterly,* No. 123 (1986), p. 38.

19   Lustiger, "The Jews and the Spanish war", p. 183.

20   Marx Memorial Library, International Brigade Memorial Archive. Box A 14, file D/3 Irish and Jewish Volunteers in the Spanish Anti-fascist War, cuttings from Francoist propaganda.

21   *ABC, Seville* (14 October 1938).

22   David Wingeate Pike, *Conjecture, Propaganda and Deceit and the Spanish Civil War* (Stanford, 1968), pp. 19–20 and pp. 30–2.

23   Judith Keene, *Fighting for Franco: International Volunteers in Nationalist Spain during the Spanish Civil War, 1936–1939* (London, 2001), pp. 149–51.

24   *Domingo* (16 January 1938).

25   *Arriba España* (16 January 1937).

26   Ibid.

27   José Pemartín, *Qué es "lo nuevo"* . . . *Consideracionses sobre el momento español presente*, 3rd edn (Madrid, 1940), pp. 322–3. See also the pamphlet *Franco's "Mein Kampf": The Fascist State in Rebel Spain: An Official Blueprint* (New York, 1939).

28   *ABC, Seville* (17 June 1939).

29   *Domingo* (12 June 1938).

30   On foreign intervention See Glyne Stone, "The European great powers and the Spanish civil war 1936–1939" in Robert Boyce and Esmonde Robertson (eds), *Paths to War: New Essays on the Origins of the Second World War* (London, 1989), pp. 199–233.

31   *ABC, Seville* (20 December 1936).

32   *Amanecer* (23 March 1937).

33   *Jewish Chronicle* (30 April 1937).

34   Pemartín, *Qué es "lo nuevo"*, pp. 322–3.

35   *Domingo* (3 April 1938).

36   Preston, *Franco*, pp.158–9.

37   Glyne Stone, "The European great powers".

38   Quoted in Christoph Eykman, "The Spanish civil war in German publications during the Nazi years", in Luis Costa, Richard Critchfield, Richard Golsan and Wulf Koepke (eds), *German and International Perspectives on the Spanish Civil War: the Aesthetics of Partisanship* (Columbia, SC, 1992), p. 167.

39   *Critica*, Buenos Aires (22 March 1937).

40   Robert H. Whealy, "Nazi propagandist Joseph Goebbbels looks at the Spanish civil war – Goebbels diaries", *Historian* (Winter 1999).

41   Herbert Rutledge Southworth, *Antifalange*, pp. 178–9.

42   Letters between Sampelayo and Fleischauer, 11 and 19 February and 4 March

1937. Archivo General de la Administracion (Alcalá de Henares), thereafter AGA. Record Groups Presidencia, Secretaria General del Movimiento 10 quoted in Wayne Bowen, *Spaniards and Nazi Germany: Collaboration in the New Order* (Columbia Missouri, 2000), p. 40.

43 Ibid., p. 41.

44 *Jewish Chronicle* (19 March 1937).

45 Hugh Thomas, *The Spanish Civil War* (London, 1990), p. 353.

46 Jonathan Steinberg, *All or Nothing: the Axis and the Holocaust 1941–1943* (London, 1991), p. 226.

47 MAEE R1460/14, Letter from Pedro Garcia Conde, Spanish Ambassador in Rome (8 September 1938).

48 On the construction of the "anti-Spain" as a mean of avoiding a class analysis of the conflict see Michael Richards, *A Time of Silence: Civil War and the Culture of Repression in Franco's Spain 1936–1945* (Cambridge, 1998), p. 27.

49 José María Pemán, *El poema de la Bestia y del Angel* (Zaragoza, 1938). Peman's antisemitism is discussed by Herbert R. Southworth, *Le mythe de la croisade de Franco* (Paris, 1964) pp. 111–13 and Gonzalo Álvarez Chillida, *José María Pemán: pensamiento y trayectora de un monarquico (1897–1941)* (Cadiz, 1996), pp. 339–66.

50 José María Pemán, *El poema*, p. 67. Calvo Sotelo had set up CAMPSA, which had a state monopoly for the distribution of oil. The oil companies, which found their installations illegally confiscated, set up a counter-campaign. See Raymond Carr, *Spain 1808–1975* (Oxford 1990) p. 579.

51 José María Pemán, *El poema*, p. 93.

52 Ernst K. Bramsted. *Goebbels and National Socialist Propaganda* (Michigan, 1965), pp. 163–4.

53 *ABC, Seville* (20 December 1936).

54 *Domingo* (3 October 1937) and (22 May 1938).

55 *Domingo* (4 April 1937).

56 *ABC, Seville* (20 December 1936).

57 *Domingo* (4 April 1937).

58 *ABC, Seville* (19 April 1937).

59 *ABC, Seville* (21 June 1938). In fact Maritain had converted from Protestantism.

60 *Domingo* (30 June 1938).

61 *Domingo* (18 December 1938).

62 *ABC, Sevilla* (9 October 1938).

63 Antonio Vallejo Nágera, *Divagaciones intranscendentales* (Valladolid, 1938), p. 140. On Vallejo-Nágera see Richards, *Time of Silence*, pp. 57–61.

64 Louis W. Bondy, *Racketeers of Hatred: Julius Streicher and the Jew-baiters International* (London, 1946), p. 210.

65 *Amanecer* (20 September 1936).

66 The notion that the Jews exhaled a bad odour was related to the view that they were demonic and that Satan himself smelled foully. According to traditional

Christian belief the Jews' horrible odour would evaporate with baptism. Kertzer, *The Popes against the Jews*, p. 209.

67   Quoted in Carlos Fernández, *Antología de 40 años* (La Coruña, 1983), p. 18

68   On Nelken see Paul Preston, "Margarita Nelken: A full measure of pain", in *Doves of War* (London, 2003).

69   Quoted in Álvarez Chillida, *José María Pemán*, p. 359.

70   Manuel Sánchez del Arco, *El sur de España en la reconquista de Madrid: diario de operaciones glosado pour un testigo*, 2nd edn (Seville, 1937), pp. 78–80 quoted in Preston, *Doves of War*, p. 356.

71   *ABC* (19 February 1939).

72   Quoted in Fernandez, *Antologia*, p. 19.

73   Quoted in Fernandez. *Antologia*, p. 13.

74   *Domingo* (11 December 1938).

75   Antonio Vallejo-Nágera, *Divagaciones*, pp. 105–6.

76   *Domingo* (11 December 1938).

77   *El ideal Gallego* (8 September 1938), quoted in Fernandez, *Antologia*, p. 65.

78   *Arriba España* (14 August 1938).

79   *American Hebrew* (24 September 1937).

80   *American Jewish Year Book* 40 (1938–1939), p. 188. In reality the *Kahal* is the Hebrew word for community.

81   Bondy, *Racketeers*, p. 210.

82   Avni, *Spain, the Jews and Franco*, pp. 48–9.

83   YIVO Institute for Jewish Research (New York), HIAS-HICEM archives, MKM 15.36. Series 245.4.12 SPAIN. Extract of Letters concerning the situation of refugees from Germany in Spain.

84   Manuel Ros Agudo, *La Guerra secreta de Franco (1939–1945)* (Barcelona, 2002), p. 181.

85   PRO FO 371/24154 W11493, letter from Consul-General Rodgers in Barcelona to the Foreign office (28 July 1939).

86   PRO FO 371/24154 W2150/2150/41, telegram from Rodgers in Barcelona to the Foreign office (6 February 1939).

87   Marx Memorial Library, International Brigade Memorial Archive. Box A 14, file D/3 Irish and Jewish Volunteers in the Spanish Anti-fascist War. A 50th Anniversary Lecture and Record Recital by Manus O'Riordan, pp. 25–6.

88   Ian Mac Dougall (ed.) *Voices from the Spanish Civil War: Personal Recollections of Scottish Volunteers in Republican Spain 1936–1939* (Edinburgh, 1986), p. 259.

89   Ros Agudo, La Guerra secreta, p. 183.

90   Balfour, *Deadly Embrace*, p. 268.

91   MAEF, Correspondance politique et commerciale. Sous-série: M Maroc. No. 207 Intérêts espagnols. Zone espagnole du Maroc (Evénements de 1936, Sédition du Maroc Espagnol), p. 196 and PRO FO371/ 20500 w12765, letter from Mr. Monck-Mason, consul in Tetuán (30 September 1936).

92   MAEF: Correspondance politique et commerciale. Sous-série: M Maroc. No. 207 Intérêts espagnols. Zone espagnole du Maroc (Evénements de 1936,

Sédition du Maroc Espagnol), p. 196 and *Democracia* (25 November 1936).

93 Driessen, *On the Spanish Moroccan Frontier*, p. 96; Lisbona, *Retorno a Sefarad*, p. 64.

94 *Democracia* (25 November 1936).

95 AAIU IV.C.II, translation of *Democraci*a (25 February, 1937) and letter from Albert Saguès (27 October, 1937).

96 *La Revue de Genève* (19 March 1937).

97 Richards, *Time of Silence*, p. 55.

98 Kamen, *The Spanish Inquisition*, pp. 200–3.

99 Archivo General de la Administración Alcalá de Henares (thereafter AGA), Sección Africa, M-2454 Information from Tangier (23 September 1936).

100 AGA, Sección Africa, M-2454, anonymous note from Tangier (27 September 1936).

101 PRO, FO371/20501 w1727, letter from Mack-Mason (25 November 1936).

102 Captain F.H Mellor, *Morocco Awakes* (London, 1939), pp. 161–3.

103 Charles Halstead, "A 'Somewhat Machiavellian' Face: Colonel Juan Beigbeder as High Commissioner in Spanish Morocco, 1937–1939", *Historian*, Vol. 37 (November 1974), p. 50 and Shannon E. Flemming, "Spanish Morocco and the Alzamiento Nacional, 1936–1939: The Military, Economic and Political Mobilization of a Protectorate", *Journal of Contemporary History*, Vol. 18 (January 1983), pp. 36–7.

104 *Jewish Chronicle* (26 March 1937).

105 AAIU, IV.C.II, letter from Moïse Levy, Director of the school in Tetuán (5 March 1937).

106 Georges Soria, *Un grave danger: L'infiltration Allemande au Maroc* (Paris, 1937), pp. 7–9.

107 Otto Katz, *The Nazi Conspiracy in Spain* (London, 1937), p. 178.

108 Preston, *Franco*, pp. 158–9.

109 AAIU IV.C.II, letter from Albert Saguès (25 February 1937).

110 *Depêche de Toulouse* (11 August 1937) in AAIU IV.C.II.

111 Katz, *The Nazi conspiracy*, p. 177.

112 See *Jewish Chronicle* (22 February 1937); *L'Univers Israélite* (29 January 1937). AAIU IV.C.II, letter from Albert Saguès (21 February 1937) and PRO FO 371/21650 C2394, letter from Monck-Mason (22 March 1938).

113 AAIU, IV.C.II, letter from Léon Aranias (21 February 1937).

114 *Domingo* (21 March 1937).

115 Balfour, *Deadly Embrace*, p. 282.

116 AGA, Sección Africa, M-2454, letter from Colonel Tomás García Figueras to the Office of Native Affairs (28 April 1937).

117 PRO FO 371/21264 w6889, weekly report of Monck-Mason to Edward Keeling British consul-general in Tangier (10 September 1937).

118 Ibid.

119 AGA, Sección Africa, M-2454, Letter from Colonel Tomás García Figueras to the Office of Native Affairs (28 April 1937).

120 AAIU, IV.C.II, letter from Saguès (27 October 1937).

121 AAIU, IV.C.II, letters from Saguès (26 August 1937) and (30 August 1937). See also MAEE R893, pamphlet from the Association Hispano-Hebrew.

122 PRO FO 371/21266 w6889, weekly report of Monck-Mason (10 September 1937).

123 AAIU, IV.C.II, letter from Saguès (27 October 1937).

124 AAIU, IV.C.II, letter from Saguès (25 February 1937).

125 AAIU, IV.C.II, letter from Saguès (27 October 1937) and AAIU, ID1, report from Moise Levy (18 July, 1938).

126 MAEE R893, pamphlet from the Hispano-Hebrew Association.

127 *Jewish Chronicle* (19 February 1937).

128 *Jewish Chronicle* (21 August 1936) and (17 December 1937).

129 AAIU, IV.C.II, Letter from Saguès (27 October 1937).

130 Rosalinda Powell Fox, *The Grass and the Asphalt* (Puerto Sotogrande, 1997) pp. 114–15.

131 Wiener Library, PC2.331E, press cutting EAJ27 (3 August 1936).

132 MAEE R895/119–120, clipping of an article from the Judeo-Spanish diary *El Mesajero* (19 March 1936).

133 Léonardo Senkman. "Maximo José Kahn: de escritor español del exilio a escritor del desastre judío", *Raíc*es, No. 27, Winter 96, pp. 44–52.

134 MAEE R895/119–120, letter from Maximo José Kahn, the Republic's consul in Salonica (28 September 1938)

135 MAEE R895/119–120, letter from Kahn (27 October 1938).

136 MAEE R1784/14, appendix to the Letter from Kahn (20 January 1938).

137 MAEE R1784/14, letter from Kahn (4 February 1938).

138 MAEE R1784/14, letter from Martín de Paúl, Spain's Consul in Amsterdam (16 May 1938).

139 MAEE R 895/103, report on the Sephardic Congress of Amsetrdam, Barcelona (4 June, 1938).

140 MAEE, R1672/1, letter from Sebastiàn Romero de Radigales, Nationalist agent in Athens (31 August 1938).

141 MAEE R1000/16, letter from Sabetay I D'Jaen, Chief Rabbi of the Sephardic community of Romania (25 May 1937).

142 MAEE R1672/1, letter from Pedro de Prat y Soutzo, Nationalist agent in Bucharest (9 May 1938).

143 MAEE R1672/1, letter from Julio Palencia, Nationalist representative in Istanbul (31 August 1938).

144 MAEE R1672/1, letter from Pedro de Prat y Soutzo (9 May 1938).

145 Romanian currency.

146 MAEE R1672/1, letter from Sebàstian de Romero Radigales (7 April 1938).

147 MAEE R1672/1, letter from Carlos de Miranda y Quartia (14 June 1937).

148 MAEE R1672/1, letter from Carlos de Miranda (24 June 1938).

149 MAEE R1672/1, note from the Ministry of Foreign Affairs (4 April 1939).

150 Ibid.

151 MAEE R1672/1, decree No. 35 (19 July 1938).

152 MAEE R1672/1, note from the Ministry of Foreign Affairs (18 April 1939).

153 Ibid.

154 MAEE R1672/1, letter from Carlos de Miranda (5 February 1938).

155 MAEE R1672/1, letter from the Ministry of Foreign Affairs in Burgos (31 August 1938).

156 *El Ideal Gallego* (30 January 1938) quoted in Fernandez, *Antologia*, p. 56.

157 Pemartín, *Qué es "lo nuevo"*, p. 322.

158 *ABC, Sevilla* (14 October 1938)

159 Graciela Ben-Dror, *La Iglesia católica ante el Holocausto, España y América Latina* (Madrid, 2003), p. 84 quoting *El Pensamiento Navarro* (24 November 1938).

160 *ABC, Sevilla* (14 October 1938).

161 On Nazi racist mysticism see George L. Mosse, *Toward the Final solution: A History of European Racism* (Madison, Wisconsin, 1985).

162 Pemartín, *Qué es "lo nuevo"*, p. 17.

163 *Amanecer* (11 November 1938).

164 MAEE R1460/14, letter from Pedro Garcia Conde to the Ministry of Foreign affairs (18 August 1938).

165 MAEE R1672/1, notes prepared by the Foreign Ministry on the expulsion of Sephardic Jews from Italy (13 October 1938) and (25 October 1938).

166 Yahil, *The Holocaust*, pp. 110–11.

167 MAEE R1672/1, letter from Antonio Magaz to the Foreign Ministry (23 November 1938).

168 MAEE R1672/1 report from Rojas (1 December 1938).

169 MAEE R1672/1, letter from Antonio Magaz to the Foreign Ministry (23 November 1938). Among the countries denying visas to the Jews were Switzerland and Sweden, both of which had asked for a distinct mark on the passports of the Jews see Yahil, *The Holocaust*, p. 109 and Paul Levine, *From Indifference to Activism: Swedish Diplomacy and the Holocaust* (Uppsala, 1998), p. 105.

170 MAEE R1672/1, letter from Espinosa de los Monteros (1 December 1938).

171 See Álvarez Chillida, *El antisemitismo en España*, Chapter 12.

172 MAEE R1672/1, report from Rojas (3 December 1938).

173 MAEE R3462/2, letter from the Spanish Minister in Bucharest, Pedro de Prat y Soutzo to the Ministry of Foreign Affairs (21 January 1939).

174 MAEE R3462/2, letter from Prat to the Foreign Ministry (3 February 1939).

4 A Policy of Contradictions: Germanophilia and the Revival of Philosephardism (1936–1939)

1 Stanley Payne, *The Franco Regime* (Madison, 1987), p. 156.

2 PRO FO 371/24507 C380, political review of Spain for 1939 compiled by Mr.Howard, First Secretary for the British Embassy and PRO FO 371/24507 C392, memorandum by the Press Attaché of the British Embassy (5 January 1940).

3   Preston, *Franco*, p. 338.

4   PRO FO 371/31277 C10096, letter from Hoare to Eden (10 October 1942).

5   *The New York Times* (13 June 1939).

6   United States National Archives and Records Administration (thereafter NARA), RG 59, General Records of the Department of State, 1930–1939 652.1115/52, letter from US Ambassador Alexander Weddell to the Secretary of State (31 August 1939).

7   Samuel Hoare, *Ambassador on Special Mission* (London, 1946), p. 50.

8   PRO FO 371/31277 C4995, memorandum on Spanish Colonial Policy prepared by the Foreign Research and Press Service, Balliol College Oxford (21 March 1942).

9   Alfred Bosch and Gustau Nerín, *El imperio que nunca existió* (Barcelona, 2001), pp. 35–8.

10 PRO FO 425/420 C10096, letter from Hoare to the Foreign Office (10 October 1942).

11 See Michel Catala, *Les relations franco-espagnoles pendant la deuxième guerre mondiale: rapprochement nécessaire, reconciliation impossible 1939–1944* (Paris, 1997), pp. 15–91.

12 Figure taken from The American Jewish Joint Distribution Committee, *Aid to Jews Overseas: Report for 1939* (New York, 1940), p. 30.

13 *American Jewish Yearbook (1940–41)*, p. 435 and *Jewish Chronicle* (15 May 1942).

14 *The New York Times* (19 December 1939).

15 Juan Segura Nieto, *¡Alerta! . . . Francmasonería y judaismo* (Barcelona, 1940), p. 32.

16 Ibid., p. 40 and pp. 47–8.

17 On the regime's cultural repression and the construction of the "Anti-Spain" see Richards, *A time of Silence*.

18 *ABC* (1 January 1940).

19 Payne, *The Franco Regime*, p. 225.

20 YIVO, HIAS-HICEM archives, MKM 15.36. Series 245.4.12 SPAIN report Augusto d'Esaguy to HICEM Paris (5 April 1940).

21 Ibid.

22 PRO/FO 371/49663, Spain's pro-German policy (1940–1942).

23 Manuel Ros Agudo, *La guerra secreta de Franco (1939–1945)* (Barcelona, 2002), p. 183.

24 MAEE R1260/3, letter from the Interior Ministry (12 May 1940) and letter from Jesus Carrero, Undersecretary to the presidency (9 June 1940).

25 Jacobo Israel Garzón, "El Archivo Judaico del Franquismo", *Raíces* No. 33 (1997), pp. 57–60.

26 Josep Benet, *Cataluña bajo el régimen franquista: Informe sobre la persecución de la lengua y la cultura catalana por el régimen del general Franco* (1a. parte) (Barcelona, 1979), pp. 275–7.

27 Lisbona, *Retorno a Sefarad*, p. 110. According to Lisbona the government

made a first file in December 1939 and a second one in June 1940.

28   NARA RG 59, General Records of the Department of State 852.4016/8 (1940–1944), Telegram from Frost (21 June 1940).

29   *American Jewish Yearbook (1941–1942)*, p. 201.

30   Juan Bautista Vilar, "Evolucion de la poblacion israelita en Marruecos Espanol (1940–1955)", *Estudios sefardies: revista del instituto Arias Montano*, No. 1, 1978, p. 91.

31   *Spain* (13 July 1939).

32   *The New York Times* (19 December 1939).

33   MAEF (Nantes), Protectorat Maroc, Direction Intérieure – questions Juives, note au sujet de la situation des israélites au Maroc (6 August 1945).

34   MAEF (Paris), Série Guerre 1939–1945, Vichy. Sous-série: Maroc, No. 32, bulletin de renseignements No. 5 Casablanca (17 January 1942).

35   *L'Univers Israelite* (12–19 January 1940).

36   Tomás Garciá Figueras, *Lineas generales de la obra de educación y cultura que se desarrolla en nuestra zona de protectorado en Marruecos*, unpublished manuscript, Biblioteca Nacional, Madrid, Colección Garciá Figueras (1940), p. 22, quoted by Geoffrey Jensen, 'Toward the "Moral Conquest" of Morocco', p. 223.

37   Tomás García Figueras, *Marruecos: La acción de España en el Norte de África* (Barcelona, 1939), p. 298.

38   AGA Seccion Africa, M-2423, note from the Office of Native Affairs in Tetuán to the Service of Information (1 May 1940).

39   AGA, Seccion Africa, M-2645, information from the Native officer in Villa Nador José Bermejo Lopez to the delegate to Native Affairs (14 May 1940).

40   MAEF (Nantes) Protectorat Maroc, Direction Intérieure – Questions Juives, Box 2, note au sujet de la situation des israélites au Maroc (6 August 1945).

41   AAIU, Maroc XI E 178, letter from Mr Almaleh to the AIU in Paris (29 November 1939).

42   MAEF (Nantes) Protectorat Maroc, Direction Intérieure, note au sujet de la situation des israélites au Maroc (6 August 1945).

43   PRO FO 371/26960 C4225, summary for 1940 of political events in Spanish zone of Morocco, prepared by Mr Monypenny (17 March 1941).

44   Hoare, *Ambassador*, p. 52.

45   Ibid.

46   PRO FO 371/26960 C4225, summary for 1940 of political events (17 March 1941).

47   Graham H. Stuart, *The International City of Tangier*, 2nd edn (Stanford, 1955), p. 144.

48   Halstead and Halstead, "Aborted Imperialism", p. 58.

49   Michael M. Laskier, *North African Jewry in the Twentieth century: The Jews of Morocco, Tunisia, and Algeria* (New York, 1994), p. 70.

50   Ibid., p. 70.

51   Blandin, "La Population de Tanger en 1940", *Revue Africaine*, Vol. LXXXXVIII (1944), p. 115.

52   NARA, RG 59, General Records of the Department of State 881.5011/1 (1940–1944) census International Zone of Tangier (7 May 1942) and Laskier, *North African Jewry*, p. 68.

53   YIVO, HIAS-HICEM archives, MKM 16.13 Series 245.5 SPAIN report Augusto d'Esaguy on Tangier (10 August 1939) and Anthony Bianco, *The Reichmanns: Family, Faith, Fortune and the Empire of Olympia and York* (New York, 1997), p. 90.

54   Archives from the American Jewish Joint Distribution Committee (thereafter JDC), collection 1933/1944 File #1045 (Tangiers, General 1940–1944) report from the Jewish Community of Tangier to the War Refugee Board (24 February 1944).

55   Ibid.

56   Bianco, *The Reichmanns*. p. 80.

57   Richard I. Cohen, *The Burden of Conscience: French Jewish Leadership during the Holocaust* (Bloomington, 1987), p. 16. See also Lisa Fittko, *Escape Through the Pyrenees* (Evanston, 1991), pp. 21–54.

58   Donna F. Ryan: *The Holocaust and the Jews of Marseille: The Enforcement of Antisemitic Policies in Vichy France* (Chicago, 1996), p. 95.

59   Susan Zucotti, *The Holocaust, the French, and the Jews* (New York, 1999), p. 93.

60   Interview with Egon Wolff; Ryan, *The Holocaust and the Jews of Marseille*, p. 131.

61   Fittko, *Escape*, p. 94.

62   Ibid., p. 96.

63   Rother, *Franco y el Holocausto*, pp. 131–2. The decree also closed Spain's doors to Spanish nationals who had supported the Republic and to the Freemasons.

64   Ibid., p. 136.

65   YIVO, HIAS-HICEM archives, MKM 17.2 Series 2 France, rapport sur mon voyage a la frontière espagnole (10 September 1940).

66   JDC collection 1933/1944 File #914 (Spain, General 1940–1942), the refugee problem in Spain (21 April 1942).

67   JDC collection 1933/1944 File #914 (Spain, General 1940–1942), memorandum from Robert Rhatz (29 December 1942).

68   Interview with Wolff.

69   Marta Feuchtwanger, "Transit" in Andreas Lixl-Purcell (ed.), *Women of Exile: German-Jewish Autobiographies Since 1933* (New York, 1988), pp. 63–7.

70   Alma Mahler-Werfel, *And the Bridge is Love: Memories of a Lifetime* (London, 1959), p. 246.

71   Darius Milhaud, *Notes Without Music: An Autobiography* (London, 1952), p. 233.

72   Varian Fry, *Surrender on Demand*, 2nd edn (New York, 1997) p. 74.

73   The American Jewish Joint Distribution Committee, *Aid to Jews Overseas, Report for 1941 and the First Five Months of 1942* (New York, 1942) see also JDC collection 1933/1944 File #914 (Spain, General 1940–1942), the refugee problem in Spain (21 April 1942).

74 Fry, *Surrender*, p. 75.
75 Cohen, *The Burden of Conscience*, p. 18.
76 Fry, *Surrender*, p. 85.
77 Fittko, *Escape*, p. 109.
78 Henny Gurland's letter from 11 October 1940 is quoted in Gershom Scholem, *Walter Benjamin: The Story of a Friendship* (New York, 2003), pp. 281–2.
79 Momme Brodersen, *Walter Benjamin: A Biography* (London, 1996), pp 253–61.
80 Antonio Marquina and Gloria Inés Ospina, *España y los judíos en el siglo XX* (Madrid, 1987), p. 148 and Rother, *Franco y el Holocausto*, p. 139. In late December the Spanish authorities decreed that military personnel, that is men between 18 and 40 years old, from Allied countries would no longer be allowed to go through Spain. The aim was to prevent them from escaping to England and enlisting in the army there. See Marquina and Ospina, *España y los judíos*, pp. 164–5.
81 Ibid., p. 94.
82 Fry, *Surrender*, pp. 86–7.
83 Robert Belot, *Aux frontières de la liberté : Vichy-Madrid-Alger-Londres s'évader de France sous l'occupation* (Paris, 1998), p. 56.
84 Fry, *Surrender*, p. 95.
85 Ros Agudo, *La guerra secreta*, p. 185.
86 Preston, *Franco*, pp. 377–8.
87 Hoare, *Ambassador*, p. 76.
88 Ros Agudo, *La guerra secreta*, p. 190.
89 Zucotti, *The Holocaust, the French*, p. 53.
90 Ibid., p. 60.
91 MAEE R1716/2, cable from Lequerica (8 November 1940).
92 MAEE R1716/2, cable from Serrano Suñer (9 November 1940).
93 MAEE R1716/2, letter from Mario Piniés (7 December 1940).
94 Ibid.
95 MAEE R1716/2, telegram from Piniés (24 December 1940) and telegram from Serrano Suñer (26 December 1940).
96 MAEE R1716/2, telegram from Piniés (4 April 1940) and telegram from Serrano Suñer (5 April 1940).
97 The figure of 4,232 comes from Serge Klarsfeld, *Vichy-Auschwitz: le role de Vichy dans la solution finale de la question juive en France 1942* (Paris, 1983) pp. 25–9. In his report to the Foreign Ministry (10 September 1941) MAEE R1716/2, Rolland writes that 7,000 Jews were arrested.
98 MAEE R1716/2, letter from Bernardo Rolland to the Foreign Ministry (10 September 1941).
99 Avni, *Spain, the Jews and Franco*, p. 80.
100 MAEE R1261/102, letter from Merry del Val to the Foreign Ministry (2 July 1940).
101 MAEE R1261/102, report from Carlos de Miranda (2 August 1940).

102 MAEE R1261/102, letter from the *Dirección General de Seguridad* to the Foreign Ministry (2 September 1940).

103 Avni, *Spain, the Jews and Franco*, p. 82 quotes a list in the Yad Vashem central archives in Jerusalem, AA-JM 2218, K-213082–93, Avni notes that because of duplication it is possible that there were only 506 Spanish Jewish nationals in Salonica.

104 MAEE R1261/73, Cable from Serrano Suñer to the Consul General in Athens (8 November 1941).

105 Avni, *Spain, the Jews and Franco*, p. 83.

106 Zucotti, *The Holocaust, the French*, p. 58.

107 MAEE R1716/1, note enclosed to the letter of Luis Orgaz (31 October 1941).

108 Bosch and Negrin, *El imperio*, pp. 56–57.

109 MAEE R1716/1, letter from Jorro, Spanish Consul in Casablanca to the Foreign Ministry (31 July 1941).

110 MAEE R1716/2, telegram from Jorro to the Foreign Ministry (22 September 1941).

111 Archives du Centre de Documentation Juive Contemporaine (thereafter CDJ) CCCLXXXVI-31, report from the French Consul in Larache (22 August 1941).

112 NARA, RG59, 881.4016/33 (1940–1944) letter from H. Earle Russell to the Department of State (29 September 1941).

113 MAEE R1716/2, letter from Luis Orgaz to the Foreign Ministry (8 October 1941).

114 MAEE R1716/1, letter from Luis Orgaz to the Foreign Ministy (31 October 1941).

115 MAEF (Paris) Série Guerre 1939–1945, Vichy. Sous-série: Maroc. Vol. 39, letter from Noguès to Darlan (4 December 1941) and note from Rabat (17 September 1941).

116 MAEF (Paris) Série Guerre 1939–1945, Vichy. Sous-série: Maroc. Vol. 31, letter from the Vice-consul in Larache to Nogués (29 October 1941).

117 MAEF (Paris) Série Guerre 1939–1945, Vichy. Sous-série: Maroc. Vol. 31, letter from François Pietri (24 December 1941).

118 Avni, *Spain, the Jews and Franco*, p. 70 quoting *Sefarad* 1 (1941).

119 Jaime de Andrade, *Raza: anecdotario para el guión de una pelicula* (Madrid, 1982), pp. 70–1.

120 Michel Abitbol, *The Jews of North Africa During the Second World War* (Detroit, 1989), p. 79 quoting *El Mundo* (20 June 1941).

121 *Amanecer* (24 June 1941)

122 Luis Carrero Blanco, *España y el mar* (Madrid, 1941), pp. 9–10.

123 Javier Tusell, *Carrero: la eminencia gris del regimen de Franco* (Madrid, 1993), p. 61 quoting "Consideraciones sobre la situacion internacional actual en orden a la actitud de España", Archivo Carrero Blanco, carpeta II, No. 1.

124 Carrero Blanco, *España y el mar*, p. 10.

125 JDC 1933/1944, File #914 (Spain, General 1940–1942), report from Virginia Chase Weddell (15 February 1941).

126 NARA, RG59 General Records of the Department of State 852.4016/10 (1940–1945), letter from AC Frost, US General Consul (8 February 1941).

127 *Associated Press* (17 January 1942) in the Wiener Library Press Archives (London). PC6. Jews in World War II, 3D: Spain and Portugal (18 December 1939–5 December 1941).

128 *Jewish Chronicle* (10 April 1942).

129 This file can be seen at the AGA in Alcalá de Henares, Seccion Africa, M-2646. The Jews were not the only ones to be put under surveillance, some Spaniards, suspected of being "Reds" and a number of Muslims were also closely watched.

130 AGA, Seccion Africa, M-242, letter from the delegation of native affairs to the service of information, Tetuán (1 May 1940) and letter from the *Dirección General de Seguridad* in Madrid (4 July 1942).

131 AGA, Seccion Africa, M-2644, note from the Chief of Police of Tangier (5 December 1942).

132 Stuart, *The International City of Tangier*, p. 145.

133 Ibid.

134 JDC, collection 1933/1944 File #1045, report from the Jewish Community of Tangier to the War Refugee Board (24 February 1944) and NARA 840.48 Refugees/5345 Airgram from Charles Burke Elbrick.

135 MAEE R1672/1, report from Lequerica to the Foreign Ministry (18 March 1942).

136 MAEF (Paris) Série Guerre 1939–1945, Vichy, Sous-série: Maroc, Vol 32, bulletin de Renseignements No 5 (17 January 1942).

137 MAEF (Paris) Série Guerre 1939–1945, Vichy, Sous-série: Maroc, Vol 39, letter from Noguès to Darlan (11 February 1942).

138 MAEE R1716/2, letter from Lequerica (16 September 1942).

139 On Gerlier's protest see Michael R. Marrus and Robert O. Paxton, *Vichy France and the Jews* (New York, 1981), pp. 270–5.

140 MAEE R1716/1, report from Lequerica in Vichy to the Foreign Ministry (15 September 1942).

141 MAEE R1716/1, report from Lequerica in Vichy to the Foreign Ministry (15 September 1942).

5 Welcoming the "Conspirators" (1939–1045)

1 MAEE R1716/4, letter from Jordana to Asensio (28 December 1943).

2 Preston, *Franco*, pp. 474–5.

3 Nerin and Bosch, *El imperio*, p. 206.

4 PRO FO425/420 C11713, letter from the British consul general in Tangier, Gascoigne to Anthony Eden (17 November 1942).

5 Preston, *Franco*, pp. 479–85.

6 Ibid., p. 487.

7 *Pueblo* (21 August 1943).

8 *La garra del capitalismo judío: sus procedimientos y efectos en el momento actual* (Madrid, 1943), p. 8.

9   Preston, *Franco*, p. 478.

10 PRO/FO 371/34779 C477, letter from S.R. Gore Edwards to Gascoigne (17 December 1942).

11 Preston, *Franco*, p. 487 and Hoare, *Ambassador*, p. 205.

12 AGA, Sección Africa, M-2423, note from the *Dirección General de la Seguridad* (4 July 1942).

13 AGA, Sección Africa, M-2644, note from the headquarters of the Tangier police (5 December 1942).

14 PRO FO 371/34779/C229, letter from JSM in Washington to War Cabinet Office (7 January 1943).

15 *The Jewish Chronicle* (11 December 1943) and *American Jewish Yearbook 1943*, p. 296.

16 PRO FO 371/34779 C1086, telegram from Gascoigne (27 January 1943).

17 *Jewish Chronicle* (9 April 1943).

18 AGA, Sección Africa, M-2423, note from the Native Office of Yerbala to the Secretary of Native Affaire (3 May 1943).

19 AGA, Sección Africa, M-2423, note from the Native office of Yerbala (1 May 1943) and note from the Native Office of Lucus (19 May 1943).

20 *Jewish Chronicle* (4 June 1943).

21 PRO FO 371/34781 C6856, letter from Gascoigne (1 June 1943).

22 PRO FO 371/34781 C6856, reports from Isaac Benguaish, Menasse Fimat and Jose Bendahan.

23 Alderman Library University of Virginia Manuscripts and Rare Books, J. Rives Childs collection, Accession No. 9256–6, Box 4, Unpublished manuscript "Operation Torch: An object lesson in diplomacy", p. 204 and Alexander Cadogan, *The Diaries of Sir Alexander Cadogan, O.M., 1938–1945* (London, 1971), p. 534.

24 *American Jewish Yearbook 1945*, p. 297.

25 AGA, Sección Africa, M-2423, from the regional office in Tangier (10 September 1943).

26 MAEE R1773/17, telegram from Orgaz to the Foreign Ministry (6 October 1943).

27 Vichy sympathizers continued to dominate the administration in Algeria after the US landings and the situation of the Jews did not improve until June 1943, see Laskier, *North African Jewry*, p. 71.

28 *El Español* (2 January 1943).

29 Alfredo Olascoaga, *El Norte de Africa cabeza de puente ¿de quien?* (Madrid 1943), p. 3 and p. 5.

30 *Mundo* (19 December 1943).

31 The situation was different in the eight departments East of the Rhone Valley, which the Italians occupied in November 1942. The Italian authorities prevented the arrest of Jews and released many of those who had been arrested. See Zucotti, *The Holocaust, the French*, p. 166.

32 PRO FO 371/32699 w15539, cable from Joseph Schwartz (17 November 1942).

33   PRO FO 371/32699 w15619, cable for Sir Samuel Hoare to Foreign Office (17 November 1942).

34   Leo Baeck Institute New York (thereafter LBI), AR 3987, folder Spain, American Friends Service Committee report from Spain (19 August 1943) and Cambridge University, Templewood Papers, Part XIII, file 5 letter from Hoare to Eleanor Rathbone (3 May 1943).

35   NARA RG 59, General Records of the Department of State 840.48/3023 (1940–1944), Telegram from Frost.

36   JDC collection 1933/1944 file 914 (Spain General 1940–1942) draft of letter to HK Travers, chief division Department of State, Washington (20 November 1942).

37   PRO FO 371/32699 w15910, cables from Dr Schwarz to Dr Kullman (23 November 1942) and PRO FO 371/32700 w17304 from Emerson to W. Randall (23 December 1942).

38   Columbia University, Rare Book and Manuscript Library, Carlton Hayes Collection, Spanish Papers, Box 1 Folder January–February 1944, Relief of Refugees in Spain (January 1944).

39   PRO FO 371/36632 w2521, letter from A.L. Easterman, WJC in London to Rev. M. L. Perlzweig, American Jewish Congress (27 January 1943).

40   Templewood Papers, Part XIII, file 26, letter from Hoare (12 February 1943).

41   LBI AR 3987, folder Spain, American Friends Service Committee report from Spain (19 August 1943).

42   LBI AR 3987, report on Miranda (27 July 1943).

43   Hoare, *Ambassador*, p. 233.

44   Ibid and Reuben Ainszten, *In Lands Not My Own: A Wartime Journey* (New York, 2002), p. 134.

45   LBI AR 3987, report from Spain (19 August 1943).

46   LBI AR 3987, report on Miranda (27 July 1943).

47   PRO FO 371/36630 w1167, letter from Sir Hoare to Jordana (8 January 1943).

48   PRO FO 371/36637 w7187, twenty six months in Miranda de Ebro by Eli Rubin.

49   Reuben Ainszten, *In Lands Not my Own*, pp. 131–2.

50   Dolf Ringel, "Safe conduct" unpublished manuscripts Archives of the United States Holocaust Memorial Museum (Washington,DC) thereafter (USHMM) RG-02.206 and PRO FO 371/36637 w7187, Eli Rubin's testimony.

51   Ainszten, *In Lands Not my Own*, p. 139.

52   JDC collection 1933/1944 File #915 (Spain, General January June 1943) unsigned report on Miranda del Ebro (24 March 1943).

53   Ringel, "Safe conduct", p. 260.

54   Ibid., p. 262.

55   LBI AR 3987, folder Spain, AFSC report from Spain (19 August 1943).

56   Peter Hart, *Journey Into Freedom: An Authentic War-Time Journey* (Hertford, 2003), p. 63.

57   LBI AR 3987, folder Spain, AFSC report from Spain (19 August 1943).

58   Ainstzen, *In Lands Not My Own*, p. 133.

59   Ibid.

60   Cambridge University, Templewood Papers, Part XIII, file 26, letter from Hoare to Eden (12 February 1943).

61   Javier Rodrigo, *Cautivos: campos de concentración en la España franquista, 1936–1947* (Barcelona, 2005), p. 263.

62   Belot, *Aux frontières*, p. 119.

63   PRO FO 371/34739 w3414, telegram Sir. S Hoare (28 March 1943).

64   Preston, *Franco*, p. 485.

65   PRO FO 371/34739 w2774, telegram Sir. S Hoare (10 March 1943).

66   MAEE R2181/3, letter from Carlton Hayes to General Jordana (29 March 1943) and PRO FO 371/36632 w3421, telegram from Hoare to the Foreign office (27 March 1943).

67   MAEE R1716/14, verbal note from the Spanish Foreign Ministry to the Consul of Belgium (25 March 1943).

68   NARA RG 59, General Records of the Department of State 840.48 Refugees/3868 Aide Mémoire from the British Embassy in Washington (13 April 1943).

69   Preston, *Franco*, p. 490.

70   Quoted in A. Lazo, *La Iglesia, la Falange y el fascismo: un estudio sobre la prensa española de postguerra* (Seville, 1995), p. 296.

71   Quoted in Genoveva García Queipo de Llano/ Xavier Tusell, *Franco y Mussolini: la política española durante la segunda guerra mundial* (Barcelona, 1985), p. 185.

72   Fernández, *Antología*, p. 133.

73   *Mundo* (19 September 1943).

74   Yahil, *The Holocaust*, p. 415.

75   MAEE R1716/2, note from the German embassy (26 January 1943).

76   Yahil, *The Holocaust*, p. 415.

77   On Doussinague's report see Chapter 1.

78   MAEE R1716/2, letter from Doussinague to Jordana (26 January 1943).

79   MAE R1716/2, letter from Doussinague to Ginés Vidal (16 February 1943).

80   MAE R1716/2, letter from Bernardo Rolland (23 February 1943) and Daniel Carpi, *Between Mussolini and Hitler: The Jews and the Italian Authorities in France and Tunisia* (Hanover, NH 1994), p. 64.

81   MAEE R1716/2, letter from Bernardo Rolland (23 February 1943) and letter from Ginés Vidal (26 February 1943).

82   MAEE R1716/2, letter from Bernardo Rolland (23 February 1943).

83   MAEE R1716/3, letter from Spanish Jews in Paris (27 February 1943).

84   MAEE R1716/3, note from the German Embassy in Madrid (6 March 1943).

85   MAEE R1716/3, letter from Doussinague (9 March 1943).

86   Avni, *Spain, the Jews and Franco*, p. 139.

87 MAEE R1716/4, letter from Doussinague (9 March 1943) and MAEE R1716/3, cable from Jordana to Vidal (19 March 1943).
88 MAEE R1716/3, letter from Doussinague to Baráibar (17 August 1943).
89 MAEE R1716/3, letter from David Blickenstaff to José Pan de Soraluce (24 March 1943).
90 MAEE R1716/3, letter from Lequerica (13 April 1943).
91 MAEE R1716/3, letter from Fiscowisch (3 July 1943).
92 YIVO, HIAS-HICEM archives, MKM 15.36. Series 245.4.12 SPAIN letter to HIAS New York from HIAS Lisbon regarding Sephardic Jews in Spain (22 September 1943) and MAEE R1716/3, letter from Germán Baráibar to Doussingague (17 August 1943).
93 MAEE R1716/3, letter from Doussinague to Baráibar (20 August 1940).
94 Archivo Historico Nacional (Madrid) Fondos contemporreanos, Ministerio Interior Policía, Exp 53553, nota Informativa (9 September 1943).
95 MAEE R 1716/3, letter from Doussinague to German Baráibar (17 August 1943).
96 MAEE R1716/1, letter from Blickenstaff to Baráibar (15 October 1943).
97 YIVO, HIAS-HICEM archives, 20.18, file 155, Rapport de M sur l'acheminement des Sepharades de Salonique en Espagne.
98 MAEE R1716/4, carpeta no3, Expediente general de los Sefarditas Españoles MAEE R2154/11, letter from Romero Radigales, Spanish Consul General in Athens to the Spanish Foreign Ministry (6 May 1944). According to Romero, the German Foreign Ministry believed that "Spain washed its hands of its Jewish subjects in Greece".
99 MAEE R2154/11, letter from Romero Radigales to (6 May 1944).
100 MAEE R1716/1, informe: estado en que se encuentra el problema sefardita.
101 MAEE R1716/3, letter from Romero Radigales to Jordana (30 July 1943) and (8 August 1943).
102 CDJ, Document CXXVII-14, translation of a document N0–NG 5030, office of counsel of war crimes.
103 MAEE R1716/5, letter signed Federico to Doussinague (20 July 1943).
104 MAEE R1716/4, letter from Jordana to Vidal (24 July 1943).
105 MAEE R1716/3, letter from Romero Radigales to Jordana (8 August 1943).
106 CDJ, Document CXXVII-14, Document No. 5050.
107 MAEE R1716/4, telegram from Vidal to Jordana (12 August 1943).
108 Preston, *Franco*, pp. 494–5.
109 University of Southampton Library, Archives and Manuscripts, MS 238/2/16, note of a conversation between the Duque of Alba, Spanish Ambassador in London, and Mr Ben Rubenstein and Mr. A. L. Easterman, at the Spanish Embassy (4 August 1943).
110 Preston, *Franco*, pp. 502–3.
111 Javier Martínez de Bedoya, *Memorias desde mi aldea* (Valladolid, 1996), pp. 224–5.
112 American Jewish Archives, Hebrew Union College, Cincinatti Ohio, World

Jewish Congress collection, Box H 309, Folder 2. Letter from Perlzweig to Wise, Goldmann, Kubowitski, Miller, Robinson, Tartakow (22 June 1943) and University of Southampton Library, MS238/2/16, Note of a conversation between the Duke of Alba, Ben Rubenstein and AL Easterman (4 August).

113 Ibid., p. 230.
114 MAEE R1716/4, Informe: salida de sefarditas de España (26 October 1943).
115 PRO FO 371/36666 w12950, minutes from E. A. Walker (20 September 1943).
116 MAEE R1716/3, letter from Blickenstaff to Baráibar (20 August 1943).
117 PRO FO 371/36666 w12950, letter from chancery (28 August 1943).
118 MAEE R1716/4, letter from Vidal to Foreign Ministry (5 November 1943).
119 PRO FO 371/36646 w16729, minutes from Walker (9 December 1943).
120 MAEE R1716/4, letter from Doussinague to the Director of the Seguridad (10 December 1943).
121 PRO FO 371/36646 w16729, letter from Hoare to Eden (24 November 1943).
122 MAEE R1716/4, letter from Jordana to Asensio (28 December 1943).
123 MAEE R1716/4, letter from Doussinague to Baráibar (27 November 1943).
124 MAEE R1773/17, letter from Jordana to Orgaz (30 December 1943).
125 MAEE R1716/3, letter from Orgaz to Jordana (10 January 1944).
126 MAEE R1716/4, carpeta no3: Expediente general de los Sefarditas Españoles. On the policy of the British government during the Holocaust see Bernard Wasserstein, *Britain and the Jews of Europe 1939–1945* (London, 1999).
127 MAEE R 1716/4, estado en que se encuentra el problema de la evacuación del último grupo de judíos sefarditas entrados en España (29 February 1944).
128 MAEE R 1716/4, telegram from Jordana to Cardenas (19 February 1944).
129 Yahil, *The Holocaust*, p. 421 and Mark Mazower, *Inside Hitler's Greece: The Experience of Occupation, 1941–1944* (London, 1993), p. 252.
130 MAEE R1716/4, letter from Romero Radigales to Jordana (26 March 1944).
131 MAEE R1716/4, letter from Isaac Weissman to the Spanish Ambassador in Ankara José Rojas y Moreno (6 April 1944).
132 NARA RG59, 840.48 Refugees/6142A, text of a communication received by the WJC, New York, from Isaac Weissman (27 May 1944).
133 Ibid., and papers of Javier Martínez de Bedoya (Madrid, Spain), Informe no. 15-E from Bedoya to José Ibáñez Martín.
134 MAEE R1716/4, letter from Bedoya to Jordana (11 April 1944).
135 MAEE R1716/3, telegram from Jordana to Vidal (11 April 1944).
136 MAEE R1716/4, letter from Vidal to Jordan (23 April 1944).
137 MAEE R1549/5, telegram form Doussinague to the Ambassador in Berlin (10 June 1944).
138 Avni, *Spain, the Jews and Franco*, pp. 160–1 and Marquina/Ospina, *España y los judíos*, pp. 204–5.
139 University of Southampton Library, MS238/2/20, Summary of work done in Lisbon by the WJC.

140 Lucien Lazare, *Rescue as Resistance: How Jewish Organizations Fought the Holocaust in France* (New York, 1996), pp. 284–8.

141 NARA RG 59, 840.48 Refugees/6105, letter from Weissman to WJC (27 May 1944).

142 Avni, *Spain, the Jews and Franco*, p. 193/ In his memoirs Bedoya claims that 19,000 Jewish children reached Spain. The number is clearly grossly exaggerated. See Bedoya, *Memorias*, p. 231.

143 Yahil, *The Holocaust*, pp. 501–12 and Dawidowicz, *The War Against the Jews*, pp. 381–2.

144 NARA RG 59, 840.48 Refugees/6163A, telegram from Hull to Hayes (24 May 1944).

145 Randolph Braham, *The Politics of Genocide: the Holocaust in Hungary* (Detroit, 2000) (Condensed edition), p. 238.

146 On Renée Reichmann's rescue plan see Bianco, *The Reichmanns*, pp. 136–45.

147 NARA RG 59, 840.48 Refugees/6190, telegram from Childs to the US Department of State (2 June 1944).

148 MAEE R1716/5, note (22 June 1944).

149 MAEE R1716/5, note verbale from the British Embassy (7 August 1944).

150 MAEE R1716/5, letter from Sanz Briz to the Foreign Minister (22 August 1944).

151 MAEE R2696/21, letter from Orgaz to the Minister of Foreign Affairs (20 September 1944).

152 Braham, *The Politics of Genocide*, pp. 181–4.

153 Ibid., p. 237.

154 MAEE R1372/2, letter from Nicola Franco (27 October 1944).

155 USHMM, RG20.004, records relating to the investigation of Giorgio Perlasca, telegram from Lequerica to Sanz Briz (24 October 1944).

156 MAEE R1716/5, sobre protección a los judíos realizada por la legación de España en Budapest (29 December 1944).

157 Enrico Deaglio, *The Banality of Goodness: The Story of Giorgio Perlasca* (Notre Dame, 1998), p. 72.

158 MAEE R1716/5, telegram from Sanz Briz (21 November 1944).

159 Deaglio, *The Banality of Goodness*, p. 82.

160 NARA RG 59, 840.48 Refugees/7–2544, copy of note to Spanish Minister of foreign affairs from W. Walton Butterworth (25 July 1944).

161 NARA RG 59, 852.00/7–2544, letter from Butterworth to the Secretary of State (25 July 1944).

162 Quoted in Lazo, *La iglesia, la falange,* p. 204.

163 MAEE R 3115/3, circular numero 2083 and MAEE R1672/1, circular numero 2.088 (10 October 1945).

164 Rother, *Franco y el Holocausto*, p. 393.

165 Bedoya, *Memorias*, pp. 249–50.

166 Papers of Javier Martínez de Bedoya, Informe no. 313-E (27 May 1946).

167 Papers of Javier Martínez de Bedoya, Informe no. 327–2 (29 July 1946).

168 Avni, *Spain, the Jews and Franco*, p. 208.

169 *Sefarad*, Vol. 9 (1949), quoted in Raanan Rein, *In the Shadow of the Holocaust and the Inquisition: Israel's relations with Francoist Spain* (London, 1997), p. 15.

170 Julio Álvarez del Vayo, "Franco as 'Friend' of the Jews: Motives behind the dictator's new policy", *The Nation* (14 February 1949), pp. 5–7.

171 Rein, *In the Shadow of the Holocaust*, pp. 16–17.

172 *Arriba* (12 May 1949) quoted in Rein, *In the Shadow of the Holocaust*, p. 138.

173 On Darquier see his interview in *L'Express* (28 October–4 November 1978) on Degrelle see José L. Rodríguez Jiménez, *Antisemitism and the Extreme Right in Spain (1962–1997)*, Acta No. 15 Analysis of Current trends in Antisemitism, 1999. The Vidal Sassoon International Center for the Study of Antisemitism, the Hebrew University of Jerusalem <http://sicsa.huij.ac.il/15spain.html>.

174 Carlos Collado Seidel, *España refugio Nazi* (Madrid, 2005), p. 52.

175 *L'Express* (28 October–4 November 1978) and José Maria Irujo, *La lista negra: los espías nazis protegidos por Franco y la Iglesia* (Madrid, 2003), pp. 154–61.

176 Uki Goñi, *The Real Odessa: How Perón Brought the Nazi War Criminals to Argentina* (London, 2002), pp. 62–70.

177 Ibid., p. 71 on Victor de la Serna's father see Chapter 3 above.

178 Goñi, *The Real Odessa*, p. 77.

179 Ibid., p. 167 quoting Daye's unpublished memoirs.

180 *L'Express* (28 October–4 November 1978.

181 "Spanish 'Friends of Europe'", *Patterns of Prejudice*, Vol. 12, No. 4 (July–August 1978), p. 14.

182 Rodriguez Jiménez, *Antisemitism and the Extreme Right in Spain*.

Epilogue   The Contradictions and Hypocrisy of Francoist Policy

1 Jeffrey Lesser, *Welcoming the Undesirables: Brazil and the Jewish Question* (Los Angeles, 1995)

2 Ibid., pp. 85–100.

3 Ibid., p. 1.

4 David G. Goodman and Masanori Miyazawa, *Jews in the Japanese Mind: The History and Uses of a Cultural Stereotype* (New York, 1995).

5 Ibid., Chapter V.

6 See Carpi, *Between Mussolini and Hitler*.

Bibliography

This study utilizes a wide range of sources – the Spanish and foreign press, documents from public and private archives as well as memoirs.

Newspapers: The study of several Spanish newspapers (*ABC*, *El Debate*, *Arriba*, *Domingo, España, El Mundo*) and a number of pamphlets written between 1898 and 1945 has shed some light on the Spanish radical right's rhetoric of the Jews during those years. News on the situation of Jews in Spain and Spanish Morocco have also been culled from the Jewish Press (*The Jewish Chronicle*, *American Hebrew*, *L'Univers Israélite*.)

Official Archives: The files containing the correspondence and memoranda of the Spanish diplomats in the Balkans, Germany, France and Italy have been consulted in the archives of the *Ministerio de Asuntos Exteriores* in Madrid. Files pertaining to the situation of Jews in Spanish Morocco have been examined in the *Archivo General de la Administración* in Alcalá de Henares. In France, the correspondence of the French consuls in Spanish Morocco has been investigated in the archives of *Ministère des Affaires Etrangères Français* (Paris and Nantes). In England, the files on Spain and Spanish Morocco during the Civil War and on the Jewish refugees during World War II have been consulted in the archives of the British Foreign Office at the Public Record Office. In the United States, files on Jewish refugees in Spain during World War II had been examined at the United States National Archives and Records Administration in College Park, Maryland.

Private Collections: In New York, the papers of the principal relief organizations, the American Jewish Joint Distribution Committee and HICEM have been investigated. The private papers of the World Jewish Congress (WJC), which are housed in Southampton University and in the American Jewish Archives, and the private papers of Javier Martinez Bedoya, which are located in Madrid, have provided some inside view on the collaboration between the WJC and the Spanish government. The account of the situation of Moroccan Jews from 1898 to 1939 has been culled from the correspondence of the teachers of the *Alliance Israélite Universelle*, which are located in the archives of the Bibilothèque de l'Alliance in Paris.

I. Primary Sources

A. Unpublished Sources

(1) Official Archives

FRANCE
Ministère des Affaires Etrangères Français (Paris).
Série: Correspondance politique et commerciale. Sous-série: M. Maroc.
Série: Guerre 1939–1945, Vichy.
Ministère des Affaires Etrangères Français (Nantes).
Protectorat Maroc.

GREAT BRITAIN
Public Record Office, Foreign Office Papers (London).
FO 371, General Correspondence.

SPAIN
Archivo General de la Administración (Alcalá de Henares).
Sección Africa.
Archivo Historico Nacional (Madrid).
Fondos contemporáneos.
Ministerio de Asuntos Exteriores (Madrid).
Archivo General: Serie de Archivo Renovado (MAE/R files).

UNITED STATES
United States National Archives (Baltimore).
RG 59, General Records of the Department of State.
United States Holocaust Museum (Washington, DC).
Dolf Ringel, "Safe Conduct" unpublished manuscript RG-02.206.

(2) Private Archives

FRANCE
Archives de l'Alliance Israélite Universelle (Paris).
Série Maroc.
Fonds Moscou.
Archives du Centre de Documentation Juive Contemporaine (Paris).
CCCLXXXVI-31.

GREAT BRITAIN
University Library (Cambridge).
Templewood Papers.
Marx Memorial Library (London).
International Brigade Memorial Archive.

Wiener Library (London).
Document Series 684: Antisemitism in Spain –Reports and Correspondence 1936–1938.
Press Archives.

University Library (Southampton).
MS 237-41 Papers of the Institute of Jewish Affairs, 1913–1991.

SPAIN
Papers of Javier Martínez de Bedoya (Madrid, Spain).

United States
Alderman Library University of Virginia Manuscripts and Rare Books (Charlottesville).
J. Rives Childs collection.

Archives of the American Jewish Joint Distribution Committee (New York).
Collection 1933/1944.

Columbia University, Rare Book and Manuscript Library (New York).
Carlton Hayes Collection.

Leo Baeck Institute (New York).
AR 3987, folder Spain.

YIVO Institute for Jewish Scientific Research (New York).
HIAS–HICEM archives.

B. Published Sources

(1) Official Documents

ACTES ET DOCUMENTS DU SAINT SIEGE relatifs à la Seconde Guerre Mondiale. Volume 9: *Le Saint Siège et les victimes de la guerre* (Vatican, 1975).
ARCHIVES OF THE HOLOCAUST, Volume 10: American Jewish Joint Distribution Committee Part 2 (New York, 1995).
TIERNO GALVAN, Enrique (ed.), *Leyes Políticas Españolas fundamentales (1808–1978)* (Madrid, 1984).

(2) Newspapers and Periodicals

ABC
ABC, Sevilla
Acción Española
Amanecer
The American Hebrew
Archives Israélites
The American Jewish Yearbook
Arriba España
B'nai B'rith magazine
The Congress Bulletin

Domingo
El Español
L'Express
Gracia y Justicia
Heraldo de Madrid
Jewish Chronicle
Jewish Guardian
La Gaceta Literaria
Libertad
Mundo
La Nacion
The New York Times
Pueblo
The Reform Advocate
Revue Juive de Genève
El Siglo Futuro
El Sol
L'Univers Israélite
La Vanguardia

(3) Memoirs, Books, Pamphlets and Monographs

AINSZTEN, Reuben. *In Lands Not My Own: A Wartime Journey* (New York, 2002).
ALBIÑANA, José Maria. *España bajo la dictadura republicana: crónica de un período putrefacto* (Madrid, 1933).
THE AMERICAN JEWISH JOINT DISTRIBUTION COMMITTEE. *Aid to Jews Overseas, Report for 1939* (New York, 1940).
THE AMERICAN JEWISH JOINT DISTRIBUTION COMMITTEE. *Aid to Jews Overseas, Report for 1941 and the First Five Months of 1942* (New York, 1942).
AMERICAN JEWISH YEARBOOK
ANDRADE, Jaime de [pseudonym Francisco Franco Bahamonde]. *Raza anecdotario para el guión de una pelicula* (Madrid, 1982).
AREILZA, José Maria and CASTIELLA, Fernando María. *Reivindicaciones de España* (Madrid, 1941).
CADOGAN, Alexander. *The Diaries of Sir Alexander Cadogan, O.M., 1938–1945* (London, 1971).
CARRERO BLANCO, Luis. *España y el mar* (Madrid, 1941).
CASABÓ Y PAGÉS, Peregín. *La España judía* (Barcelona, 1891).
DIPLOMATIC INFORMATION OFFICE OF THE SPANISH MINISTRY OF FOREIGN AFFAIRS, *Spain and the Jews* (Madrid, 1949).
FERNÁNDEZ, Africano. *España en África y el peligro judío: Apuntes de un Testigo* (Santiago, 1918).
FITTKO, Lisa. *Escape Through the Pyrenees* (Evanston, 1991).
FRANCO, Francisco. "Xauen la triste", *Revista de Tropas Coloniales*, No. 19 (July 1926), pp. 145–148.

FRANCO, Francisco. *Textos de doctrina política: palabras y escritos de 1945 a 1950* (Madrid, 1951).

FRANCO'S "Mein Kampf": The Fascist State in Rebel Spain: An Official Blueprint (New York, 1939).

FRY, Varian. *Surrender on Demand* (New York, 1997).

GARCÍA FIGUERAS, Tomás. *Marruecos: La Acción de España en el Norte de África* (Barcelona, 1939).

GAY, Vincente. *Estampas rojas y caballeros blancos* (Burgos, 1937).

GERMAN EMBASSY in Salamanca. *La Eterna cuestion judia* (Salamanca, 1938).

GIMÉNEZ CABALLERO, Ernesto. *Notas marruecas de un soldado* (Madrid, 1923).

GIMÉNEZ CABALLERO, Ernesto. *Genio de España. Exaltaciones a una resurrección nacional y del mundo*, 8th edition (Barcelona, 1938).

GIRÓN Y ARCAS, Joaquín. *La cuestión judáica en la España actual y la Universidad de Salamanca* (Salamanca, 1906).

GONZÁLEZ RUANO, César. *Seis meses con los Nazis* (Madrid, 1933).

HART, Peter. *Journey into Freedom: An Authentic War-Time Story* (Hertford, 2003).

HAYES, Carlton J.H. *Wartime Mission in Spain* (New York, 1945).

HOARE, Sir Samuel. *Ambassador on Special Mission* (London, 1946)

LA GARRA del capitalismo judio: Sus procedimientos y efectos en el momento actual (Madrid, 1943).

LLANAS DE NIUBÓ, René. *El Judaismo* (Madrid, 1935).

MAEZTU, Ramiro De. *Defensa de la Hispanidad* (Madrid, 1941).

MAEZTU, Ramiro de. *Frente a la República*, 8th edition (Madrid, 1956).

MAHLER-WERFEL, Alma. *And the Bridge Is Love: Memories of a Lifetime* (London, 1959).

MARTINEZ DE BEDOYA, Javier. *Memorias desde mi aldea* (Valladolid, 1996).

MILHAUD, Darius. *Notes Without Music: An Autobiography* (London, 1952).

MOLA, Emilio. *Tempestad, calma, intriga y crisis*, 2nd edition (Madrid, 1932).

OLASCOAGA, Alfredo. *El Norte de Africa cabeza de Puente ¿de quien?* (Madrid, 1943).

ORTEGA, Manuel L. *El Doctor Pulido* (Madrid, 1922).

ORTEGA, Manuel L. *Los Hebreos en Marruecos* (Malaga, 1994).

PALABRAS del Caudillo, 19 Abril 1937–7 Diciembre 1942, 3rd edition (Madrid, 1943).

PEMÁN, José María. *El poema de la Bestia y del Ángel* (Zaragoza, 1938).

PEMARTÍN, José. *Qué es "lo nuevo" . . . Consideraciones sobre el momento español presente*, 3rd edition (Madrid, 1940).

PEREZ, LESHEM (Fritz Lichtenstein). "Rescue Efforts in the Iberian Peninsula", *Leo Baeck Institute Year Book 14* (1969), pp. 231–256.

POWELL FOX, Rosalinda. *The Grass and the Asphalt* (Puerto Sotogrande, 1997).

PULIDO FERNÁNDEZ, Ángel. *Españoles sin patria y la raza sefardí*, 4th edition (Granada, 1993).

RODA, Rafael De. *La politica Hispano-Sefardi en nuestro protectorado de Marruecos* (Tetuan, 1920).

SANGRÓNIZ, José Antonio de. *Marruecos : sus condiciones físicas, sus habitantes y las instituciones indígenas* (Madrid, 1921).

SANGRÓNIZ, José Antonio De. *La Expansión Cultural de España en el extranjero y principalemente en Hispano-América* (Madrid, 1925).

SANTA CLARA, Baron of. *El judaísmo* (Burgos, 1938).

SEGURA NIETO, Juan. *¡Alerta! . . .Francmasonería y judaismo* (Barcelona, 1940).

SEVILLANO CARBAJAL, Virgilio. *La España {. . .} de quién? Ingleses, franceses y alemanes en este pais* (Madrid, 1936).

VALLEJO-NÁGERA, Antonio. *Eugenesia de la Hispanidad y Regeneración de la Raza* (Burgos, 1937).

VALLEJO-NÁGERA, Antonio. *Divagaciones intranscendentales* (Valladolid, 1938).

VÁZQUEZ DE MELLA Y FANJUL, Juan. *Obras Completas, Vol. 3: Ideario* (Madrid, 1932).

VÁZQUEZ DE MELLA Y FANJUL, Juan. *Obras Completas Vol. 7: Discursos Parlamentarios* (Barcelona, 1932).

II. Secondary Sources

(1) Books

ABITBOL, Michel. *The Jews of North Africa During the Second World War* (Detroit, 1989).

ALMOG, Shmuel. *Nationalism and Antisemitism in Modern Europe 1815–1945* (Oxford, 1990).

ÁLVAREZ CHILLIDA, Gonzalo. *José María Pemán: Pensamiento y Trayectora de un Monarquico, 1897–1941* (Cadiz, 1996).

ÁLVAREZ CHILLIDA, Gonzalo. *El antisemitismo en España: La imagen del judio 1812–2002* (Madrid, 2002).

ARONSFELD, Cesar C. *The Ghosts of 1492: Jewish Aspects of the Struggle for Religious Freedom in Spain, 1848–1976* (New York, 1979).

AVNI, Haim. *Spain, the Jews and Franco* (Philadelphia, 1982).

BALFOUR, Sebastian. *Deadly Embrace Morocco and the Road to the Spanish Civil War* (Oxford, 2002).

BALFOUR, Sebastian and PRESTON, Paul (eds), *Spain and the Great Powers in the Twentieth Century* (London, 1999).

BARRACHINA, Marie-Aline. *Propagande et culture dans l'Espagne Franquiste* (Grenoble, 1998).

BELOT, Robert. *Aux Frontières de la liberté : Vichy–Madrid–Alger–Londres S'évader de France sous l'Occupation* (Paris, 1998).

BEN-AMI, Shlomo. *The Origins of the Second Republic in Spain* (Oxford, 1978).

BENBASSA, Esther and RODRIGUE, Aron. *The Jews of the Balkans: The Judeo-Spanish Community, 15th to 20th Centuries* (Oxford, 1995).

BEN-DROR, Graciela. *La Iglesia Católica ante El Holocausto, España y América Latina* (Madrid, 2003).

BENET, Josep. *Cataluña bajo el régimen franquista: Informe sobre la persecución de la lengua y la cultura catalana por el régimen del general Franco* (Barcelona, 1979).

BERNSTEIN, Serge. *Le 6 Fevrier 1934* (Paris, 1975).

BIANCO, Anthony. *The Reichmanns: Family, Faith, Fortune and the Empire of Olympia and York* (New York, 1997).

BIRNBAUM, Pierre. *Antisemitism in France: A Political History from Léon Blum to the Present* (Oxford, 1992).

BLINKHORN, Martin. *Carlism and Crisis in Spain, 1931–1939* (London, 1975).

BÖCKER, Manfred. *Antisemitismus ohne Juden : Die Zweite Republik, die antirepublikansische Rechte und die Juden. Spanien 1931 bis 1936* (Frankfurt, 2000).

BONDY, Louis W. *Racketeers of Hatred: Julius Streicher and the Jew-baiters International* (London, 1946).

BOSCH, Alfred and NERÍN, Gustau. *El imperio que nunca existió* (Barcelona, 2001).

BOWEN, Wayne. *Spaniards and Nazi Germany: Collaboration in the New Order* (Columbia Missouri, 2000).

BRAHAM, Randolph. *The Politics of Genocide: The Holocaust in Hungary* (Detroit, 2000) (condensed edition).

BRAMSTED, Ernst K. *Goebbels and National Socialist Propaganda* (Michigan, 1965).

BRODERSEN, Momme. *Walter Benjamin: A Biography* (London, 1996).

BRONNER, Stephen Eric. *A Rumor about the Jews: Reflections on Antisemitism and the Protocols of the Elders of Zion* (New York, 2000).

BUCKLEY, Henry. *Life and Death of the Spanish Republic* (London, 1940).

CARCEDO, Diego. *Un español frente al Holocausto: Así salvó Ángel Sanz Briz a 5.000 judíos* (Madrid, 2000).

CARPI, Daniel. *Between Mussolini and Hitler: The Jews and the Italian Authorities in France and Tunisia* (Hanover, NH, 1994).

CATALA, Michel. *Les relations franco-espagnoles pendant la deuxième guerre mondiale: rapprochement nécessaire, réconciliation impossible 1939–1944* (Paris, 1997).

CHOURAQUI, André. *L'Alliance Israélite Universelle et la renaissance juive contemporaine* (Paris, 1965).

COHEN, Richard I. *The Burden of Conscience: French Jewish Leadership during the Holocaust* (Bloomington, 1987).

COHN, Norman. *Warrant for Genocide: The Myth of the Jewish World Conspiracy and Protocols of the Elders of Zion* (London, 1967).

COLLADO SEIDEL, Carlos. *España refugio nazi* (Madrid, 2005).

DAWIDOWICZ, Lucy. *The War against the Jews, 1933–1945* (London, 1975).

DEAGLIO, Enrico. *The Banality of Goodness: The Story of Giorgio Perlasca* (Notre Dame, 1998).

DELGADO GÓMEZ-ESCALONILLA, Lorenz, *Imperio de papel: acción cultural y politica exterior durante el primer Franquismo* (Madrid, 1992).

DIAMANT, David. *Combattants juifs dans l'armée républicaine espagnole, 1936–1939* (Paris, 1979).

DRIESSEN, Henk. *On the Spanish Moroccan Frontier: A Study in Ritual Power and Ethnicity* (Oxford, 1992).

ELLIOT, J.H. *Imperial Spain: 1469–1716* (London, 1990).

FERNÁNDEZ, Carlos. *Antología de cuarenta años 1936–1975* (La Coruña, 1983).

FERRER BENIMELI, José. *El contubernio judo-masónico-comunista. Del Satanismo al escándalo de la P-2* (Madrid, 1982).

FOARD, Douglas W. *The Revolt of the Aesthetes: Ernesto Gimenez Caballero and the Origins of Spanish Fascism* (New York, 1989).

GARCÍA QUEIPO DE LLANO, Genoveva and TUSELL, Xavier. *Franco y Mussolini: la política española durante la Segunda Guerra mundial* (Barcelona, 1985).

GIL PECHARROMAN, Julio. *Conservadores subversivos: La Derecha Autoritaria Alfonsina 1913–1936* (Madrid, 1991).

GILMAN, Sander. *The Jew's Body* (London, 1991).

GIRARDET, Raoul. *Mythes et mythologies politiques* (Paris, 1986).

GLICK, Thomas F. and SÁNCHEZ RON, José M. *La España posible de la Segunda República: la oferta a Einstein de una cátedra extraordinaria en la Universidad Central* (Madrid, 1983).

GONDI, Olivio. *La hispanidad franquista al servicio de Hitler* (Mexico, 1979).

GOÑI, Uki. *The Real Odessa: How Perón Brought the Nazi War Criminals to Argentina* (London, 2002).

GONZÁLEZ GARCÍA, Isidro. *La cuestion judía y los origenes del sionismo (1881–1905): España ante el problema judío* (Madrid, 1988).

GONZÁLEZ GARCÍA, Isidro. *Los judíos y la Segunda República, 1931–1939* (Madrid, 2004).

GOODMAN, David G. and MIYAZAWA, Masanori. *Jews in the Japanese Mind: The History and Uses of a Cultural Stereotype* (New York, 1995).

GRAUMANN, Carl F. and MOSCOVICI, Serge. *Changing Conceptions of Conspiracy* (New York, 1987).

HARRISON, Joseph. *The Spanish Economy in the Twentieth Century* (London, 1985).

HASSÁN, Iacob M. (ed.), *Actas del primer simposio de estudios sefardíes* (Madrid, 1976).

IRUJO, José Maria. *La lista negra: Los espías protegidos por Franco y la iglesia* (Madrid, 2003).

KAMEN, Henry. *The Spanish Inquisition: A Historical Revision* (London, 1997).

KATZ, Otto. *The Nazi Conspiracy in Spain* (London, 1937).

KEENE, Judith. *Fighting for Franco: International Volunteers in Nationalist Spain during the Spanish Civil War, 1936–1939* (London, 2001).

KENBIB, Mohammed. *Juifs et Musulmans au Maroc 1859–1948* (Rabat, 1994).

KERTZER, David. *The Popes against the Jews: The Vatican's Role in the Rise of Modern Antisemitism* (New York, 2001).

KLARSFELD, Serge. *Vichy-Auschwitz: Le role de Vichy dans la solution finale de la question Juive en France* (Paris, 1983).

LANGMUIR, Gavin I. *History, Religion and Antisemitism* (Berkley, 1990).

LANGMUIR, Gavin I. *Towards a Definition of Antisemitism* (Berkeley, 1996).

LANNON, Frances. *Privilege, Persecution and Prophecy: The Catholic Church in Spain, 1875–1975* (Oxford, 1987).

LASKIER, Michael. *The Alliance Israélite Universelle and the Jewish Communities of Morocco, 1862–1962* (Albany, New York 1983).

LASKIER, Michael. *North African Jewry in the Twentieth century: The Jews of Morocco, Tunisia, and Algeria* (New York, 1994).

LAZARE, Lucien. *Rescue as Resistance: How Jewish Organizations Fought the Holocaust in France* (New York, 1996).

LAZO, Alfonso. *La Iglesia, La Falange y el Fascismo: Un estudio sobre la prensa Española de posguerra* (Seville, 1995).

LESSER, Jeffrey. *Welcoming the Undesirables: Brazil and the Jewish Question* (Los Ángeles, 1995).

LEVINE, Paul. *From Indifference to Activism: Swedish Diplomacy and the Holocaust* (Uppsala, 1998).

LIPSCHITZ, Chaim U. *Franco, Spain, the Jews and the Holocaust* (New York, 1984).

LISBONA, José Antonio. *Retorno a Sefarad: La politica de España hacia sus judíos en el siglo XX* (Barcelona, 1993).

MACDOUGALL, Ian (ed.), *Voices from the Spanish civil War: Personal Recollections of Scottish Volunteers in Republican Spain, 1936–1939* (Edinburgh, 1986).

MARQUINA, Antonio and OSPINA, Gloria Inés. *España y los judíos en el siglo XX* (Madrid, 1987).

MARRUS, Michael R. and PAXTON, Robert O. *Vichy France and the Jews* (New York, 1981).

MASERAS, Alfons. *La Nostra Gent Francesc Macià* (Barcelona, 1946).

MAZOWER, Mark. *Inside Hitler's Greece: The Experience of Occupation (1941–1944)* (London, 1993).

MELLOR, F.H. *Morocco Awakes* (London, 1939).

MORODO, Raúl. *Los origenes ideologicos del franquismo: Acción Española* (Madrid, 1985).

NOGUÉ, Joan and VILLANOVA, José Luis. *España en Marruecos (1912–1956). Discursos geográficos e intervención territorial* (Madrid, 2001).

PABÓN, Jesús. *Cambó: Parte primera (1918–1930)* (Barcelona, 1969).

PAYNE, Stanley G. *The Franco Regime, 1936–1975* (Madison, 1987).

PAYNE, Stanley G. *Spain's First Democracy: The Second Republic, 1931–1936* (Madison, 1993).

PENNELL, C.R. *Morocco Since 1830: A History* (London, 2000).

PIKE, David Wingeate. *Conjecture, Propaganda and Deceit and the Spanish Civil War* (Stanford, 1968).

PRESTON, Paul. *The Coming of the Spanish Civil War: Reform, Reaction and Revolution in the Second Republic 1931–1936*, 2nd ed. (London, 1994).

PRESTON, Paul. *Franco: A Biography* (London, 1995).

PRESTON, Paul. *Comrades* (London, 1999),

PRESTON, Paul. *Doves of War: Four Women of Spain* (London, 2003).

PUERTOLAS, Julio Rodriguez. *Literatura fascista española* (Madrid, 1987).

RAMSDEN, H. *The 1898 movement in Spain. Towards a Reinterpretation with Special Reference to En Torno al Casticismo and Idearium Español* (Manchester, 1974).

REIN, Ranaan. *In the Shadow of the Holocaust and the Inquisition: Israel's Relations with Francoist Spain* (London, 1997).

RICHARDS, Michael. *A Time of Silence: Civil War and the Culture of Repression in Franco's Spain, 1936–1945* (Cambridge, 1998).

RODRÍGUEZ JIMÉNEZ, José. *Historia de la Falange Española de la JONS* (Madrid, 1980).

RODRÍGUEZ-PUÉRTOLAS, Julio. *Literatura fascista española: volumen I historia* (Madrid, 1987).

RODRIGUO, Javier. *Cautivos: Campos de concentración en la España franquista, 1936–1947* (Barcelona, 2005).

ROS AGUDO, Manuel. *La guerra secreta de Franco, 1939–1945* (Barcelona, 2002).

ROTHER, Bernd. *Franco y el Holocausto* (Madrid, 2005).

RYAN, Donna F. *The Holocaust and the Jews of Marseille: The Enforcement of Antisemitic Policies in Vichy France* (Chicago, 1996).

SCHOLEM, Gershom. *Walter Benjamin: The Story of a Friendship* (New York, 2003).

SEIDMAN, Michael. *Republic of Egos: A Social History of the Spanish Civil War* (Madison, 2002).

SEMOLINOS, Mercedes. *Hitler y la prensa de la II Republica* (Madrid, 1985).

SERELS, M. Mitchell. *A History of the Jews of Tangier in the Nineteenth and Twentieth Century* (New York, 1991).

SMITH, Anthony D. *Myths and Memories of the Nation* (Oxford, 1999).

SORIA, Georges. *Un grave danger: L'infiltration allemande au Maroc* (Paris, 1937).

SOUTHWORTH, Herbert Rutledge. *Le mythe de la croisade de Franco* (Paris, 1964).

SOUTHWORTH, Herbert Rutledge. *Antifalange: Estudio crítico de 'Falange en la Guerra de España, la Unificación y Hedilla', de Maximiano Garcíja Venero* (Paris, 1967).

STEINBERG, Jonathan. *All or Nothing: the Axis and the Holocaust 1941–1943* (London, 1991).

STUART, Graham H. *The International City of Tangier*, 2nd edition (Stanford, 1955).

THOMAS, Hugh. *The Spanish Civil War* (London, 1986).

TUDOR, Henry. *Political Myths* (London, 1972).

TUSELL, Javier. *Historia de la democracia cristiana en España. Los antecedents, la CEDA y la II República* (Madrid, 1974).

TUSELL, Javier. *Carrero: La eminencia gris del regimen de Franco* (Madrid, 1993).

VINCENT, Mary. *Catholicism in the Second Spanish Republic: Religion and Politics in Salamanca, 1930–1936* (Oxford, 1996).

YAHIL, Leni. *The Holocaust: The Fate of European Jewry* (Oxford, 1990).

YSART, Federico. *España y los judíos en la Segunda Guerra Mundial* (Barcelona, 1978).

WASSERSTEIN, Bernard. *Britain and the Jews of Europe, 1939–1945* (London, 1979).

WILSON, Stephen. *Ideology and Experience: Antisemitism in France at the Time of the Dreyfus Affair* (Rutherford, New Jersey, 1982).

ZUCOTTI, Susan. *The Holocaust, the French, and the Jews* (Lincoln, New England, 1999).

(2) Articles

ALAN, Ray. "Spanish antisemitism today", *Commentary* Vol. 38, No. 2 (August 1964), pp. 64–66.

ÁLVAREZ CHILLIDA, Gonzalo. "El mito antisemita en la crisis española del siglo XX", *Hispania*, Vol. 194 (Sept.–Dec. 1996), pp. 1037–1070.

ÁLVAREZ JUNCO, José. "The nation-building process in nineteenth century Spain", in Clare Mar-Molinero and Angel Smith (eds), *Nationalism and the Nation in the Iberian Peninsula: Competing and Conflicting Identities* (Oxford, 1996)

ÁLVAREZ DEL VAYO, Julio. "Franco as 'Friend' of the Jews: Motives behind the dictator's new policy", *The Nation* (14 February 1949), pp. 5–7.

AVNI, Haim. "Los judíos y España en 1949. Un desencuentro mistificado", in F. Ruiz Gomez M and M. Espadas Burgos (eds), *Encuentros en Sefarad. Actas del congreso internacional "Los Judíos en la historia de España"* (Ciudad Real, 1987), pp. 137–152.

BACHOUD, Andrée. "Franco et les Juifs", *Nationalismes, feminismes, exclusions: Mélanges en l'honneur de Rita Thalmann* (Berlin, 1999), pp. 87–97.

BALFOUR, Sebastian. "Spain and the Great Powers in the aftermath of the Disaster of 1898", in Sebastian Balfour and Paul Preston (eds), *Spain and the Great Powers in the Twentieth Century* (London, 1999)

BALFOUR, Sebastian and LA PORTE, Pablo. "Spanish Military Cultures and the Moroccan Wars 1909–1936", *European History Quarterly* Vol. 30, No. 3 (July 2000), pp. 307–333.

BAUTISTA VILAR, Juan. "Evolucion de la poblacion israelita en Marruecos Espanol (1940–1955)", *Estudios sefardies: Revista del Instituto Arias Montano*, No. 1 (1978).

BAUTISTA VILAR, Juan. "L'ouverture a l'occident de la communauté juive de Tétouan 1860–1865", in Sarah Leibovici (ed.), *Mosaiques de notre mémoire: Les Judéo Espagnols du Maroc* (Paris, 1982), pp. 85–127.

BLANDIN. "La Population de Tanger en 1940", *Revue Africaine*, Vol. LXXXXVIII (1944), pp. 89–115.

BLIN, Pascale. "Franco et les juifs du Maroc: Une approche historique", in Abramson, Pierre-Luc and Martine Berthelot (eds), *L'Espagne contemporaine et les juifs* (Perpignan, 1991), pp. 33–57.

BOTTI, Alfonso. "L'Antisemitismo in Spagna durante la Seconda Repubblica (1931–1936)" in Catherine Brice et Giovanni Miccoli (eds), *Les racines chrétiennes de l'antisémitisme politique* (Rome, 2003), pp. 183–213.

BOWIE, Leland. "An aspect of Muslim–Jewish relations in late nineteenth-century Morocco: A European diplomatic view", *International Journal of Middle East Studies* 7 (1976), pp. 3–19.

BRAUDE, Benjamin. "The myth of the Sefardi economic superman", in Jeremy Adlman and Stephen Aron (eds), *Trading Cultures: The Worlds of Western Merchants Essays on Authority, Objectivity and Evidence* (Turnhout, 2001).

CHANDLER, James A. "Spain and Her Moroccan Protectorate 1898–1927", *Journal of Contemporary History*, Vol. 10 (1975), pp. 301–322.

EFRON, John M. "Scientific Racism and the Mystique of Sephardic Racial Superiority", *Leo Baeck Institute Yearbook* Vol. 38 (1993), pp. 75–96.

EYKMAN, Christoph. "The Spanish civil war in German publications during the Nazi years", in Luis Costa, Richard Critchfield, Richard Golsan and Wulf Koepke (eds), *German and International Perspectives on the Spanish Civil War: the Aesthetics of Partisanship* (Columbia, SC, 1992).

FEUCHTWANGER, Marta. "Transit" in Andreas Lixl-Purcell (ed.), *Women of Exile: German-Jewish Autobiographies Since 1933* (New York, 1988), pp. 63–66.

FLEMING, Shannon. "Spanish Morocco and the *Alzamiento Nacional*, 1936–1939: The military, economic and political mobilization of a protectorate", *Journal of Contemporary History*, Vol. 18 (1983) pp. 27–42.

FRIEDLANDER, Robert. A. "Holy Crusade or Unholy Alliance? Franco's National Revolution and the Moors", *The Southwestern Social Science Quarterly*, Vol. 4, No. 4 (March 1964), pp. 346–356.

GARZÓN, Jacobo Israel. "Judios en España en los años treinta: Segunda República y Guerra Civil", *Raíces*, No. 26 (1996), pp. 61–70.

GARZÓN, Jacobo Israel. "Racismo antisemita en la literature española 1931–1945", *Raíces*, No. 11 (1997), pp. 27–32.

GARZÓN, Jacobo Israel, "El Archivo Judaico del Franquismo", *Raices*, No. 33 (1997), pp. 57–60.

GODA, Norman. "Franco's Bid for Empire: Spain, Germany, and the Western Mediterranean in World War II", in Raanan Rein (ed.), *Spain and the Mediterranean since 1898* (London, 1999).

GONZÁLEZ GARCÍA, Isidro. "El problema del racismo y los judios en el fascismo italiano y su incidencia en el gobierno de Burgos en el ano 1938", *Hispania*, Vol. 165 (1987) pp. 309–335.

GONZÁLEZ GARCÍA, Isidro. "España y los Judios del Norte de Africa, 1860–1900", *Aportes Revista de Historia del Siglo XIX* (6 September 1987), pp. 3–17.

GONZÁLEZ GARCÍA, Isidro. "L'Antisemitisme en l'Espanya Contemporània", *L'Avenç*, No. 198 (1995), pp. 56–62.

GUERSHON, Isaac. "La Revista de la Raza: Organo del filosefardismo español", *Raíces*, No. 8 (1994) pp. 58–61.

GUERSHON, Isaac. "The foundation of Hispano-Jewish associations in Morocco: Contrasting portraits of Tangier and Tetuan", in Harvey E. Goldberg (ed.), *Sephardi and Middle Eastern Jewries: History and Culture in the Modern Era* (Bloomington, 1996).

HALSTEAD, Charles. "A 'somewhat Machiavellian' face: Colonel Juan Beigbeder as High Commissioner in Spanish Morocco, 1937–1939", *Historian*, Vol. 37 (November 1974), pp. 44–66.

HALSTEAD, Carolyn and HALSTEAD, Charles "Aborted imperialism: Spain's Occupation of Tangier 1940–1945", *Iberian Studies*, Vol. 7, No. 2 (Autumn 1978), pp. 53–71.

HOROWITZ, Irving Louis. "Philo-Semitism and Antisemitism: Jewish Conspiracies and Totalitarian Sentiments", *Midstream*, Serie 36, pp. 17–27.

JENSEN, Geoffrey. "Toward the 'moral conquest' of Morocco: Hispano–Arabic education in early twentieth-century North Africa", *European History Quarterly*, Vol. 31, No. 2 (April 2001), pp. 205–229.

KALMAR, Ivan Davidson and PENSLAR Derek J., "Orientalism and the Jews: an Introduction," in Kalmar and Penslar (eds), *Orientalism and the Jews* (Lebanon, NH: 2004).

LAZO, Alfonso. "Un antisemitismo sin judíos", *La Aventura de la Historia*, Año 1, Numero 5 (20 March 1999), pp. 16–20.

LUSTIGER, Arno. "The Jews and the Spanish war", in Ricardo Izquierdo Benito, Uriel Macías Kapón and Yolanda Moreno Koch (eds), *Los judíos en la España Contemporánea: Historia y Visiones 1898–1998, VIII curso de Cultura Hispanojudía y Sefardí de La Universidad de Castilla-La Mancha* (Castilla la Mancha, 2000).

MARTÍNEZ SANZ, José Luis. "Reflejo en España del antijudaismo Aleman prehitleriano", in F. Ruiz Gomez M and M. Espadas Burgos (eds), *Encuentros en Sefarad. Actas del congreso internacional "los judíos en la historia de España"* (Ciudad Real, 1987), pp. 347–367.

MORCILLO-ROSILLO, Matilde. "España y los sefarditas de Salónica durante el incendio de 1917", *Sefarad*, Vol. 59, No. 2 (1999), pp. 353–369.

NASH, Mary. "Social eugenics and nationalist race hygiene in early twentieth century Spain", *History of European Ideas*, Vol. 15, No. 4–6 (1992), pp. 741–748.

OLIVARES Javier Vidal and ORTUÑEZ Pedro Pablo "The internationalisation of ownership of the Spanish railways companies, 1858–1936", *Business History*, Vol. 44, No. 44 (October 2002), pp. 29–54.

ORTIZ, Carmen. "The uses of folklore by the Franco regime", *Journal of American Folklore*, Vol, 112, No. 446 (Autumn, 1999), pp. 479–496.

PARRY, D.L.L "Articulating the Third Republic by conspiracy theory", *European History Quarterly*, Vol. 28, No. 2 (1998), pp. 163–188.

PRAGO, Albert. "Jews in the International Brigades", in Alvah Bessie and Albert Prago (eds), *Our Fight: Writings by Veterans of the Abraham Lincoln Brigade* (New York, 1987).

PRESTON, Paul. "Alfonsist monarchism and the coming of the Spanish civil war", in Martin Blinkhorn (ed.), *Spain in Conflict: Democracy and its Enemies* (London, 1986), pp. 160–182.

RAY, Alan. "Spanish antisemitism today", *Commentary*, Vol. 38, No. 2 (August 1964), pp. 64–66.

RODRÍGUEZ JIMÉNEZ, José L. "Antisemitism and the Extreme Right in Spain (1962–1997)", Acta No. 15 *Analysis of Current trends in Antisemitism*, 1999. The Vidal Sassoon International Center for the Study of Antisemitism, the Hebrew University of Jerusalem, <http://sicsa.huij.ac.il/15spain.html>.

RODRÍGUEZ JIMÉNEZ, José L. "Los Protocolos de los Sabios de Sión en España", *Raíces*, No. 38, (1999), pp. 27–40.

SENKMAN, Leonardo. "Maximo Jose Kahn: De Escritor español del exilio a escritor del desastre judío", *Raíces*, No. 27 (1996), pp. 44–52.

SHINDLER, Colin "No Pasaran: the Jews who fought in Spain", *Jewish Quarterly*, No. 123 (1986), pp. 34–41.

SHUBERT, Adrian. "The epic failure: The Asturian revolution of October 1934", in Paul Preston (ed.), *Revolution and War in Spain (1931–1939)* (London, 1985).

STONE, Glyne. "The European Great Powers and the Spanish civil war 1936–1939" in Robert Boyce and Esmonde Robertson (eds), *Paths to War: New Essays on the Origins of the Second World War* (London, 1989).

THOMAS, Martin. "French Morocco–Spanish Morocco: Vichy French Strategic Planning against the "Threat from the North", in Christian Leitz and David J. Dunthorn (eds), *Spain in an International Context (1936–1959)* (New York, 1999).

TOFIÑO QUESADA, "Spanish Orientalism: Uses of the Past in Spain's Colonization in Africa", *Comparative Studies of South Asia, Africa and the Middle East*, Vol. 23, No. 1&2, 2003, pp. 141–8.

VINCENT, Mary. "The Spanish Church and the Popular Front: the experience of Salamanca province", in Martin S. Alexander and Helen Graham (eds), *The French and Spanish Popular Fronts: Comparative Perspectives* (Cambridge, 1989).

WHEALY, Robert H. "Nazi propagandist Joseph Goebbbels looks at the Spanish civil war – Goebbels diaries", *Historian* (Winter 1999).

(3) Unpublished theses

BLIN, Pascale. *Franco et les juifs. Paroles et actes. De sa rencontre avec les juifs à la reconnaissance de la communauté juive d'Espagne (1968): Un itineraire controversé* (Paris: Sorbonne Nouvelle Paris III, 1988).

GOODE, Joshua Seth. *The Racial Alloy: the Science, Politics and Culture of Spain, 1875–1923* (Los Angeles: University of California Press, 1999).

LICHTENSTEIN, Joseph Jacob. *The Reaction of West European Jewry to the Reestablishment of a Jewish Community in Spain in the 19th Century* (New York: Yeshiva University, 1962).

Index

122, 139, 142–3, 148–50, 154, 159
Athens, 90, 91, 114–15, 142–3,
148–50
Salonica, 16, 18, 26, 28, 29, 30, 89–90,
91, 114, 142–4
Guedalla, Haim, 13
Guernica, 80

Hassan, Augustus, 89
Hassan, Joe, 119, 125
Hayes, Carlton J. H, 125, 140, 144, 147,
150
Hedilla, Manuel, 77
HICEM, 58, 101
Himmler, Heinrich, 102, 110
Hispanidad, 4, 54, 145
Hispano-Jewish association, 17, 18, 22,
24, 46, 88
Hitler, Adolf, 4, 39, 47, 56, 57, 59, 66,
76, 77, 86, 92, 93, 94, 98, 110, 131,
157
Hoare, Samuel, 99, 105, 125, 133, 134,
136, 137, 142, 148
Horthy, Miklós, 152
Hungary, 36, 150–3

Informaciones, 54, 56, 57, 59
Inquisition, 5, 7, 11–12, 14, 28, 32, 33,
51, 66, 79, 82, 85, 101, 157
International Brigades, 65, 73–4, 106, 133
International Red Cross, 143, 151
Isabella I, Queen of Castile, 4, 6, 11, 12,
30, 39, 52, 56, 68, 79, 93, 101, 103,
157
Israel, 2, 46, 154, 155, 159

Japan, 9, 36, 144, 159
Jews
Ashkenazi, 16, 17, 29, 31–2, 73, 98,
117, 119
Jewish refugees, 2, 3, 7, 39, 47–9,
58–60, 63, 95, 97, 101, 102,
105–10, 119–20, 122, 123, 125–6,
131–8
Jewish volunteers in the International
Brigades, 73–4
of Morocco, 6, 9, 10, 13, 19, 20, 21–2,
23, 28, 34, 41, 47, 52, 68, 85, 88,
96, 103, 116, 118–21, 131, 158,
Sephardic, 2, 7, 8, 10, 15–37, 40–6, 58,
73, 89–91, 98, 100, 101, 102, 104,
105, 114–18, 122, 138, 142, 145,
149, 152, 153, 154

stateless, 100, 107, 109, 120, 126, 132,
135, 136
Jordana y Sousa, Count Francisco Gómez,
22, 91, 96, 98, 134, 136, 137, 138,
141
Jorro, Jaime, 115–16, 120
Jouin, Ernest, 36, 51

Kahn, Maximo José, 89–90
Kemal, Mustafa (Ataturk), 43
Kristallnacht, 93, 94

La Gaceta Literaria, 28–30, 45, 59, 89
Langenheim, Adolf, 76, 86
Lapuya, Isidro López, 14
Largo Caballero, Francisco, 40, 58
Lazar, Hans, 155
League of Nations, 26, 48
Ledesma Ramos, Ramiro, 50
Lequerica, José Félix, 50, 111, 120, 121,
141, 150, 152, 156
Lerroux, Alejandro, 40, 41, 61, 62,
63
Lerroux, Aurelio, 61
Lesca, Charles, 156
Lorca, Yzugardia, 82
Ludendorff, Erich, 76
Luna, José, 119

Macià, Francesc, 58, 62
Madariaga, Salvador de, 48
Maeztu, Ramiro de, 53–4, 56
Magaz, Antonio, 94–5
Mahler-Werfel, Alma, 108
Marina Vega, José, 22
Maritain, Jacques, 80
Martínez de Bedoya, Javier, 144–5, 149,
153–4, 159
Marx, Karl, 36, 52, 54
Maurras, Charles, 50, 53, 74–5
Mayalde, Conde de, 102, 109–10
Melilla, 12, 58, 84, 85, 86, 104, 106, 125
Menéndez Pelayo, Marcelino, 10, 32
Merry del Val, Alfonso, 113–14
Milhaud, Darius, 108
Miranda de Ebro, 2, 108, 119, 133–6
Miranda, Carlos de, 91–2, 114, 119
Mola Vida, Emilio, 67–8
Montesinos y Espartero, Pablo (Duque de
la Victoria), 50
Moors, 4, 6, 12, 13, 30, 32, 35, 39, 52,
53–5, 66, 67, 78, 81, 86–7, 99, 117,
158